MADE HOLY: IRISH WOMEN
RELIGIOUS AT HOME AND ABROAD

MADE HOLY: IRISH WOMEN RELIGIOUS AT HOME AND ABROAD

YVONNE McKENNA
University of Limerick

Foreword by
Margaret MacCurtain

IRISH ACADEMIC PRESS
DUBLIN • PORTLAND, OR

First published in 2006 by
IRISH ACADEMIC PRESS
44, Northumberland Road, Dublin 4, Ireland

and in the United States of America by
IRISH ACADEMIC PRESS
c/o ISBS, Suite 300, 920 NE 58th Avenue
Portland, Oregon 97213-3644

WEBSITE: www.iap.ie

British Library Cataloguing in Publication Data
An entry can be found on request

ISBN 978-0-7165-3341-3 (cloth)
ISBN 978-0-7165-3341-2
ISBN 978-0-7165-3342-1 (paper)
ISBN 978-0-7165-3342-9

Library of Congress Cataloging-in-Publication Data
An entry can be found on request

Typeset in 10.5/13pt Palatino by FiSH Books, Enfield, Middx.
Printed by MPG Books Ltd, Bodmin, Cornwall.

For Monica, Neil and Lorraine,
and in memory of Dennis

[It] is human beings who are, in the ultimate analysis, the
subjects of history, despite their appearance as 'catatonics'.

Luisa Passerini

Contents

Foreword

Despite considerable research on twentieth-century Ireland, there are sections of its society which remain hidden from history. Yvonne McKenna, in *Made Holy: Irish Women Religious at Home and Abroad*, rescues from oblivion the lives of a group of Irish women particularly neglected. In selecting the period before and after the Second Vatican Council (1962–65) and in choosing a sample of thirty young Irish women who became members of religious orders that placed them in an English environment and later, for fourteen sisters of her chosen sample, in mission enterprises in Africa, Asia and Latin America, McKenna presents a complex and vivid narrative of less travelled roads.

The population census of Ireland accorded professional status to members of religious orders in twentieth-century Ireland. As such, women religious formed the largest and most powerful group of professional women in Ireland. McKenna, however, sidesteps the task of attempting a national portrait that would require exhaustive research and would need to build on specialised research topics not yet undertaken. Instead, she examines a group of women in the Diaspora. In her Introduction, she writes that the origins of her study began while she herself was living in England, with a 'desire to research the experiences of Irish female emigrants to England', having observed the significance of religion in the lives of Irish women. From that vague starting point, her inquiry grew into a research project which involved two separate though related branches of inquiry: how did an Irish woman come to be a sister or nun (the terms are interchangeable) living in England and what were the experiences of migration for Irish women religious in England and the missions? All her other questions, including the sisters' reflections when they retuned to Ireland, derived from this initial two-step exercise.

McKenna points out that her examination of Irish women religious in the period she reviews is not so much about Catholic sisters or nuns as it is about women and the specific roles they adopted. She offers her study as an exercise in identity-formation. It is much more than that, of course, but she aims to explore the 'ways in which Irish women religious have inhabited, negotiated and contested a sense of self as Irish, as women, as Catholics and as religious. Using the methodology of oral history, the taped recording of a face-to-face conversation, McKenna raises intriguing and important questions: for instance, are the responses to her inquiry coloured by race, by ethnicity, or even, subconsciously, by colonial inferiority, expressed in the give-away Irish 'brogue' or accent. Read all of *Made Holy*, including the footnotes!

This is one of the few studies I know that attempts to uncover the mentality of Irish women religious in England, an invisible and largely overlooked group. In so doing, McKenna joins a widening collection of studies that are coming-into-being of a new historical narrative. Her book takes Suellen Hoy's 'The Journey Outward: the recruitment and emigration of Irish religious women to the United States 1812-1914' into new territory.[1] Similarly, Deirdre McMahon's investigation of the mission of the Irish Presentation Sisters in India (a research project Yvonne McKenna is also involved in) makes an interesting contrast to the diaries of Nora Prediville and Alice Nolan, two Kerry girls who travelled to New Orleans in the late 1880s to enter a convent of white and mainly Irish women in a racially-segregated city.[2]

The women in McKenna's study come from a society where Catholic values were foundational to Irish identity as they understood it. Their pre-Vatican families and neighbours regarded religious vocation as a normal calling in a society where the vocational element was an important one in career choices. She explains, 'Vocations for the religious life in the period the women of this study entered were understood as a calling that was extended to some, though not all, individuals'. McKenna captures the mood of those pivotal years around the Second Vatican Council as she follows here women religious into self-imposed exile and listens to them as older women reflecting on their experiences in England and as missionaries. This is a book where the voices of those who inhabit the pages linger in the memory long after the reader has put the book aside.

Margaret MacCurtain
June 2006

NOTES

1   S. Hoy 'The Journey Out: the Recruitment and Emigration of Irish
    Religious Women to the United States, 1812-1914', *Journal of
    Women's History*, 6, 4 (1995), pp. 64–98.
2   McMahon, D. 'Irish Catholic missionaries in India, an oral
    history', lecture given to the National Library of Ireland History
    Society, 15 February 2006. S. Hoy and M. MacCurtain *From Dublin
    to New Orleans: The Journey of Nora and Alice* (Dublin: Attic Press,
    1994).

Acknowledgements

This book is based on the oral history testimonies of thirty Irish women religious and I take pleasure in acknowledging the debt owed to each of them, for giving so generously of their time and for making the collection of their narratives such a hugely interesting, exciting and enjoyable experience. I hope this book does some justice to their fascinating stories.

Since first conceiving of this project for a doctoral thesis, through to finishing it during the course of post-doctoral research, there were many others who provided help and support. In England, I am very grateful to Maria Luddy and Caroline Wright, whose guidance and encouragement played no small part in the completion of the original thesis. I am grateful also to colleagues and friends at Warwick University including Joan Haran, Marsha Henry, Anne-Marie Kramer, Joanna Liddle, Terry Lovell, Gilma Madrid and Marianne Tortell and to Annie Phizacklea and Bronwen Walter for turning a daunting prospect into an almost relaxing and enjoyable experience. Special thanks are also due to Ewan Pearson and members of the WOIRN, especially Louise Ryan.

Back home, an IRCHSS Government of Ireland Research Fellowship enabled me to continue my research at the University of Limerick and I acknowledge gratefully the support of the Centre for Women's Studies at UL. Most especially, I am indebted to Breda Gray for her insightful perspectives and unflinching encouragement, and also her sense of humour. Beyond academia, I am thankful to all in Belmarino and its diaspora, as well as 11 Thirlestane Terrace, and to Aisling Dillon, Nadine Early and Eoin Ó Broin for helpful comments on earlier drafts and entirely unrelated matters.

Parts of Chapters 2, 4 and 5 have been published previously. A section of Chapter 2 was first published as 'A Gendered Revolution: Vatican II and Irish Women Religious' *Irish Feminist Review* 1, 1

(January 2006), pp. 75–93. A version of a section of Chapter 4 was first published as 'Forgotten Migrants: Irish Women Religious in England, 1930s–1960s' in *The International Journal of Population Geography* 9, (2003) pp. 295–308, while a section of Chapter 5 was first published as 'Entering Religious Life, Claiming Subjectivity: Irish Nuns, 1930s–1960s', *Women's History Review*, vol. 15 no. 2, April 2006, pp. 189–211. All reprinted by permission and with thanks.

Introduction

'We need to hear the voices of women religious, the self
which is no longer annalist but the *subject* of the testimony'[1]

The first post-independence census taken of the Irish Free State
population in 1926 recorded a figure of 9,564 female religious – nuns
and sisters, choir and lay[2] – living in the twenty-six counties, a further
279 in the six counties of Northern Ireland. At the time, this
represented almost seventy per cent of the total number of religious,
male and female, then resident in Ireland. Between the foundation of
the state and the fiftieth commemoration of the 1916 Rising, the
number of Irish women entering religious life rose continuously and
by the late 1960s their number had increased to almost 15,500.[3] In
addition, there were, it was estimated, a further 15,000 Irish nuns
living as members of both Irish and foreign congregations outside
Ireland, throughout the Irish and European diaspora and on the
mission fields of Africa, Asia and Latin America.[4] As the census in
Ireland considers religious life to be an occupation in itself, and
accords religious professional status, for much of the twentieth
century women religious formed the largest and most powerful group
of professional women in Ireland. Though their number has been in
decline since the latter 1960s, at the close of the twentieth century
there were still over 10,000 nuns living in Ireland.

There are several reasons why women religious should form a
vital part of the study of twentieth-century society and womanhood
in Ireland, its diaspora and beyond. These include the number of
Irish women who entered religious life, the role they have played in
the provision of health, education and welfare, their significance in
the development of the Irish state and its national identity and the
fact that that convents provided a means of training, education,
travel and in- and out-migration for women. And yet, they remain
curiously under-explored. Indeed, until now, no full-length study on
Irish nuns in the twentieth century existed. While filling an
increasing amount of space on the shelves of university libraries as

1

the subject of under- and post-graduate theses, research on Irish nuns in the twentieth century remains curiously thin on the ground, especially regarding availability to the general public, beyond the hallowed walls of academia. Notwithstanding the letters, memoirs and memories nuns have left behind, the correspondence and conversations they continue to have, in fact we know very little about a group of women who have touched the lives, indirectly if not directly, of the vast majority of Irish women, if not Irish men also, as well as the lives of a significant number of non-Irish people. Though nuns were a common and familiar sight in Ireland and else- where throughout the last century, a much utilised icon of Ireland, Irishness and Irish womanhood, in reality we know very little about their personal lives and experiences therein. This book marks a first step towards alleviating these lacunae in our knowledge.

As Margaret MacCurtain has pointed out, women religious represent numerous, if not endless, possibilities for the researcher.[5] There are the obvious historical biographies of individual founders. In addition, religious, their convents and associated institutions are a rich resource for exploring work, work practices and management; the development of health, education and welfare services; state and semi-state bodies and infrastructure; religio-state relations, religious architecture, spirituality. Migration, class, elitism and the family are other less obvious areas that would be well served by attention to religious life.

Then there are the women themselves. The individuals who entered religious life worked in various forms of employment, lived in convents and religious houses of varying size, in numerous locations at home and abroad. Based on the collected oral testimonies of thirty Irish women religious, it is women religious themselves who form the focus of this enquiry. Shifting the balance from icon to person, its aim is to give voice to women generally ignored in explorations of Irish womanhood and to hear them speak about aspects of their lives of which women's few religious leave public record. Drawing on their oral histories, this book explores what the women's narratives reveal about the their experiences of being women, of being Irish women and of being Irish women religious, both inside and outside Ireland.

The genesis of this book lay in a desire, while living there, to research the experiences of Irish female emigrants to England.[6] A rudimentary literature review had underlined the significance of religion as a theme in the lived experience of Irish women, regardless of their particular religious beliefs or absence thereof. From this grew a more specific interest in women religious themselves, truly overlooked in the then limited sources, still overlooked in the now much larger body of material that exists on Irish migration to Britain.[7] As part of that study, in addition to Irish women religious living in England, the narratives of Irish sisters who had returned to live in Ireland were collected. As is often the case, this did not add the desired 'finishing touch' to that research but rather served to open up several new lines of enquiry which became the focus of a second piece of research, undertaken upon my own return to Ireland, to collect oral history testimonies from returned Irish female missionary religious. This book, then, is the result of two separate though related inquiries which together offer a picture beyond the initial scope of each. That objective was, very simply, to ask of one group: how did you come to be an Irish nun living in England? To ask of the other: What drew you to the missions, what were your experiences of them and what has been your experience of returning to live in Ireland? From these two starting points, all other questions fell.

Perhaps less simply, this is a book about identity. More specifically, it is about subjectivity and identity formation, about the ways in which Irish women religious have inhabited, negotiated and contested a sense of self as Irish, as women, as Catholics and as religious. It is about how they have done this over the course of their lives and in the context of the societies in which they have lived. It looks at the complex ways in which subjectivities are formed and displayed, taking account of the role the women play in constructing a self identity, as well as other contributing factors, including how the women feel positioned by others, their socio-historical situation, the cultural and political climate in which they live. In addition to exploring the inter-dynamics and occasional tensions that occur within and between subjectivities, this book is equally concerned to examine the connection between identity formation and context, without suggesting a determining relationship between the two. Such is the importance of context that place is given special attention. In this case, specific places: Ireland, England, the missions.

But this is not to deter the reader! It is merely a high-falutin' way of saying what has already been said: that the main enquiry of this book is to explore the experiences of a group of Irish women religious, and their various identities, at home and abroad. This book does not seek to deconstruct gendered, ethnic, religious or migrant identities as concepts but to investigate further the lived reality of these identities. In as much as it does this, it is a book about Irishness, womanhood, and Irish womanhood both within Ireland and outside it. As it relates to these themes, and in exploring them, this book focuses on several aspects of the women's lives: their background and training, their working lives and spirituality, their relationship with congregation, co-religious, family and friends.

Methodology is a bit of an ugly word. It suggests an almost purely scientific approach which belies the very human basis of this research. Although all religious communities are required by law to maintain archives (which they do, many to an exceptionally high standard), these were unlikely to house the kind of personal information this research sought to uncover. Therefore, women religious themselves were asked to be involved by consenting to take part in one or more semi-structured, conversational-style interviews which more often than not began with one or other of the questions posed above.[8]

Certain criticisms have been levied against oral history as a method of historical research. One such criticism is that it is particularly open to bias, omission and distortion. In fact, no form of record is 'pure', capable of offering a truth untouched by author, intended audience or context. Before they are written about, events are first seen or experienced and so can be distorted before they are even committed to paper. In response to such criticisms, however, oral historians have become more aware and more reflexive about the production of knowledge within their discipline and become more accountable as a result.

On the other hand, there were many appealing aspects about oral history. As Paul Thompson has pointed out, one of the great contributions made by oral history has been its role in democratising history through admitting the voices of those traditionally excluded from the 'mainstream'.[9] Certainly, it was the way that oral history had been used with respect to including women in history that particularly impressed me.[10] Feminist researchers have embraced oral history because it integrates women's lives and experiences, traditionally ignored or obscured, into scholarship, testing reigning definitions of what is 'important' and 'worthy' of study. Oral history puts women's voices at the centre of research, helps shape its agenda and enables gender to be used as a category of analysis.[11] As the purpose of my research was to uncover the voices of women religious, oral history seemed the obvious choice – particularly since religious tend not to keep public account of their personal lives and were, until the latter decades of the twentieth century, specifically trained *not* to think or talk about themselves.[12]

Equally appealing was oral history's close connection to subjectivity, precisely the area I wanted to explore. As Alessandro Portelli has said, 'The unique and precious element which oral sources force upon the historian and which no other sources possess in equal measure ... is the speaker's subjectivity ... They tell us not just what people did, but what they wanted to do, what they believed they were doing, what they now think they did.'[13] Significantly, oral history tells us less about events themselves than about their meaning and how it is individuals experience and make sense of them in their own lives. Experiences are central to the construction of self and it is through exploring women's experiences that we might better understand how women occupy the category 'woman'.[14] Like Beverly Skeggs, I did not believe that experience created or fixed subjectivity or that it could offer some essential or authentic 'truth' about either womanhood or the self, but rather that it 'informs our take up and production of [subject] positions'.[15]

Oral history is also, of course, fundamentally about memory. It involves giving – and, in effect, creating – a version of the past. Using these terms might suggest I am talking about inventing stories, telling tales. This is far from the case. It is an acknowledgement, however, of the dynamics of oral history and the reality that the product of the oral history encounter, the interview itself, is always contingent upon a range of factors from the mood of the interviewer and the respondent and the relationship between them, to the present circumstances of the interviewee and their assessment, at that moment, of their own past. Added to this are a host of other mitigating factors too numerous to mention, even if they could all be identified. This is also true of other forms of record, the difference being that oral histories tend not to be re-edited by their subjects and remain, therefore, fixed in one moment.[16] But oral history is no less valuable because of this. What it prompts in addition is to think more deeply about memory, about how people remember and why they remember certain events or moments, the tropes and devices they use to explain or make sense of their own memories to themselves and others. The fact that memory is always a 'looking back' does affect the hows and whys of remembering, but it does so without negating the value of what is said.

Few of the thirty women who took part in this study had experienced accounting for themselves in the manner an interview requires, had, as it were, fixed accounts of themselves to offer the relative stranger. That said, we all have 'versions' of ourselves or events in our memory bank, which we tap into. These can be challenged in the course of an interview when something is asked from a different perspective, one our particular version might not have taken account of. Our experience of an event, or memory of it, might have been formed in the context of one subjectivity over another. Thus, for example, an individual's experience of migration might be different depending on their assessment of it as an Irish person, as a woman or as a religious. Even when there were 'stories to tell', and these were told, different renderings of them could be revealed through the course of the same or subsequent interviews.

This book spans several decades, a timescale dictated by the age of the women themselves, who were born between 1911 and 1950 and were aged between 49 and 86 when interviewed.[17] It is a timeframe that incorporates several key moments in the history of Ireland, of Irish women and of religious. Over the period, (partial) Irish independence was achieved, attendant nation building taking place in its wake. The country witnessed economic boom and bust and boom again. It experienced waves of large-scale emigration in the 1950s and 1980s, smaller-scale immigration of Irish nationals in the 1970s and, more recently, increased immigration, including the immigration of non-Irish nationals. The Catholic Church and Catholicism grew and then declined in both stature and power as the state began to urbanise, modernise and secularise.

The women who took part in this study were as much part of this society as they were a product of it. Their entry into the convent was to some degree representative of the more general pattern of Irish women's entry into religious life. Five of them entered in the 1930s, nine in the 1940s, eight in the 1950s, seven in the 1960s (although only one in the second half of that decade) and one in the 1970s. However, in many other respects the women were *not* representative. They did not represent all Irish women. Having remained within religious life, they did not represent all Irish women who entered into religious life during the period. Crucially, they did not represent all Irish women religious still within religious life. Drawing on the oral histories of a self-selecting group of women religious, this book aims to tell much about the experiences of thirty women religious without ever claiming to be a definitive study of all religious or even of *these* women religious. The women's stories do reflect, however, on issues beyond themselves, even beyond religious life, to national identity, gendered structures within Irish society, the family, marriage and motherhood.

Aside from wanting to collect and examine the experiences of a group of women thus far overlooked in academic inquiries of Irish womanhood and migration, the research for this book did not begin with any agenda or hypothesis to test. Unavoidably, however, it was influenced by the role I played in the collection of the interviews and, naturally, my interpretation and analysis of them. Oral histories are, as such, jointly produced and it was for this reason, as much as in the interests of anonymity, that the women and their congregations, as well as some place names, are given pseudonyms.

Having transcribed the interviews, interpretation of them involved a dialogue between myself and the interview narratives, a process by which the women's accounts were transformed from spoken word into this, *my* book. The women and myself did not engage over the interview transcripts or my interpretation of them,[18] and I am sure that any further involvement on their part would have resulted in a very different written piece. As it stands, the interpretation is my own and I take full responsibility for it. There is no suggestion that this book represents the 'authentic' or 'true' voice of Irish women religious, or even the women religious who took part – nor was it the aim of the project to do so. More accurately, it is my interpretation of the partial accounts given by them, which I had helped to create. This is not to say, however, that the women did not influence how I interpreted their accounts. As Skeggs has said, 'their knowledge enabled my knowledge [and] I was constantly learning from them'.[19] Nor was it the case that I regarded the women as research 'objects'. Indeed, their subjectivity is something that is highlighted throughout the chapters that follow.[20]

The book is in four parts, which follow a largely chronological trajectory. Part I explores the women's lives before entering religious life, which they did between the ages of 17 and 28. A background chapter provides the context in which to place the women's accounts, upon which the second and all subsequent chapters are based. While not offering a complete analysis of events in Ireland between the 1910s and the 1960s, Chapter 1 offers a brief overview of the society in which the women were born and raised, influenced by topics and themes suggested within the interviews themselves. These include the significance of Catholicism in Ireland; the gendered nature of that society and the gendered structures at work within it; the lived realities of married motherhood for Irish women; and the extent to which national identity and emigration were elemental to the experience of growing up in the newly independent state. Chapter 2 explores the women's experience and interpretation of the society they lived in, their attraction to religious life and familial responses to their religious vocation.

Part II explores the women's entry into and life within religious life, which occurred predominantly in the pre-Vatican II era, during which a particularly strict and rule-bound form of governance prevailed. Chapter 3 explores how this system worked in practice and the women's retrospective judgement of it, as well as the difficulties and rewards they associated with it. How the women experienced this regime outside Ireland, how it was experienced differently by women in one place, and the implications of being closer to or further from the 'core' of the Roman Catholic Church is the focus of Chapter 4, which draws attention to important differences in the ways in which women occupy and assert an identity as 'religious' or 'missionary religious'.

Vatican II is the name given to the second meeting of the Catholic Church's Vatican Council, which took place between 1962 and 1965. It heralded a cycle of change and modernisation within the Church and a major reorganisation of the practise of Catholicism which particularly affected those who had taken vows to live within it. Vatican II was both a dominant theme and an important reference point in the women's narratives as well as an important prism through which to understand their accounts and is the focus of Part III. Chapter 5 explores the impact of Vatican II on the women's sense of self as religious, their individual and collective response to it and the contestations and negotiations that occurred around it, while Chapter 6 looks once more at the specificity of place, in particular the impact of Vatican II in England and on the missions. It also explores how the greater freedoms brought about within religious life did not always equate to greater liberty and could, in fact, expose inequalities which served to threaten the sense of community within congregation.

The final part, Part IV, brings the story back to Ireland. Chapters 7 and 8 explore the experiences of returning to Ireland for, respectively, women from England and the missions. They draw attention to the changes that have occurred both within Ireland and within the women themselves, altered as they have been by the personal journey each has made, and continues to make, out of and back to Ireland. Putting the emphasis on Ireland and Irishness in its many forms, the focus remains also on womanhood and religious identity. The chapters provide a neat but complicated finale: taking the reader back to where it all began, without any sense of returning to the beginning.

A random survey undertaken by myself during the course of writing this introduction collected the opinions of over 100 Irish people: men and women, of various ages, living both in Ireland and outside of it. In it, I asked respondents to tell me the one word they associated with nuns. I gave no suggestions except to outline that it could be a the first word that popped into their head, or one that came to them after deeper examination; it could be a noun, an adjective or a verb; a colour, an emotion, an expletive. Their personal reflections received revealed the myriad associations, many incompatible, that are made around women religious.

Associated with wisdom, power, knowledge and employment, religious are equally considered as innocents, unworldly, over-protected and idle. Remembered, both positively and negatively, as individuals, they tend also to be thought of as a collective, an indistinguishable, be-habited group who think and act in unison. Nuns are associated with achievement, their own and others', as much as achievement inhibited, their own and others. They are seen as both the victims and perpetrators of repression and abuse; represent the seizure of opportunity as much as its denial. They are considered strict and harsh; friendly and maternal. They are loved and loathed; respected and dismissed. They conjure up feelings of safety, but also of fear. Significant to the past, they are deemed irrelevant in con-temporary Ireland, invisible in its future. They are strong and weak, meek and firm, caring and uncaring, dedicated and misguided. They are at once both intimately familiar and entirely remote.

Without making any claims to scientific legitimacy – or, more importantly, suggesting that religious could be 'summed up' in one word – this informal poll served to highlight the many and varied opinions people hold about religious, a fact also evidenced in the responses received when I have told people I was writing a book about nuns. While few have been shy to share their opinions, most were more interested to find out what *I* had found out, what truth I might have to impart about a group of women who have had a profound impact on Ireland and beyond, but who remain at some level unknown and unknowable.

In the chapters that follow, the reader will be introduced to thirty women religious from a range of congregations, whose experiences vary as much as could be expected of any group of women. Through their stories, the reader will be informed and enlightened, have their opinions confirmed, reinforced and challenged. There are times, perhaps, the reader will be moved by the women's testimonies, find themselves sympathising with one, some or all of their accounts. Likely, there are times they will be frustrated or angered by them, as much by the admissions as the omissions. Despite its limited aims, the value of this book will be limited further if the reader expects to find in these pages every individual religious they have ever known, every representation of religious life they ever conceived of. This book does not tell 'The Whole Story'. Rather, it attempts to tell a part of it, as all histories do. It provides a tentative first step towards uncovering the lives of a small number of a much larger group of women integral to but overlooked in studies of Irish history, Irish womanhood and Irish diaspora studies.

NOTES

1   M. MacCurtain, 'Late in the Field: Catholic Sisters in Twentieth-Century Ireland and the New Religious History', in M. O'Dowd and S. Wichert (eds) *Chattel, Servant or Citizen: Women's Status in Church, State and Society* (Belfast: Institute of Irish Studies, Queen's University, 1995), pp. 34–44, p. 43.

2   The terms 'nun' and 'sister' have distinct meanings in canon law (the law of the Catholic Church). Strictly speaking, nuns are members of religious orders, take formal vows and are enclosed while sisters are members of religious congregations who take simple vows and are not enclosed. Previously referred to as 'active' religious, sisters are allowed to work and move outside their congregation. The distinction between the terms is rarely maintained in the vernacular, however, and for stylistic reasons, 'female religious', 'woman religious', 'sister', 'nun', and their plurals, will be used interchangeably throughout this book, although its focus will be on 'active' religious.

3   This number is for the island of Ireland. Figures of religious have been collected from the following sources: the 'Survey of Catholic Clergy and Religious Personal, 1971' carried out by the Research and Development Unit of the Catholic Communications Institute of Ireland and published in *Social Studies/Irish Journal of Sociology*, 1, 1 (1972), pp. 137–234; the Census of Ireland 1926–1991; and the Catholic Directory 1922–2004. (The Research and

Development Unit and the Catholic Directory collect figures for the island of Ireland while the Census records only that of the twenty-six counties).

4   'Survey of Catholic Clergy and Religious', p. 205.

5   MacCurtain, 'Late in the Field', p. 38.

6   A note on terms: the focus of my initial inquiry was limited to the experiences of women in England, specifically within the context of relations between England and Ireland and constructions of Irishness and Englishness in and between each place. Though, as Bronwen Walter has argued, 'the identity of Englishness has colonised Britishness' (B. Walter, *Outsiders Inside, Whiteness, Place and Irish Women* (London: Routledge, 2001), p. 94), 'England' and 'Englishness' are more specific and distinct terms than 'Britain' and 'Britishness'. Throughout this book, I use both terms but try to make clear why I use one term over another. If Britain is used in a quote to refer more specifically to England, I have let it stand. When I talk about state relations, I use the term Britain rather than England. However, when referring to post-colonial Irish identity and attitudes towards the former colonial power, I use the term England because it was England that was seen as the traditional 'enemy' and it was in relation to a particular notion of England and Englishness that Ireland and Irishness was constructed in the nineteenth and twentieth centuries (although England/Englishness and Ireland/ Irishness were not constructed only in relation to each other).

There is also a politics around the terms emigration and migration, as well as some debate concerning the efficacy of each term when referring to Ireland. Given the changed relationship between Ireland and Britain, there is also some confusion about how it might best be applied to discuss movement between the two before and after 1921. Migration, according to its dictionary definition, means 'to pass from one place to another' (Chambers, 1998). Emigration, according to the same dictionary, implies movement from 'one country or state to another as a place of abode'. Migration can, of course, also mean this.

In the Irish context, David Lloyd chooses to use the term emigration because he believes it evokes memories 'of famine, of eviction, of dispossession and of economic depression, [serving as] a reminder of the political and economic legacies of colonialism' ('Making Sense of the Dispersal', *Irish Reporter*, 13, 1 (1994), pp. 3–4, p. 4.). By contrast, Patrick O'Sullivan regards emigration as too 'emotionally freighted a term' (*Irish Women and Irish Migration, Volume 4, The Irish World Wide Series* (London: Leicester University Press, 1995), p. 2), and there is no doubt that it is a loaded word in Ireland, having chiefly negative associations of forced exile. Thus, O'Sullivan considers migration a more appropriate and inclusive term, one that can incorporate both in- and out-migration. Likewise, David Fitzpatrick considers migration capable of encompassing the complexities of movement with the continued possibility of further movement and/or return (*Oceans of Consolation, Personal Accounts of Irish Migration to Australia* (Cork: Cork University Press, 1994), p. 534.

In this book, both migration and emigration will be used although the latter will be used more often, especially to refer to movement across national borders for the purposes of changing abode. All the women of this study who left Ireland for England did so after 1921, eliminating that confusion. While cognisant of the associations around emigration (indeed, wanting to explore them), using emigration as it is popularly conceived, but in reference to a group it is not generally attributed to provides an interesting perspective from which to consider the term and its usage.

7   See, for example, B. Gray, *Women and the Irish Diaspora* (London: Routledge, 2004) and Walter, *Outsiders Inside*.

8   In total, thirty women were interviewed, between one and three times. A total of forty-eight interviews took place which, when transcribed, ran to over half a million words. Respondents were found by sending letters and making follow-up telephone calls to a number of congregations in London and Dublin. The sample was mostly self-selecting: either the women responded directly to a letter or 'phone call or were co-opted by those already involved. A few women were asked by their superiors to take part.

9   P. Thompson, *The Voice of the Past, Oral History* (Oxford: Oxford University Press, 1988), pp. 101–150 (first published 1978.

10   See, for example, E. Roberts, *A Woman's Place, An Oral History of Working-Class Women 1890–1940* (Oxford: Basil Blackwell, 1984) and *Women and Families, An Oral History 1940–1970*, (Oxford: Blackwell, 1995)

11   See, for example, J. Sangster, 'Telling our Stories: Feminist Debates and the Use of Oral History', *Women's History Review*, 3, 1 (1994), pp. 5–28.

12   A chance discovery, while reading a rule book (the written constitution each religious congregation is required by canon law to have) brought home the extent of this. *The Directory of the Religious of the Congregation de Notre-Dame de Sion* was dated 1946 but was in use until the late 1960s. In the margin of one page, in the same pencil script used to make amendments in the book (thus suggesting it was the hand of whomever religious once used it), a note was written. It read: 'try never to bring yourself into your conversations'.

13   A. Portelli, 'The Peculiarities of Oral History', *History Workshop*, 12 (1981), pp. 96–107, pp 99–100.

14   See, for example, J. W. Scott, 'The Evidence of Experience', *Critical Inquiry*, 178, 3, (1991), pp. 773–797 and B. Skeggs, *Formations of Class and Gender, Becoming Respectable* (London: Sage, 1997).

15   Skeggs, *Formations of Class*, p. 27.

16 This is not necessarily the case. The same and subsequent interviews often provide an opportunity, by accident or design, to re-edit.

17 See Appendix I for brief biographies.

18 Those women who were involved in the initial research did receive a copy of the doctoral thesis, after it had been completed and were invited to respond.

19 Skeggs, *Formations of Class*, p. 30.

20 If the subjectivities of the women who took part in this study, as well as my interpretation of them, form the basis of what follows, then I need to account for my subjectivity also. My material background is Irish and middle-class. I was raised Catholic, attended Catholic schools but am not practising Catholic. To this I can add my experiences of being an Irish woman in Britain and a returned Irish migrant. Being an Irish woman in London, I became more aware than was ever the case before how significant (though not how *exactly*) my background as a Catholic and my position as a white, Irish, non-national was to my experience of England. Returning to Ireland in 2003, I became aware of being Irish in Ireland and the complexities of returning to a much-changed nation. The significance of my gender had been something I had ruminated on for some time already, having undertaken both an academic and personal interest in feminism. This interest no doubt informed much of my intellectual biography as well as my approach to research. While these are the points of my material and intellectual biography that I can name, I am sure there are many other relevant factors that are invisible to me.

Part I

Ireland 1910s–1960s

CHAPTER 1

Irish Society, 1910s–1960s

'The State recognises that by her life within the home, woman gives to the State a support without which the common good cannot be achieved' [1]

INTRODUCTION

Through their oral histories, this book looks back over the lives of thirty women who were born in Ireland between 1910 and 1950 and entered religious life between 1930 and 1970. It is often said that the past is a foreign land, where people do things differently. With this in mind, it seems necessary, before considering the accounts of the women themselves, to look for a moment at the society they were born and grew up in and, in particular, the issues, events and process that helped shape their lives within it. To that end, this chapter provides a general historical overview of certain aspects of that Irish society, one that is informed by the narratives themselves and the topics the women choose to cover in delivering and constructing them. Of necessity, this chapter offers a limited outline, being no more than an attempt to give flesh to the bones of the women's testimonies without trying to explain, or explain away, those narratives.

NATIONAL IDENTITIES, SYMPATHIES AND SENTIMENT

During the period in which the women of this study were born and grew up, the position and status of Ireland changed fundamentally. When the oldest respondent, Bernadette, was born in 1911, Ireland was still officially part of the United Kingdom of Great Britain and Ireland. Following rebellion in 1916 and a war of independence fought against Britain between 1919 and 1921, a treaty was signed at the end of 1921 which gave partial independence to twenty-six of the thirty-two counties of Ireland. The remaining six counties in the north-east, known as Northern Ireland, remained under British rule. The legal connection between Britain and Ireland was challenged by successive Irish governments and in 1949, one year before the youngest respondent, Josephine, was born, the Irish Free State, as the twenty-six counties had been known, became a completely independent republic.

Of the women in this study, only Bernadette had any living memory of Irish independence. The rest of the women were born either in the heady period between 1918 and 1921 when independence was being fought for or after it had been achieved. They were too young to remember the actual and violent transfer of power from one government to another. As will be seen, however, they were each influenced by attitudes towards England that took hold in the newly post-colonial society and an Irish national identity that was defined in opposition to England, as *not* English, if not anti-English.[2]

CATHOLICISM AND THE CATHOLIC CHURCH IN IRELAND

Catholicism had played a vital role in the struggle for independence and the construction of a national identity in the late nineteenth and early twentieth century. When independence was achieved, it became one of the most important ways of defining what it meant to be Irish and was equally important as an organising structure in the society that was shaped in its wake. Catholicism influenced and helped shape not only spiritual but social, cultural, political and familial forms in Irish society and for several decades following independence, was regarded as a cornerstone of Irish identity. Numerically, Catholics have dominated the population of Southern Ireland. When independence was achieved, almost 93 per cent of the population were Catholic, rising to 95 per cent in the 1960s. In 2002, still almost 90 per cent of the population of Ireland were registered as Catholic in census returns.[3]

The regulation of Catholic devotion

Although commonly referred to by the women of this study as the 'traditional' Irish faith, Irish Catholicism was a more recent construction than their use of the term suggested. The religion of the masses, which had been a mix of quasi-pagan, quasi-Christian practices, was formalised and regulated only in the nineteenth century, particularly under a movement known latterly, though still debated by historians, as the devotional revolution. It is estimated that in the 1830s, only 30 per cent of Irish Catholics attended mass. By 1895, this had risen to over 90 per cent.[4] More in addition to, rather than distinct from, formal religious practice, Catholicism also began in the nineteenth century to be more closely associated with an Irish national identity that stood in opposition to English Protestantism.

Catholic social teaching was reflected in the legislation of the newly independent state. J. H. Whyte gives several examples of laws introduced following direct consultation with or recommendation from bishops and describes a Catholic moral code as being 'enshrined in the law of the state'.[5] Examples include censorship laws introduced in the 1920s, prohibition of divorce (1925) and the Criminal Law Amendment Act of 1935, which, among other things, made it an offence to import or sell contraception in Ireland.[6] Catholic principles were also reflected in the 1937 Constitution of Ireland, which recognised the 'special position of the Holy Catholic Apostolic and Roman Catholic Church as the guardian of the Faith professed by the great majority of the citizens'.[7]

While the influence of the Catholic Church in Ireland was significant, it was not total. The Catholic Church was never established' as the Church of England was in England and confusion even surrounded the juridical meaning of its special position.[8] In fact, the Catholicity of Southern Ireland should be regarded not solely in terms of the strength of the Church but as reflecting the religious principles and beliefs of a significant portion of the population and, vitally, those in power. As Whyte argues, it was not only that Ireland was predominantly Catholic but that for much of this period Catholics in Ireland were 'committed and practising.[9]

The Catholic Church in Ireland took its self-appointed position as moral guardian of the state seriously and asserted its right to prescribe social behaviour by instigating or involving itself in initiatives designed to curb what it saw as increased incidences of immorality. Chrystel Hug suggests that after independence, immorality replaced England as Ireland's 'enemy' and, quoting Margaret O'Callaghan, described the Church's response to this as 'almost hysterical puritanism'.[10] Between the formation of the state and the 1960s, the Church campaigned on several issues and was actively opposed to jazz music and dancing, unregulated dance halls, many published works of literature, foreign films, public courting and styles of dress deemed unsuitable. These campaigns were directed against what the Church considered to be the importation of anti-Christian, foreign lifestyles, against which it posited its own specifically Irish model of morality.[11]

J. S. Donnelly Jnr argues, convincingly, that the devotional revolution in Ireland reached its peak between 1930 and 1960, drawing on the Church's hugely successful campaign of Marian worship in the period to support his argument.[12] Certainly, the women of this study grew up in a period of very strong Marian devotion, although the worship of Mary was neither a twentieth-century nor an Irish invention. Organised events included public prayer meetings and processions, some of which were attended by several thousand people, and pilgrimages to Fatima, Knock and Lourdes. In addition, the Church espoused individual and familial prayer to the Virgin in the form of rosaries and novenas.

As was the case elsewhere, the Catholic Church in Ireland drew upon the figure of the Virgin Mary as a model for Irish women to emulate. This contributed to an idealisation of womanhood that was both intimately associated with motherhood and detached from sex or sexuality. The Virgin had been central to notions of Irish womanhood in the nineteenth century,[13] but she became more pertinent in the post-independence period as the Church became increasingly concerned with morality, especially female morality. The Church in Ireland was particularly anxious about the low and late rate of marriage, which was causing young people to spend longer periods of time single, outside the sanctity of marriage and in danger from corrupting behaviour. It also became increasingly concerned with the moral fate of Irish women emigrants.[14]

A church-going people

Acceptable social practice in Ireland became so not solely because the Church decided that was how it should be but because society accepted this in return. Although the general Catholic public were not as vociferous as the Church in campaigning around issues of morality, they tended not to publicly question the Church's authority over it either. Inevitably, there were those who dissented, but this was generally done in private, hidden away to avoid what could be brutal consequences. Women who contravened sexual norms faced 'exceptionally severe censure from public opinion'[15], while those who became pregnant outside marriage received no welfare, were stigmatised by illegitimacy laws (as were their children) and were often excluded by a judgmental society.[16] Unmarried pregnant women were usually sent away by parents to give birth elsewhere. Publicly, the Irish people had to be seen to be behaving in accordance with the Church's pronouncements. What is more, local communities could prove more effective than legislation at policing themselves, ostracising individuals who were seen to behave in ways contrary to social norms.

Seeds of change

If the 1930s to the 1960s marked the zenith of the devotional revolution in Ireland, it was in the 1960s that it began to decline. Socio-economic and attitudinal changes in Irish society combined with modernisation within the Catholic Church itself to create the conditions by which this could occur. Internally, the Church was transformed by the Second Vatican Council, which met between 1962 and 1965.[17] The aims of Vatican II, as it became known, were to identify, modernise and clarify the position of the Catholic Church with respect to the changed and changing realities of the modern world. Arising from the Vatican Council meetings, the Church issued sixteen documents promulgating its position on various issues from ecumenicalism to religious freedom. Significantly, the status of the laity was improved and recommendations were made to the clergy to be less authoritarian with their flock. Vatican II inspired more open and frank discussion within Catholicism in Ireland and led to what one of the women in this study described as a 'lighter' attitude to Catholicism.[18] As will be seen, it had an especially profound effect on those in religious life.

The other significant development occurred within Irish society itself. The economic fortunes of independent Ireland, depressed since its inception, began to take a turn for the better due to policies introduced after Sean Lemass assumed leadership of Fianna Fail and the government in 1959. In the 1960s, Ireland experienced record economic growth, rising employment levels, spreading urbanisation, increased consumerism and reduced emigration. By the end of the decade, it had become, for the first time, a predominantly urban, rather than rural, country. Social changes, as they often do, accompanied economic change. One of the great catalysts for this was television, which served to bring issues previously confined to the domestic and private sphere into the open, including marital relations and sexuality. In contrast with earlier periods, there was a marked increase in the marriage rate, which rose by 20 per cent between 1966 and 1970. Fertility rates, previously the highest in Europe, declined by one-third over the course of the decade.[19]

These demographic changes reflected changing attitudes amongst Irish Catholics. More and more women were, for instance, using contraception.[20] The 1960s was, in essence, the first decade of the twentieth century in which a significant number of Irish Catholics began to openly question the authority of the Church, especially in matters considered private, and to make decisions about personal morality that were at odds with the teachings of the Church. As Terence Brown describes, religion was becoming less an 'all embracing reality within which life must be ordered, an immutable aspect of Irish national identity', and more 'a personal expression of individual communities and values'.[21]

Attitudinal change, especially that which occurred in the 1960s, should not be exaggerated. The Catholic population in Ireland remained more publicly devout than in other western European countries and the Church continued to maintain a position of strength within Irish society, especially with respect to education and health. There was, however, a perceptible alteration in the position of the Church which was, significant to this study, also reflected in changing attitudes towards religious life.

WOMEN AND IRISH SOCIETY

It would be impossible to précis, either at one moment or over the period in which the women of this study were born and grew up, 'the' position of women in Ireland. To do so would suggest an homogeneity of experience, aspiration and access to resources which could never exist. Notwithstanding this, however, it is possible to explore dominant ideologies surrounding womanhood that held currency during the period, as well as some of the material realities of women's lives.

Legislation, limitation and opportunity

Despite the role women played in the struggle for independence,[22] their claim to equal citizenship following it was challenged by various pieces of gender-specific legislation which assumed women's primary place within the home and sought to protect it. Examples of this include the Civil Service Amendment Act (1925), which gave the civil service the power to limit women's access to more senior positions within it and legislation introduced in 1927 which automatically exempted women from jury service (although they were able to volunteer their services if they so wished). Significantly, the debates that surrounded the jury bills, both within and outside parliament, focused on women's 'natural role' and the limited extent to which it was claimed women could be expected to fulfil the obligations of citizenship given their commitments in the home.[23]

This is not to suggest that women were completely denied, or allowed themselves to be denied, any public role whatsoever. In 1922, early by European standards, women over the age of twenty-one in Ireland were given the right to vote equally with men. Although no woman held a ministerial post in either the Free State or the Republic until 1979, women were involved in formal politics as members of both houses of the Oireachtas (the Irish Parliament) throughout the period and organised themselves politically on various issues including the living conditions of women in Ireland.[24]

Legislation was also introduced which limited women's access to paid employment. In addition to the Civil Service Act, in 1933, a bar on married women's employment was introduced in many industries, including public sector employment. Two years later, the Conditions of Employment Act gave certain industries the right to impose a maximum proportion of women workers or prohibit them entirely if deemed necessary. In 1938, the statutory age of retirement for women was lowered from 65 to 60 but remained unchanged for men. A 1953 Department of Education memo on women and public sector teaching stated that 'the care and direction of a home and the rearing of family constitute a whole-time assignment sufficient to tax the strength and energy of the normal woman' adding that pregnant teachers would create an 'unhealthy curiosity' amongst school children.[25] The suggestion was that marriage and motherhood (rarely was there a distinction made between the two) were not only physically but morally incompatible with paid employment.

Although schooling was compulsory between the ages of 6 and 14, and provided free of charge, secondary and further education was reserved for those who could afford it. Free, post-primary education was not introduced until 1966. While no formal obstacles with the exception of resources prevented women entering the professions, research shows that promotion to higher levels was more difficult for women than men.[26]

Until the 1950s, women who were 'gainfully employed' worked predominantly in agriculture or domestic service, though these industries had been in decline since the 1920s. In fact, the number and proportion of women in paid work declined overall in the three decades prior to the 1960s. Though women's employment in some sectors did increase over the period, this was not sufficient to absorb the number of women leaving or choosing not to enter agriculture and domestic service.[27]

Agriculture and domestic service were predominantly low-paid, low-status jobs so it was not surprising that women were choosing to leave these areas of employment. At the same time, however, alternative industries were not being created in which women might be employed. Until the 1960s, Ireland was a predominantly rural society and opportunities for women to take on respectable and acceptable work were limited. Moreover, the policies pursued by successive governments were not geared towards creating jobs for women, though there was a demand for them. In the 1920s, and increasingly thereafter, women were already choosing emigration over low-status and under-paid jobs in Ireland.[28]

In contrast to other European states, the number and proportion of women 'engaged in home-duties' in Ireland, which is to say women working in the home for no pay, including farmer's wives, rose between 1926 and 1961. Caitriona Clear cautions against assuming this to be the consequence of a monolithic gender ideology which forced women back into the home after independence. Highlighting that the numerical increase in women engaged in home duties was far less dramatic than was their decline in agriculture or domestic service, she argues that women were not, in fact, being *forced* back into the home but *choosing* to leave home-based employment, be it domestic or agricultural.[29]

It could be argued, however, that equivalent numbers of women were not engaged in home duties because it had become a less viable and, in some cases, less attractive option for women. The shift in farming methods from sub-division of land to impartible inheritance, which occurred in the wake of the Great Famine of the 1840s, meant that farms were usually passed on intact from father to son rather than divided up amongst siblings. Fewer women were inheriting land themselves and there were also fewer men inheriting land, with fewer eligible bachelors as a result. The lack of alternative employment in Ireland led to rising emigration amongst 'surplus' men and women. As many farmers were reluctant to pass on their land until late in life, inheriting sons could be middle-aged at least before they took over management of the farm and would be in a position to marry. Moreover, with generally only one farmhouse per farm, prospective wives faced sharing their new home with their in-laws.[30]

As a consequence, Irish marriage rates, until the 1960s, were among the lowest in the world, while the proportion of those never-married was amongst the highest. Although in the 1940s there was a surplus of single women relative to single male farmers in rural Ireland, by the 1950s women's migration to urban areas in Ireland and, more often, outside it had reversed this ratio.[31] Ironically, at a time when marriage and motherhood were idealised and enshrined in the constitution of the state, fewer women in Ireland were actually getting married.

The socio-economic advances of the 1960s improved women's opportunities for work and marriage. Industrialisation and urbanisation created jobs for men, but especially for women. The proportion of women in paid employment increased by 10 per cent in the 1960s, although more significant was women's movement into the newer industries and the fact that more married women were taking up paid employment.

Although women were not literally chased back into the home in the decades following independence, it is true to say that complementing ideologies, amongst them Catholic social teaching, nationalist rhetoric and idealised notions of womanhood, combined with the realities of a depressed economy to limit their opportunities outside it.[32] This is not to suggest, however, that opposition did not exist. Women, as well as some men, challenged constructions of womanhood publicly – and privately, in the form of leaving Ireland.[33] Marriage and motherhood was, however, the dominant form of womanhood.[34] It was idealised in society, enshrined in the Constitution and was the path followed by most women in Ireland. In the following section, some of the realities of motherhood in the period are explored.

Models of womanhood I: marriage and motherhood

Until recently, accepted wisdom suggested that the experience of life within the home for women between the 1930s and the 1960s was

chiefly negative due to the difficult conditions under which they
lived, women's low status within society and the prevalence of
patriarchy. It was considered especially so for rural women. Clear, on
the other hand, offers a more complex picture showing that there was
sympathy for women's position in Ireland amongst various sectors of
society, including some male politicians, and attempts, some
successful, to improve their situation.[35] While recognising the failure
of successive governments and Irish feminists to properly address
some of the main issues affecting women, including their health, she
challenges the notion that the 'woman of the house' was without
status or agency. Be that as it may, the reality was that for many
women, working in the home amounted to very hard work.

By 1946, the majority of urban homes had electricity but few rural
ones did, while fewer than 40 per cent of the population lived in urban
areas. The drive for rural electrification was successful, however, such
that by 1956 over half of rural homes were connected, although many
electrical household appliances remained prohibitively expensive.[36]
The speed with which rural Ireland was connected was not matched
by the introduction of piped water. In 1946, over 90 per cent of urban
homes had piped water, while more than one-third had a fixed bath.
By contrast, over 90 per cent of rural homes relied on a pump or well
for water and fewer than 5 per cent had a fixed bath.[37] Only one in five
rural homes had any form of toilet and just one in twenty had one
indoors.[38] The situation was slow to improve. By 1961, just over 12 per
cent of rural homes had piped water.[39] Ten years later, fewer than half
of rural homes were still without running water and one-third were
without a fixed bath.[40] The realities of cooking and cleaning in these
conditions, often for large families, would be arduous by modern
Western standards, though it should not be taken as read that urban
living was necessarily easier. The problems of overcrowding and bad
housing for those who lived on low incomes in urban areas could be
just as overwhelming, water equally heavy whether it was carried up
tenement stairs or from a local well.

Notwithstanding the recognition given to women as mothers in the
Constitution of 1937, very little practical support was offered to them
in the form of child allowance, health care or home help. In addition,
women had very few rights under family law, were not entitled to
welfare payments and were in a vulnerable position if their marriage
broke down. Over the period, attempts were made to ease the burden
women faced. Non-contributory widows' pensions were introduced

in 1936, although not for deserted wives until 1976.[41] Statutory weekly family allowance payable for all children after the second was introduced in 1944, though this was paid to the 'head of the household', who was, more often, male. In 1952, second children became eligible for allowance and in 1963 all children were included in the scheme.[42]

Without doubt, the most positive impact on women's living conditions in Ireland came as a result of the economic advances of the 1960s. Not only did a more buoyant economy stimulate urbanisation but it generated money which could be spent on improving homes or investing in modern conveniences.[43] Some women took on paid employment themselves, using the money they earned to improve their domestic situation.

The living conditions of women cannot tell us everything about the experience of marriage or motherhood, positive or negative, or about the levels of happiness within marriage. Nor is it the intention to suggest they could. The aim of this chapter is to draw attention to some of the practical realities women faced as married mothers. While the living conditions of most women in Ireland did improve over the period, and continued to advance after it, the reality of marriage and motherhood was very difficult for many women and far removed from idealised notions of it espoused by the Catholic Church.

Models of womanhood II: religious life

Arguably the most important model of womanhood outside marriage and motherhood was religious life. Certainly, it was the only other form of womanhood the Church publicly advocated, conforming, as it did, with Catholic ideologies of de-sexualised womanhood.[44] Unlike employment, which tended to be regarded as a precursor to marriage and motherhood, religious life presented an alternative to it. Though women were able to amass a degree of cultural capital through certain kinds of employment, especially teaching and nursing, it was expected that they would give up work upon marriage. On the other hand, women who remained outside both marriage and religious life had very little status in Irish society.[45]

Active religious congregations as we now know them first appeared in Ireland towards the end of the eighteenth century. Mirroring growth elsewhere in Europe, the number of women's congregations increased substantially in Ireland in the nineteenth century and continued also to do so into the twentieth century. The number of religious in Ireland rose from 120 in 1800 to 1,500 in 1851 and stood at over 8,000 in 1901.[46] As a proportion of total Catholic religious in Ireland, male and female, women represented 6 per cent in 1800, just under 40 per cent in 1850 and over 70 per cent in 1901.[47] In the twentieth century, the number of women religious in Ireland continued to increase, as the population of the Free State/Republic declined, such that by 1967 there were almost 15,500 of them.[48] This figure does not take account of the large number of Irish women who entered congregations outside Ireland, including non-Irish and missionary congregations, a path followed by many Irish women. The number of religious in Ireland reached its peak in 1967 and has been in decline since then.[49]

During the period in which the women of this study were growing up, women religious were a revered and accepted part of Irish society. They dominated and controlled women's health and education, as well as taking care of the elderly, the insane and 'the fallen'. Religious themselves were a common sight in society. Their buildings and institutions were dotted across the villages, towns and cities of Ireland and they formed a numerous, easily identifiable and powerful group of women in Ireland. Due to the position and importance of Catholicism in Irish society and the predominance of religious in the provision of education and health, not to mention redemption, religious congregations were intimately associated with the embourgeoisement of Irish society in the nineteenth century, and respectability and class mobility in the twentieth. In census returns, religious were (and still are) categorised as members of the 'professional classes'. Mary Peckham Magray has suggested that religious life was the 'most culturally privileged position women could hold in the nineteenth century'.[50] Given the limited opportunities open to women and the continued, indeed expanding, importance of the Church, at least in the period up to the 1960s, the same might be said for much of the twentieth century.

The position of religious in Irish society began to decline in the late 1960s, as did Irish women's attraction to the religious life. Vocations from women declined from 1,409 in 1966 to 547 in 1975. During the 1970s, there was an overall decline in vocations by 70 per cent.[51] The relationship between Vatican II and declining vocations is difficult to quantify but it is likely that the most significant factor affecting the declining number of entrants was the socio-economic and attitudinal changes that took place in Irish society from the 1960s. Greater access to work and education increased the opportunities available to women, which had a positive impact on the material reality of marriage and motherhood. Perhaps more significantly, social changes produced a more open and questioning society, including of matters religious, and one in which a more positive expression and awareness of sexuality began to emerge, albeit tentatively.[52] Dominant notions of womanhood began to be questioned, challenged and debated more openly. Increasingly, and despite the changes of Vatican II, religious life became associated with a form of womanhood considered less appealing and, for many, passive and repressive. Simply put, religious life became less and less attractive, as a life path to follow, a fact reflected in declining vocations.

In exploring marriage and motherhood and religious life as models of womanhood, the intention has not been to suggest that these were the only options available to Catholic women in Ireland. Women, depending on their resources, might stay on in education, become trained and qualified, enter the job market. Denied these opportunities, they might have been able to secure other sorts of work or leave Ireland to seek opportunities elsewhere. They could choose to marry or not, although spinsters were stigmatised. It was married motherhood and religious life, however, that were idealised by the Catholic Church and within Irish society, representing the hegemonic notions of womanhood that existed during the period in which the women of this study were born and grew up.

EMIGRATION AND DIASPORA

'Emigration,' remarked Liam Ryan, 'is at the centre of the Irish experience of being modern'.[53] To speak of Irish society in the twentieth century without attending to it, would, according to Diarmaid Ferriter, be to deny 'one of the great formative factors in modern Irish history'.[54] Such was the scale and impact of emigration in Ireland, that it is impossible to conceive of the nation within its borders alone, while the fact of it disallows the charge of insularity often levelled at mid-twentieth-century Ireland: it may have tended to gaze inwards, but it could never be said to stand alone. As many of their generations did, each of the women in this study lived outside Ireland, all of them having grown up within a 'culture of emigration'.

Though not insignificant beforehand, large-scale emigration became a feature of Irish society in the wake of the Great Famine of the 1840s and has had a profound effect on the demography, not to mention the psychology, of the country since then. Due to both mortality and emigration, the population of Ireland declined from 8.2 million in 1841 to 5.4 million in 1871. It is estimated that during and immediately after the Great Famine, over 2 million people left Ireland.[55] Between 1871, when records first began, and 1926, when the first post-independence census was taken, a further 1.8 million people departed.[56] Throughout this period, the most popular destination for emigrants was the United States, although a great many also went to Britain.[57] Emigration rates peaked during and immediately after the Famine, abated to some extent in the 1870s, rose again in the 1880s and maintained a high, if declining, rate from then until independence. This represented the first 'great wave' of Irish emigration.

The second great wave, which reached its peak in the 1950s, occurred between the 1930s and the 1960s, almost exactly the period in which the women of this study left Ireland. In contrast to the pre-independence period, the most popular destination for those leaving after it was Britain, especially England.[58] Irish census returns between 1926 and 1971 suggest a net out-migration figure of 1.14 million overall, although during the 1950s alone over 400,000 people left Ireland.[59] Most of the 1950s emigrants went to England, a fact reflected in subsequent census returns for England and Wales which record a marked increase of Irish-born people, especially from the Republic.[60]

Emigration declined in the 1960s while, in the 1970s, net immigration figures were recorded for the first time. Recession in the 1980s precipitated another rise in the levels of emigration, establishing a third great wave. While Britain remained the most popular destination in the 1980s, a greater proportion of Irish people were also choosing to go elsewhere, including, illegally, to the United States.[61] Although the number of Irish-born people in Britain was shown to have declined in recent census returns, their number is still consider-able. What is more, when second- and third-generation estimates are taken into account, the Irish form Britain's largest immigrant group.[62] In the 1990s, Irish migration underwent further change. Emigration declined between 1991 and 1995 and net immigration rates have been recorded since 1996, both of Irish and foreign nationals. The majority of those returning have come fom Britain, illustrating the continued importance of the migration flow betwen Britain and Ireland, albeit in a different direction.[63]

For the most part, emigration has negative connotations in Ireland and is chiefly associated with a form of enforced exile from the homeland which, prior to independence, was blamed on the occupying power and, in the immediate decades following it, symbolised the failure of the new state. Perhaps for this reason emigration did not become part of Irish public discourse until the 1950s. While greater recognition then began then to be paid to the significance of emigration, it was never matched with constructive measures to alleviate it. Hence, emigration has remained an important, if periodic, 'safety-valve' for the Irish economy. Attempts in the 1980s to re-conceptualise emigration in more positive terms never held water and, though it would seem the great waves of emigration are behind us now, its scale and impact on several generations of Irish people has left a residual uneasiness concerning the price paid for the relief provided.[64]

Apart from its scale, one of the most significant features of Irish migration in the modern era has been its gendered composition. Between 1871 and 1926, over half those who left Ireland were women. More women than men left Ireland in the inter-war period, immediately following the Second World War and in the 1960s. Fewer women returned to Ireland during the spell of immigration in the 1970s, although more men left in the 1980s.[65] Setting Irish migration apart from European patterns, Irish women have left Ireland often in equivalent or greater numbers than men. In addition, for the most part they have left not as male appendages but as young single women, their remittances, at least until the earlier part of the twentieth century, facilitating the migration of other females.[66] Census figures from the immediate post-Famine period record more Irish women than men living in Britain[67] while, since 1921, they have consistently out-numbered their male counterparts in Britain.

The fact of women's emigration was particularly difficult for the new state to accept. In the 1930s and 1940s, women themselves were seen to be the problem. Their 'female flightiness' ajudged to be providing them with fanciful ideas of the splendours that awaited them elsewhere.[68] The *Report on the Commission on Emigration and other Population Problems*, reporting in 1954, suggested instead that women left Ireland not only for economic but 'psychological' reasons which included dissatisfaction with their lot; paucity of attractive marriage opportunities and frustrations with social or religious aspects of Irish society.[69] Robert E. Kennedy, writing in 1973, argued that the low status of women in rural society had a negative impact on their health and longevity and suggested this as a reason for their leaving.[70] More recently, Enda Delaney has returned to economics as the prime motivation for Irish women's emigration.[71]

Irish emigration to England

Due not only to its scale, but also because it was to England that over half the women of this study migrated to, it is worth considering in greater detail the reality of life in England for Irish people during the twentieth century, recognising at the same time the extent to which those experiences were individually varied. Irish migration to England was already a significant part of the relationship between the two countries before Irish independence. The large-scale immigration of Irish people into Britain in the nineteenth century was not received positively. Concerns were raised, for example, that Irish people 'threatened the British way of life, the level of wages and the moral standards of the population'.[72] As Celts, the Irish were considered racially different to the native populations. As Celts and Catholic, with possible nationalist tendencies, they were considered potentially if not already disloyal to the Crown. Though various governments considered imposing restrictions on Irish immigration, this was deemed unworkable prior to 1921, because Ireland was still officially part of the United Kingdom, and, after it, because it remained within the Commonwealth.[73]

During the Second World War and for its post-war reconstruction, England relied on Irish immigrants for labour, just as Irish people and the Irish economy relied on migration to and remittances from England (and elsewhere) for survival. The relationship between Ireland, as a migrant sending, and England, as a migrant receiving, nation entered a new phase, however, with increased migration into Britain of other non-nationals, especially from India, Pakistan and the West Indies. As immigration and the fears surrounding it became increasingly associated with race and colour, Irish migrants, predominantly white and English-speaking, became less problematic as a group. Although deemed of lower stock than the indigenous population, they were no longer considered racially distinct from it. As one parliamentary report succinctly stated: 'The Irish are not –

whether they like it or not – a different race from the ordinary inhabitants of Great Britain'.[74] Racially re-appointed, the Irish became officially 'invisible'. Despite Ireland's exit from the Commonwealth in 1949, Irish people were granted a curious status in Britain, enabling them to retain their Irish citizenship while enjoying the full rights of subjecthood. Citizens of Ireland were also excluded from legislation introduced to control immigration in 1962, 1968 and 1971.

Official invisibility, however, did not guarantee wider acceptance in society and the level of Irish immigration in the 1950s did not go unnoticed.[75] Hostility continued to be focused around specific issues such as crime, disorderly behaviour and low living standards and was embodied in the 'No Irish' signs attached to accommodation and job vacancies common throughout the 1950s and 1960s.[76]

Although Irish migration declined once more in the 1970s, the presence of Irish people already living in England became the cause of concern, as did increased immigration in the 1980s. In 1973, shortly after the outbreak of 'the troubles' in Northern Ireland, the reformed Irish Republican Army (IRA) embarked on a military campaign in England which lasted until 1994 and contributed to a heightened anti-Irish feeling throughout the period. In 1974, the Prevention of Terrorism Act was introduced. Designed to combat IRA terrorism, it led to the collective criminalisation of Irish people and created what Paddy Hillyard has described as a 'suspect community' of Irish people living in Britain.[77] The IRA ceasefire in 1994 and subsequent peace process has given rise to better relations between the two countries and eased the situation for Irish people living in England. Without doubt, the success of the Irish economy since the early 1990s has contributed to a more positive representation of Ireland and Irishness, although this should not be overstated. The Commission for Racial Equality, in a report published in 1997, found that anti-Irish racism was endemic in British society and ingrained in certain state structures such as policing and the criminal justice system.[78] Problematically, the report further found that anti-Irish racism was generally accepted as natural or justified in society.[79] Notwithstanding this, the position of Irish people in England, for the reasons touched upon here, has been altered and, for many, much improved since the 1930s.

Irish women in England

Despite the scale of Irish migration to Britain in the nineteenth and twentieth century, with some notable exceptions, it remained curiously ignored by scholars. It is only in recent decades that much attention has been turned to exploring the experiences of Irish women. As a very brief overview, what can be said with some certainty about women who left Ireland for England during the second great wave of Irish emigration is that, whatever opportunities they were seeking, they provided England with a migrant labour force, especially in areas from which the indigenous population were turning away. From the late nineteenth to mid-twentieth century, the single most important source of employment for Irish women in the UK was domestic service, although they were also to be found in factories and other areas of industrialised employment.[80] The 1951 census of England and Wales showed a clustering in the professions, chiefly nursing but also teaching, and 'personal services' (cleaning and cooking). Two-thirds of all Irish women in paid employment were involved in these areas, although less than one-third of the total British female population was.[81] The proportion of Irish women working in personal services fell between 1951 and 1971 signifying their movement into white-collar and clerical work although nursing retained its importance as a source of employment. Reflecting the better education levels of 1980s migrants, the 1991 census revealed a discontinuity in the working patterns of younger Irish women and a sharp increase in the proportion of Irish women in managerial and professional employment.[82]

Revealing though this information is, it cannot tell us anything about the personal experiences of Irish women migrants. Thankfully a growing body of literature is emerging which attempts to explore a history too long obscured in general accounts. Nor do these figures provide any insight into the numbers of migrant Irish women who were or became religious. Unrecorded in census returns, untallied by the Catholic Church, we simply do not know how many Irish women moved to England as professed sisters or nuns, or entered congregations in England to become them. The limited research conducted thus far suggests that a significant portion of the populations of convents in England and Wales was Irish-born or of Irish descent, at least in the nineteenth century and up to the Second World War.[83] There is no obvious reason why the pattern would have altered considerably thereafter, at least until vocations began to decline in Ireland also. While more research needs to be conducted on the subject, it is reasonable to suggest, as Walsh does, that Irish nuns represent 'a hidden Irish diaspora' in Britain.[84]

The other diaspora

While not generally included within the category 'migrant' or considered in discussions of emigration, religious missionaries were certainly part of the Irish national consciousness, perhaps no more so than in the period during which the women of this study were growing up and making the decision to enter religious life. There is a distinction to be made, organisationally and ideologically, between religious who left Ireland to work for Irish emigrant communities or in predominantly Christian countries and those whose ministry was to the non-Christian world. For that reason, an indigenous Irish missionary movement cannot be said to have begun until the establishment of the Maynooth Mission to China in 1916, late by European standards.[85] The roots of this movement, however, were clearly located in the nineteenth century, and both in the minds of the Irish public and missionaries in the field, what amounted to an indigenous movement and what went previously was not so easy to set apart. Some of the outposts of Ireland's diaspora, from Jamaica to Bombay, were far enough removed from any general understanding of the term to complicate the distinction. Added to this was the fact that the work of Irish religious abroad often extended beyond Irish and/or Christian communities. In addition, Irish religious were deeply involved in the continental mission to non-Christian nations as members of European, especially French, religious organisations, a number of whom recruited directly in Ireland and had also established formation houses there also.

Thus, from about the 1830s then, and not unconnected to Catholic emancipation, a growing number of religious left Ireland to mission abroad. From the beginning, women formed a significant portion of those leaving. As members of Irish organisations which included the Mercy, Dominican, Presentation and Loreto congregations, and as sisters of non-Irish organisations which included the Good Shepherd, Holy Family and Cluny congregations (to name but a few), Irish women religious travelled to Asia, the Americas and the Antipodes in greater numbers than their male counterparts. During the peak of the missionary movement in Ireland, which occurred in the decades following the establishment of the Maynooth Mission to China (renamed the St Columban's Foreign Mission Society) and during which a number of indigenous religious missionary congregations were established,[86] women religious maintained their proportional significance as they increased their numerical advantage. By the early 1960s, there were as many Irish priests abroad as there were at home (2,000).[87] At the same time, there were twice that number of Irish sisters (that is, members of Irish congregations) abroad, which was still less than a quarter of the number of women religious then in Ireland.

Though living elsewhere, Irish missionaries were a fundamental part of society at home in Ireland. In order to survive, religious congregations involved in missionary work, whether indigenous or not, needed support in the form of money and personnel and were much involved in promoting themselves and their work in Ireland. Using slides and films, individual religious, often missionaries on home leave, brought the exoticism of the missions within reach of the Church and school audiences to which they spoke. Their message was at once urgent, idealistic, romantic and heroic: outside the Church, there was no salvation. The souls of millions hung in the balance. In addition to the oral testimonies were the written appeals, usually in the form of accounts from the field. A vast publishing press developed. The Society of African Missions produced six issues of *African Monthly* per year, the St Columban Fathers' *Far East* and the Holy Ghost Fathers' *Missionary Annals* appearing monthly. In addition, women's congregations published their own magazines while articles about missionaries and missionary organisations appeared in the Catholic, regional and national press.

Irish people proved hugely receptive, not only in terms of the monetary contribution they made and in the numbers of individuals who entered religious life with the expressed intention of going 'on the missions', both significant, but also the degree to which the laity involved itself in the wider mission project. Devotees turned out in great numbers to hear missionaries speak, distributed and sold missionary magazines on their behalf and helped organise charitable events, as well as collecting money directly for the missions. The combined circulation of *African Monthly*, *Far East* and *Missionary Annals* was estimated to be 130,000 per issue.[88] While the amount of money the laity contributed is not known, the childhood recollections of more than a few generations of Irish people, including the women of this study, would be incomplete without reference to the missions.

The missionary movement appealed because it captured the spirit of the times. It was both utterly modern and intrinsically linked to the past. In particular, Ireland's glorious past. It provided the laity, finally confident in its own identity, with an opportunity to profess itself as

Irish and as Catholic while at the same time taking part in and, indeed becoming frontrunner of, an international, supra-national and supernatural project. It provided heroes and heroines, living and deceased, from home and abroad: Fathers Daniel O'Sullivan, Joseph O'Leary and William Shine; Bishops Shanahan, Galvin and Broderick; Mother Kevin and Mother Marie Martin; Blessed Martin de Porres, Thérèse of Lisieux, Maria Goretti and Gemma Galgani. The mission project extended Ireland's frame of reference beyond Ireland, itself, providing an alternative and more positive conception of Irish migration which, perhaps for that reason, has yet to be fully recognised or researched.

CONCLUSION

The societal context in which the women of this study lived as girls, women and religious is fundamental to understanding the choices they made and the subjectivities they have inhabited. The Ireland that took shape in the wake of independence was influenced by a range of factors, not least its colonial past, violent inception, and the socio-cultural and religious beliefs which underpinned it. In addition, it was formed in response to the realities of its own situation, which included, for many decades, a depressed economy and large-scale emigration.

A shelf of books would fail to do justice to the four topics touched upon in this chapter, which claims to do no more than provide a brief overview of national identity, Irish Catholicism, womanhood and migration in the decades following independence. The aim here has been to provide a context in which to place the narrative accounts of a group of thirty women whose testimonies form the basis of this study. In addition, however, its purpose has been to re-locate the women within their own historical biographies: as Irish, as laity, as women and as migrants, identities not generally associated with nuns whose identity as religious tends to subsume all others within it.

NOTES

1   Article 41, Bunreacht na hEireann, (Dublin: 1937), p. 136, which states in its entirety:

The State recognises the Family as the natural primary and fundamental unit group of Society, and as a moral institution possessing inalienable and imprescriptible rights.

In particular, the State recognises that by her life within the home, woman gives to the State a support without which the common good cannot be achieved.

The State shall, therefore, endeavour to ensure that mothers shall not be obliged by economic necessity to engage in labour to the neglect of their duties in the home.

2   See, for example, S. Lambert, *Irish Women in Lancashire 1922–1960: Their Story* (Lancashire: Centre for North-West Regional Studies, University of Lancaster, 2001), p. 1; and J. J. Lee, *Ireland, 1912–1985* (Cambridge: Cambridge University Press, 1989) p. 669.

3   According to census in 1991, there were 3,228,327 Catholics living in Ireland, which represented almost 92 per cent of the total population. By 2002, while the numbers of Catholics rose to 3,462,606, their proportion of the total population had fallen slightly. It is worth noting also that in 1991, 66,270 individuals registered themselves as having no religion, though this figure had risen to 71,994 by the 2002 census.

For an historical analysis of Catholicism over the period see, for example, T. Inglis, *Moral Monopoly, The Rise and Fall of the Catholic Church in Modern Ireland* (Dublin: University College Dublin Press, 1998) (first published 1987); G. Meany, 'Sex and Nation: Women in Irish Culture and Politics', in A. Smyth (ed.), *Irish Women's Studies Reader* (Dublin: Attic Press, 1993), pp. 230–44; A. Rossiter, 'Bringing the Margins into the Centre: a Review of Aspects of Irish Women's Emigration', in Smyth (ed.), *Irish Women's Studies Reader*, pp. 177–202; and J. H. White, *Church and State in Modern Ireland, 1923–1979* (Dublin: Gill and Macmillan, 1980).

4   A. K. Martin, 'The Practice of Identity and an Irish Sense of Place', *Gender, Place and Culture, A Journal of Feminist Geography*, 4, 1 (1997), pp. 89–113, p. 93.

5   Whyte, *Church and State*, p. 24.

6   It was already an offence under the 1929 Censorship Act to publish, sell or distribute literature advocating birth-control. The 1935 Act merely closed potential loopholes.

7   Whyte, *Church and State*, p. 54.

8   Ibid., p. 54, 61.

9   Ibid.

10 C. Hug, *The Politics of Sexual Morality in Ireland* (Hampshire: Macmillan Press, 1999), p. 77.

11 Of course, there was nothing especially or intrinsically Irish about this. On this, see J. S. Donnelly Jnr, 'The Peak of Marianism in Ireland, 1930–60', in

S. J. Brown and D. W. Miller (eds), *Piety and Power in Ireland, 1760–1960* (Indiana: University of Notre Dame Press, 2000), pp. 252–83 and L. O'Dowd, 'Church, State and Women: the Aftermath of Partition', in C. Curtin, P. Jackson and B. O'Connor (eds), *Gender in Irish Society* (Galway: Galway University Press, 1987), pp. 3–36.

12 See, for example, Donnelly, 'The Peak of Marianism'.

13 Nor did the Catholic Church have a monopoly on notions of de-sexualised womanhood, which had, for instance, formed the basis of middle-class or elite Victorian womanhood.

14 See, for example, E. Delaney, *Demography, State and Society, Irish Migration to Britain, 1921–71* (Liverpool: Liverpool University Press, 2000); and L. Ryan, 'Irish Female Emigration in the 1930s: Transgressing Space and Culture', *Gender, Place and Culture*, 8, 3 (2001), pp. 271–82.

15 Whyte, *Church and State*, p. 32.

16 J. Beale, *Women in Ireland, Voices of Change* (Bloomington and Indianapolis, IN: Indiana University Press, 1987), pp. 57–62.

17 The First Vatican Council had been convened in 1869 and proclaimed papal infallibility.

18 See, also, T. Brown, *Ireland A Social and cultural History 1922–2002* (London: Harper Perennial, 2004) (first published in 1981), p. 283.

19 See Brown, *Ireland*, p. 247, M. E. Daly, '"Oh, Kathleen Ni Houlihan, Your Way's a Thorny Way!" The Condition of Women in Twentieth-Century Ireland', in A. Bradley and M. G. Valiulis (eds), *Gender and Sexuality in Modern Ireland* (Massachusetts: University of Massachusetts, 1997), pp. 102–25, p. 116 and Lee, *Ireland 1912–1985*.

20 Although it was believed that the Catholic Church would change its position on contraception, an encyclical, *Humanae Vitae*, issued in 1969 reiterated the Church's opposition to any 'un-natural' form of contraception. See, also, D. Keogh, *Twentieth-Century Ireland: Nation and State* (Dublin: Gill and Macmillan, 1994), p. 267.

21 Brown, *Ireland*, p. 289. See, also, J. H. Whyte, 'Church, State and Society, 1950–70', in J. J. Lee (ed.), *Ireland 1945–70* (Dublin: Gill and Macmillan, 1979), pp. 73–82 and *Church and State*.

22 M. Ward, *Unmanageable Revolutionaries* (London: Pluto Press, 1989) and 'National Liberation Movements and the Question of Women's Liberation: The Irish Experience', in C. Midgley (ed.), *Gender and Imperialism* (Manchester: Manchester University Press, 1998), pp. 104–22.

23 See M. G. Valiulis, 'Power, Gender, and Identity in the Irish Free State', in J. Hoff and M. Coulter (eds), *Irish Women's Voices Past and Present* (Bloomington and Indianapolis, IN: Indiana University Press, 1995), pp. 117–36, 'Neither Feminist nor Flapper: the Ecclesiastical Construction of the Ideal Irish Woman' in M. O'Dowd and S. Wichert (eds), *Chattel, Servant*

or Citizen, pp. 168–78, and 'Engendering Citizenship: Women's Relationship to the State in Ireland and the United States in the Post-Suffrage Period', in M. G. Valiulis and M. O'Dowd (eds), *Women and Irish History* (Dublin: Wolfhound, 1997), pp. 159–72.

24   See, for example, C. Beaumont, 'Women and the Politics of Equality: the Irish Women's Movement, 1930–1943' in Valiulis and O'Dowd (eds), *Women and Irish History*, pp. 173–88; 'Gender, citizenship and the state in Ireland, 1922–1990', in S. Brewster, *et al.* (eds), *Ireland in Proximity: History, Gender, Space* (London: Routledge, 1999), pp. 94–108; C. Clear, *Women of the House: Women's Household Work in Ireland, 1922–1961 Discourses, Experiences, Memories* (Dublin: Irish Academic Press, 2000); L. Connolly, *The Irish Women's Movement from Revolution to Devolution* (Hampshire and New York: Palgrave. 2002); and M. Cullen and M. Luddy (eds), *Female Activists, Irish Women and Change 1900–1960* (Wicklow: The Woodfield Press, 2001).

25   Quoted in Keogh, *Twentieth-Century Ireland*, p. 281.

26   See P. O'Connor, *Emerging Voices, Women in Contemporary Irish Society* (Dublin: Institute of Public Administration, 1998).

27   Due to changing farming techniques, the number of farm hands needed declined over this period. The demand for domestic service was not, however, sated (Clear, *Women of the House*, p. 16).

28   See Daly, 'Oh, Kathleen'.

29   Clear, *Women of the House*, p. 15.

30   Beale, *Women in Ireland*, pp. 20–62.

31   See M. E. Daly, '"Turn on the Tap": the State, Irish Women and Running Water', in M. G. Valiulis and M. O'Dowd (eds), *Women and Irish History*, pp. 206–19, p. 206. See also P. Travers (1995), '"There was Nothing for me There": Irish Female Emigration, 1922–71', in P. O'Sullivan (ed.), *Irish Women and Irish Migration* (London: Leicester University Press, 1995), pp. 146–67.

32   However, it is worth noting (as Clear, Daly, and O'Dowd, have) that ideologies of womanhood in Ireland as predominantly home-based were little different to those elsewhere in Europe.

33   On this, see Beaumont, 'Women and the Politics of Equality'; Clear, *Women of the House*; Connolly, *The Irish Women's Movement*; Daly, 'Oh, Kathleen'; Rossiter, 'Bringing the Margins' and Valiulis, all references.

34   Of course, some married women did not have children. However, contraception was banned in Ireland until the 1970s and reproduction was part of both Catholic and nationalist ideology which both contributed to high fertility rates in Ireland over the period.

35   Clear (*Women of the House*, p. 171) suggests such discourses to be explicit or implicitly assumed in much of the literature concerning the position of women in Ireland. She takes issue, in particular, with Beale, *Women in Ireland*, and Valiulis, 'Power, Gender and Identity' and 'Neither Flapper nor

Feminist'. See also C. M. Arensberg and S. T. Kimball, *Family and Community in Ireland* (Massachusetts, MA: Harvard University Press, 1940 and 1968)

36 Daly, 'Turn on the Tap', p. 207; Clear, *Women of the House*, p. 151.
37 Daly, 'Turn on the Tap', p. 207.
38 Beale, *Women in Ireland*, p. 21.
39 Clear, *Women of the House*, p. 143.
40 Daly, 'Turn on the Tap', p. 218.
41 Clear, *Women of the House*, p. 51–2.
42 Lee, *Ireland 1912–1985*, p. 280.
43 Beale, *Women in Ireland*, p. 42–50.
44 Walter, B., *Outsiders Inside*, p. 18.
45 On this see, for example, A. Byrne 'Single Women in Ireland: A Re-Examination of the Sociological Evidence', in A. Byrne and M. Leonard (eds), *Women and Irish Society: A Sociological Reader* (Belfast: Beyond the Pale, 1997), pp. 415–30.
46 T. Fahey, 'Nuns in the Catholic Church in Ireland in the Nineteenth Century' in M. Cullen (ed.), *Girls Don't Do Honours: Irish Women in Education in the 19th and 20th Centuries* (Dublin: WEB, 1987), pp. 7–30, p. 7.
47 M. P. Magray, *The Transforming Power of the Nuns: Women, Religion and Cultural Change in Ireland, 1750–1900* (New York: Oxford University Press, 1998), p. 45.
48 J. Lennon, *et al.*, 'Survey of Catholic Clergy and Religious Personnel, 1971', *Irish Journal of Sociology*, 1, 1 (1972), pp. 137–234. Census returns show that religious accounted for 2 per cent of single women above the age of 15 in 1922, almost 4 per cent by the mid-1960s.
49 Inglis, *Moral Monopoly*, p. 213. According to the Catholic Directory of Ireland and based on figures collected by itself and the Council for Research and Development, there were 13,246 women religious living in Ireland in 1988. By 1998, this had declined to just over 11,000. The latest figures from 2004 record 8,853 female religious living in Ireland.
50 Magray, *Transforming Power of Nuns*, p. 45.
51 Inglis, T., 'Decline in Numbers of Priests and Religious in Ireland: Report on Recent Surveys', *Doctrine and Life*, 30, 2 (1979), pp. 79–98, p. 81.
52 Inglis, *Moral Monopoly*, p. 157.
53 L. Ryan, 'Irish Emigration to Britain since World War II' in R. Kearney (ed.), *Migrations, The Irish at Home and Abroad* (Dublin: Wolfhound Press, 1990), pp. 45–68, p. 45.
54 D. Ferriter, *The Transformation of Ireland, 1900–2000* (London: Profile Books, 2004), p. 44.
55 Ó Gráda, C., *Ireland Before and After the Famine: An Exploration in Economic History, 1800–1925* (Manchester: Manchester University Press. 1993), pp. 104–5.

56 As official registers were never kept, the figures given are *net* rates of emigration only. Figures given are taken from the *Report on the Commission on Emigration and other Population Problems* (Dublin: 1954), p. 250.

57 National Economic and Social Council (NESC), *The Economic and Social Implications of Emigration* (Dublin: NESC, 1991).

58 Delaney, *Demography*, p. 45.

59 NESC, *Economic and Social*, p. 58.

60 It was not until the 2001 census that 'Irish' appeared as a distinct ethnic category. As a result, census reports prior to 2001 record only the number of Irish-born, not the number of people born of Irish parents or of Irish lineage who consider themselves to be Irish.

61 Due to undocumented migration to the United States, the figures we have of 1980s migration are likely to be understated. See B. Gray, 'From "Ethnicity" to "Diaspora": 1980s Emigration and "Multicultural" London', in A. Bielenberg (ed.), *The Irish Diaspora* (Essex: Longman, 2000), pp. 65–88, p. 66.

62 M. J. Hickman and B. Walter, *Discrimination and the Irish Community in Britain: A Report of Research Undertaken for the Commission for Racial Equality* (London: Commission for Racial Equality, 1997), p. 19.

63 B. Gray, 'Gendering the Irish Diaspora: Questions of Enrichment, Hybridization and Return', *Women's Studies International Forum*, 23, 2, (2000), pp. 167–85, p. 183.

64 As was evidenced in the reaction to 'Prime Time' reporter Paul Rouse's exploration on that programme of the position of and conditions under which some Irish male migrants to Britain in the 1950s currently live ('Prime Time', RTE 1, 22 December 2003).

65 Gray, 'From "Ethnicity" to "Diaspora"', p. 68.

66 See, for example, M. Murphy, 'The Fionnuala factor: Irish Sibling Emigration at the Turn of the Century' in Bradley and Valiulis (eds), *Gender and Sexuality*, pp. 85–101.

67 Walter, *Outsiders Inside*, p. 119.

68 Lee, *Ireland, 1912–1985*, p. 376.

69 *Commission on Emigration, 1948–1954, Reports* (Dublin: The Stationery Office, 1955), p. 303.

70 R. E. Kennedy Jnr, *The Irish: Emigration, Marriage and Fertility* (California: University of California Press, 1973), pp. 66–85.

71 Delaney, *Demography*, p. 184.

72 J. A. Jackson, *The Irish in Britain* (London: Routledge & Kegan Paul, 1963), p. 40.

73 For a discussion on these debates see Delaney, *Demography*; and K. Paul, *Whitewashing Britain: Race and Citizenship in the Post-War Era* (New York: Cornell University Press, 1997).

74 Quoted in Delaney, *Demography*, p. 209.

75 See, for example, C. Holmes, (ed.), *Immigrants and Minorities in British Society*

(London: George Allen & Unwin, 1978) and *John Bull's Island: Immigration and British Society, 1871–1971* (Hampshire: Macmillan, 1988).

76   See L. Curtis, *Nothing But the Same Old Story* (Dublin: Information on Ireland, 1984); and M. Lennon, M. McAdam and J. O'Brien, *Across the Water: Irish Women's Lives in Britain* (London: Virago, 1988).

77   P. Hillyard, *Suspect Community: People's Experience of the Prevention of Terrorism Act in Britain* (London: Pluto, 1993)

78   Hickman and Walter, *Discrimination*, p. 190, 235.

79   Ibid., p. 213.

80   Walter, *Outsiders Inside*, p. 148.

81   Ibid., p. 150.

82   Gray, 'From "Ethnicity" to "Diaspora"', p. 68.

83   B. Walsh, *Roman Catholic Nuns in England and Wales, 1800–1937: A Social History* (Dublin: Irish Academic Press, 2002).

84   Ibid., p. 141.

85   The Irish missionary movement of the medieval period in fact bore no resemblance or relation to the modern movement and should not, as it tends to, be regarded as an extension of it (E. M. Hogan, *The Irish Missionary Movement, A Historical Survey, 1830–1980* (Dublin: Gill & Macmillan, 1990), p. 6, n. 11.

86   Including the Missionary Sisters of St Columban in 1922; the Sisters of the Holy Rosary in 1924; St Patrick's Missionary Society in 1932; and the Medical Missionaries of Mary in 1937.

88   D. Fennell, *The Changing Face of Catholic Ireland* (London: Geoffrey Chapman, 1968), p. 139.

89   Hogan, *The Irish Missionary Movement*, p. 40.

CHAPTER 2

Growing Up

'It was a very traditional Irish Catholic background, like
everybody else...Everybody was the same'[1]

INTRODUCTION

While the previous chapter focused on aspects of Irish society
generally, this ones moves on to examine more specifically the
women's narrative account of their youth. As previously illustrated,
much has been written about the limitations that faced women in post-
independence Ireland. Historians of gender have further drawn
attention to the myriad ways in which women worked within and
around these limitations to carve a space for themselves in society.
This exploration of women's agency has not, however, been extended
to include the thousands of Irish women who entered religious life,
either in Ireland or outside it. Drawing on their testimonies, this
chapter seeks to present the women of this study as active agents. As
their accounts reveal, they were cognisant of the society around them
and their place within it, formed an attraction to religious life in the
context of it, and claimed a subjectivity in doing so not generally
accorded them.

NATIONAL IDENTITY

Given the period the women of this study were born and grew up in,
it was not surprising that their notions of Irishness were influenced
by discourses of national identity which constructed Ireland and
Irishness in opposition to England and Englishness. Many of the
women were exposed from an early age to anti-English sentiments
befitting the newly post-colonial state. They were taught to think of
England and Britain as Ireland's 'other': not only Protestant in
contrast to Catholic Ireland but more urban, less pious and more
dangerous. Some of the women received a similar message in the

44

home. Josephine's mother, for example, pleaded with her daughter not to emigrate to England: 'I'd rather see you dead at my feet than in that place'. Growing up, the women were aware of Anglophobic sentiment and could identify their own or their family's position in relation to it. Several of them absorbed anti-English sympathies themselves, for example, Hannah: 'I was very interested in History and, of course, we were taught it with a bias against England. I remember saying to an uncle, "I'd prefer to have the Germans here rather than the English". And he said, "You don't realise what you're saying". But I thought I knew what I was saying'. On the other hand, some women received a 'different education', as Pauline put it, at home where 'you could not say a *thing* against England'. Frances described her mother as 'Anglophile' while Eileen 'never had any problem about England' because her ('pro-British') father had been in the British civil service and 'hadn't much time for the kind of graft that went on when the Free State was declared'.

RELIGIOUS IDENTITY

More significant as a source of communal identity was the women's religion. By their own admission, the women grew up surrounded by Catholicism: at home, at school, in society. Ireland was experiencing, as Aisling put it, 'a great age of faith' during the time she grew up. Clearly, the women's Catholicism was important in their young lives. Catholicism 'meant everything' to Elaine and May, was 'vital' to Kate and was 'a way of life' for Irene. Often, the women used organic terms to talk about Catholicism, suggesting not only that they were surrounded by it but that they were imbued with it. As Elaine put it, 'it was natural, a part of you'.

Catholicism and national identity were not, in fact, easily separable. For many of the women, Catholicism was fundamentally about being Irish. Hannah, Lillian and Kate talked about being raised as 'traditional Irish Catholic[s]', Irene spoke of growing up in the 'good old-fashioned Irish faith', Elaine in the 'traditional Irish faith'. Using the terms Catholic and Irish interchangeably suggested the women made no distinction between the two. In some quotes the nation itself was invoked. May described Catholicism as 'absolutely embedded in the country' while in the following quote Kate makes a connection between Catholicism and nature:

'Prayer…and God was part of the warp and weft of everybody's life, especially in the country because you depended on God for fine weather, for everything…You didn't want [farm animals] to die because that was money lost and you prayed to God for them to get better and so on.

In revealing this more dependent relationship, it was as though the land itself might be Catholic.

Catholicism in the period the women were talking about and in the form they understood and practised it had been a 'tradition' in Ireland for less than half of a century. The established discourse of Irish Catholicism as a tradition, however, represented the success of Catholicism in establishing itself as a fundamental part of Irish national identity in the late nineteenth and early twentieth centuries. By the time the women of this study were growing up, Catholicism had become an element of national identity and worked in a similar way to it, binding the nation together and drawing boundaries between who belonged within and who remained outside. The women presented their practice of religion in the context of a society in which everyone was the same. Winnie, for example, described her family as 'a very normal kind of Irish Catholic family' while Josephine and Catherine portrayed their family's practice of the faith as typical, Josephine remarked that her family was 'like everyone else in the street' while Catherine described her family as 'like most Irish families, most Irish households'.

Catholicism was practised by the women in very specific, ritualistic, often public ways which gave a certain rhythm to their lives: rosary every evening, Mass daily or on Sundays, fasting on Fridays, confession once a month and so on. In addition to conforming to this pattern themselves, the women were aware of others practising their religion in the same way. This created a sense of community which was both real (local), as Josephine's quote suggests and imagined (national), as Catherine's does.[2]

The intractability of Catholicism and national identity was revealed also in a story Barbara told about her school days with the Mercy sisters, a number of whom she described as 'patriotic': 'They spoke of the 1916 Easter Rising and how we would meet people such as Pearse and Plunkett in heaven. That was very evident. We were all conscious of that'. Further, the nuns suggested that, as good patriots, neither the girls nor their families should buy goods in Protestant shops, Barbara noted, however, that they were 'never successful' in this regard. Despite their failure, the nuns' attitude drew attention to religious cleavages in Irish society. Many women conceived of non-Catholics only as 'the other', whether they be the 'heathens' Irish missionaries were abroad 'saving', English Protestants in England or, especially, the minority Protestant population of Ireland. As Hannah remarked: 'There were very few non-Catholics in the surrounding [area but] you could tell who were the Catholics when the Angelus[3] went...The funny thing is you remember and you were *conscious* of it'. Likewise, Aisling remembered the 'one Protestant' who lived in her parish:

> He was always referred to as 'the Jumper'. Now, they didn't boycott him or anything, but he was the odd man at the end of the parish. You know what 'Jumper' means? He jumped from one religion to the other. That was the phrase that we used in our part of the world'.

There were, of course, situations and circumstances which served to disrupt the assumed division between Irish Catholics and 'the rest'. These included communal ties that were based on factors other than religion, such as economics or trade (Barbara's cohesive community was an example of this), demography or social class. Growing up in Derry, Margaret was aware from a young age of her own positioning as 'the other' in relation to the ruling Protestant class. Rebecca also grew up Catholic in Northern Ireland, though in the majority Protestant county of Tyrone. Their elevated class position distinguished herself and her family from other Catholics and led to them feeling a greater sense of community with the local Protestant elite. Although living in the Free State/Republic, Vera's social position, also firmly middle-class, distinguished her from 'traditional, Irish Catholics', something she seemed keen to emphasise. While 'traditional, Irish Catholic' was a term the women used freely and frequently, it was both a more recent and less stable category than its common usage suggested.

CATHOLICISM AND THE FAMILY

Catholicism was integral also to the women's experience of family life; it was from the family that they received their religion. In describing the roots of their Catholicism, the family was invariably mentioned. Catholicism was important for Catherine 'because it was important to my family' while Brenda remarked that she had come 'from a very good religious family...[a] very good Catholic family. [We] said the rosary every night and that sort of thing. And a very good setting and wonderful home. I think that made a big impression on me'.

Religion was also something the family did together, through the rituals of prayer, Mass and so on: '[the family] met together and said morning and evening prayers' (Bernadette). While religion was deemed to unite the nation on a macro level, it was also understood to join the family on a micro level. If, as Tom Inglis suggests was the case,[4] Irish society segregated the sexes to such an extent that even when married men and women lived largely independent lives, meeting for prayer might have been an important way in which the family came together as a family. For Bernadette, prayer became especially significant after her family was forced to separate following the early death of her father. When her family met during school holidays, they prayed together. This served to verify that they were still a family, although they lived apart.

Religion could also connect individuals to their family after they left home. Frances moved to boarding school in England at the age of 10 and used Catholicism as the essential link ('lynchpin') between 'spotty' Liverpool and home. Training as a nurse in Dublin, Elaine felt 'lonely for home', alienated from her fellow students whose preferred forms of entertainment ('ballet and the pictures') were quite different to her own ('Irish dancing'). She sought refuge in the Church, eventually developing a vocation for religious life. For these women, religion was a staple in their lives and served to re-connect them with a sense of belonging they associated with home.

Although the women described their religion as something that was innate and natural, the patterns and rituals associated with it had, in fact, to be learned – usually, in the first instance, in the home. The women were generally able to identify the importance of their parents in this regard. While the practice of Catholicism could be said to bring the family together, there were distinct gendered roles that women and men took on as mothers and fathers in passing religion on to their children. Moreover, while male and female children were taught together, they would probably have recognised the different roles they would eventually be expected to inherit as adults. For the women of this study, it was predominantly their mothers who were in charge of passing on the rituals of devotional religion. Several of the women remarked that it was their mother more than their father who physically organised them for prayers, led them in the rosary, prepared them for Mass and so on. Norah suggested that religion was matrilineal when she remarked that 'the mother hands on an awful lot of the faith in the home...That's where I got my own faith really, from my mother and grandmother'. Likewise, Bernadette had learned her religion 'at my mother's knee'.

While it was the women's mothers' responsibility to pass on the rituals of Catholicism, religion was by no means unimportant to their fathers. Some fathers took at least an equal interest in making sure religion was passed on to them, although the role they assumed in doing so was usually distinct: 'My mother led us [in prayer] but my father was the one to whom it mattered most. It mattered to him a lot that this rosary was said. But he wouldn't lead it. It was her role to lead it' (Geraldine). Geraldine's father's role was, as she later described it, to 'inspire' the family and this seemed a common responsibility for fathers to take on. While they were bound by the rules and obligations of Catholicism themselves, fathers tended not to take on the extra burden of teaching.

Inglis has made much of the special relationship that existed between the Catholic Church and Irish mothers and explored the manner in which this special role as religious educator within the home was established and maintained.[5] The women's testimonies confirm that mothers and fathers had distinct roles in this regard but not, as Inglis' work might be taken to suggest, that women were more 'religious' figures than men. They were, however, associated with a different form and interpretation of religion.[6] Mothers tended to be associated with the serious business of rituals, while fathers were more spiritual, a term used by many of the women to describe their father. Spiritual suggests otherworldly, ethereal and more free, in contrast to their mothers whom they associated with the more man-made, institutional and earth-bound Church, as well as its clearly defined set of rules. The exception was Catherine's mother whose approach Catherine described as 'more light-hearted' but who was admonished by her husband, who felt she should 'give better example to the kids'. As fathers tended to 'join in' rather than organise prayers in the family home, they had to 'work' at religion less, but were not any less associated with it as a result. The only example given of a father taking a more active role came from Geraldine, whose father was called upon to recite a particular prayer in October in honour of St Joseph 'because it was a specialist role!'.

Importantly, fathers influenced daughters in matters religious. In the following quote, Josephine sums up the different functions, albeit both effective, that her parents had assumed:

> I suppose my mother had the most influence but my father had the most conscientiseing influence. He was the one who brought in the other side of religion which was [that] you were responsible for the poor...He would talk to us about that and how people didn't have the basics of life and as Christians you were kind of obliged to look at that too.

A binary is set up between the ritualistic mother and the father's spirituality. Although mothers were religious, they were not deemed to reach the deep spirituality of their husbands.[7] Their fathers' interpretation of religion was arguably more attractive than the ritual and pedagogy associated with their mothers.

The women described their religion as a religion of hardship and of fear, but it was also associated with comfort and pleasure. These conflicting discourses could co-exist around the one experience. Elaine, for example, vividly described the difficulties of conforming to the obligations of Catholicism, but also of the rewards to be had from the investment:

> If you went to the parish church you were taken by my father in the trap. [He] picked up everybody on the way so we were absolutely crowded up. People were standing on your leg and your toes and everything. Anyway, we eventually got to the service as it was just about starting. [We] rushed in. And...there was such crowds...If you were really in early you [still] wouldn't be able to get a seat. So most of the time we stood. And the huge crowd! All women on one side and the men on the other. And I was with my mother and my sisters. And my father and my brother used to go to the other side. I couldn't see a thing except the only thing that I was able to see was one of the stations of the cross. It was St Veronica wiping our Lords face and, as I say, I used to keep looking at this at Mass and Sunday after Sunday. And I wouldn't miss it for anything. And all that hardship.

Because, more than despite of, this hardship there was for Elaine 'nothing else...that gave you so much consolation at the time but your religion'. It was in the suffering of religion that the reward lay while the pain associated with it was a source of strength.

Religion was also based on fear, of hell predominantly but also of the imposing figure of the priest and the authority of the Church. As Vera remarked, 'we had...Archbishop McQuaid[8] who was similar to Pope Pius XII[9] and between them, you were indoctrinated to such an extent...that you could only think one way'. The Church and its priests were powerful figures in Irish society, whose authority the women would have had little space to question. It was, Elaine commented 'how...we were brought up. To reverence authority in the people who had [it]'. Indeed, some of the women were 'encouraged' by priests in their religious vocation, either to enter religious life itself or in their choice of congregation.[10]

The Church's authority was based partly on the divine knowledge it had and administered about the possible outcome of not conforming to its teachings. Fear was, according to Frances, 'drummed into us'. May was especially worried not about this life but the next: 'You wouldn't miss Mass for fear that you would be knocked down in the street and down you went to hell...I was brought up on a religion of fear but it meant a lot to me'.

The elevated status of the Church as well as its otherworldly authority meant a certain wonder and mystery was attached to it and May described herself as being 'in awe' of it. Likewise, there was a sense of awe in Elaine's memory of her first Holy Communion. Although this event had taken place close to seventy years before our interview, she was able to describe in startling detail the 'candle and nice flowers' that she had held during the procession. It was also clear that receiving communion had continued to be a significant event, requiring memorable preparation. As Elaine recalled 'You had to be washed...Your chest...your back...your feet and hands. It was an outward sign of the wonder of what you were receiving.' The cleanliness associated with preparing for this event contrasted significantly with the day-to-day drudgery of life as she described it on the family farm.

Religion was the cause of celebration, especially at Easter and Christmas, and could also be the source of domestic revelry. Both Frances and Joan remarked upon the sense of occasion that accompanied a relative priest's visit to the home to say Mass. For Frances, the rewards were spiritual: 'There was something very intimate about having...the most sacred moment of religion just for the family'. But they were also material involving large family gatherings and a great feast.

In addition, Catholicism was associated with social events and fraternising outside the home. Josephine recalled going to Mass with friends in the 1960s, as well as 'skiv[ing] off Holy Hour[11] on a Sunday night'. Likewise, Geraldine, born five years earlier, recalled her youth: 'When I think back...our entertainment was sort of going to the Holy Hour. We wouldn't [have] thought of saying "[I'm] going to the cinema" but if I could say "I'm going to Holy Hour", it got you into town. [Religion] was socially *right'*.

The positive associations the women made around faith, even its hardship, helped influence their sense of religious identity as well as shaping their attraction to pursuing a religious life. Though it would be impossible to identify the precise connection between the strength of Catholicism in Ireland and the large number of religious vocations from Irish people, it seems fair to propose that a relationship existed between the two. Many of the women in this study connected their vocation to their 'religious upbringing' (Bernadette), both social and familial. Indeed, Kate remarked that there was 'very little chance of a vocation [without] prayer in the home'.

The type of Catholicism that existed in Ireland during the period the women of this study were growing up was institutional, authoritative and ritualistic. This formal institution with its specific rituals and practices was experienced, however, more as an organic culture into which the women were born. Although the women learned the particular conventions and procedures associated with Catholicism, it was an almost unconscious learning. As everyone around them was practising their religion in the same way, it felt 'natural': natural as opposed to constructed; natural as good and wholesome; natural in terms of being intrinsic to the body; and natural to do with land and soil.

GENDER

It was as they were growing up that the women of this study became aware of the particular roles women and men, girls and boys had in Irish society. Margaret, the eldest girl in a family of nine, observed, for example, that 'the girls helped mother and did the housework and the boys ... were free to do what they wanted!' Likewise, Josephine recalled being 'expected to do things that the boys were *never* expected to do'. The lives of their mothers provided a model of marriage and motherhood for the women, for which they were being groomed. Some of them not only assisted their mothers but were themselves required to take over the job of mothering: 'My two youngest brothers were thirteen and fourteen years younger than me so, I mean, I brought them up. My mother was worn out with childbearing so she used to take to her bed ... and I ran the house. I did. I knew how to do it' (Margaret).

The women also became aware of the particular expectations associated with Irish Catholic motherhood. Frances described large families as 'part of the ethos of the time' while Elaine implied a degree of social pressure to conform to this code when she said: 'My mother had six [children]. All around us had eight, nine and ten. And she was always disappointed ... always felt bad because she didn't have more'. Conforming to the stereotype of the self-sacrificial Irish Mother,[12] the women portrayed their own mothers as hardworking, uncomplaining and put-upon. Margaret's mother was almost a martyr to motherhood while Catherine described her mother as:

> Just great. Wonderful. She married late in life ... and had eight children. One after the other, right up into her forties. And she was a small, thin, little woman. And a marvellous worker. We'd a farm and she worked inside the house and outside the house, because my father was quite delicate ... She used to do half the work and she was never down! ... She was so enduring. So patient ... So sacrificing.

As Catherine did, the women tended to depict their mothers as strong figures, Frances describing her own mother as 'the real live wire and ruler of the roost'. Despite this, some of them experienced firsthand the vulnerability of their mother's position in a society that officially exalted the role of motherhood but offered women who were mothers very little practical support. When Bernadette's father died, her mother was forced to put the six children into care and seek paid work. Similarly, Frances and her ten siblings were sent to schools across England and Ireland when their benefactor, an uncle, died.

Furthermore, the women were also familiar with nuns. All but one of them had attended convent schools, some as boarders, so they were in daily contact with religious. Although nuns groomed Irish girls to become 'proper' mothers,[13] the irony was that their own lives represented an alternative path to this. It was the sight of nuns that first attracted Annette, Irene and Bernadette to religious life. Annette and her young friends 'used to see the nuns go around saying the rosary...We'd come home ...dress up as nuns [and] say the rosary [ourselves]. It was a life ambition. Almost from the cradle'.

Perhaps the most influential figure in this regard was the missionary nun. Several of the women recalled religious missionaries visiting their schools, among them Margaret: '[A missionary sister came to visit and] talked about her work in Africa...I was only eight at the time and I remember saying..."I want to do what you're doing." It was almost like I always had the idea, I never thought of anything else'. Likewise, it was a visit from two missionary sisters to Pauline's school (when she was aged 'nine or ten') that 'started it for me'. Certainly, it would be difficult to overestimate the impact of an energetic, youthful and unfamiliar woman disrupting the day's classes to tell pupils about her life in an exotic land.

Notwithstanding the presence of nuns in their lives, however, the women could not have 'known' religious life in the same way they knew motherhood. Canon law and the rules surrounding enclosure excluded laity such that the non-professional, private lives of nuns remained just that. Perhaps as a consequence, the women of this study tended not to associate religious with the domestic space or the work involved therein. Though religious did domestic chores, they were not generally seen engaging in them, at least to the extent that the women saw their own mothers involved in such work. In addition, it was mostly outside religious' domestic space that the women came into contact with them. This proved an important distinction between how the women conceived of married motherhood and religious life. In addition, some of the women – though not all – had been positively influenced by the nuns they had come into direct contact with Eileen, for example, acknowledged that nuns had given her 'a great sense of personal worth'.

Marriage and religious life were not the only options available to the women of this study, but they were the only paths seriously considered by them. Unsurprisingly, none of them considered spinsterhood as an attractive path to follow. During the period they grew up, spinsterhood was regarded as an unfortunate situation foisted upon a woman, not a condition she might willingly choose. Tellingly, Joan's cousin, a priest, had advised her: 'Get married. Or be a nun. Don't be an old maid. They don't make good women'. Employment, on the other hand, tended to be seen as a temporary state, a precursor to marriage or religious life, not an endgame in itself. The message the women received growing up was that women were legitimated by the institutions to which they belonged. Although women were valued for taking on certain kinds of work before marriage (especially teaching and nursing) ultimately power, prestige and respect, however complex, resided in the institutions of the family (land, property, children) or religious life. Outside this lay the marginality and 'misery' of spinsterhood or the deviance and depravity of the 'fallen woman'.[14]

FORMING AN ATTRACTION TO THE RELIGIOUS LIFE

Although some of the women harboured ambitions to enter religious life from a young age, it was generally as teenagers that they gave it more serious consideration, entering finally between the ages of 17 and 28. The women framed their attraction to religious life in varied and various ways, oftentimes giving more than one reason for their entry. Collectively, their responses revealed the wide range of possibilities, as well as the very particular opportunities, the women believed religious life offered.

The desire for adventure and heroism

Many of the women discussed their attraction to religious life in terms of a desire for adventure which was, more often than not, associated with going on the missions. As May put it: 'the missions ... that's what most of us wanted'. The influence of mission film and literature was especially obvious in this regard, some of the terminology and language associated with those media evident in the women's reflections, which were replete with references to saving 'pennies for the black babies' or a desire to work, as Rosemary put it 'with the coloured people in an African country'. Claire was particularly inspired by the visits of missionary sisters to her school and remembered especially the films they brought with them: 'The one thing that always stayed in my mind were scenes of Africa and the sisters with big sun helmets ... and they were trekking through the thick, dense, tropical forest with bags in their hands. And I thought, "Oh my goodness! Aren't they great warriors for Christ! …I'd love to be one of those!"'.

The missions represented an alternative to religious life at home. Barbara's interest was influenced by returned missionaries who 'spoke of the place and their life in such a way that conveyed to me …a great sense of freedom and relaxation, …[one] denied…to those religious…working in Ireland'. The missions gave women an opportunity to get involved in an important international project that took them out of Ireland without the negative connotations of emigration. The missions were also exotic. In addition to Africa (Aisling, Barbara, Pauline, Rosemary, Angela, Claire and Deirdre), desirable destinations included California (Margaret), Louisiana (Vera), Texas (Sarah) and South America (Norah).

Missionaries were also important figures back home, their sacrifice highly regarded. As Lillian put it, 'the most wonderful thing you could do was to go abroad and save…children that were [otherwise] doomed to hell'. Many of the women shared the romantic picture of missionary life Vera held: 'That it's all sunshine and sitting under palm trees and teaching little children.' Invariably, those little children were an adoring audience, while 'saving' them may have appealed to the maternal instincts the women had been groomed to develop. In describing missionary life, the setting was all important: the sun was always shining and it was never cold. The reference to palm trees completes this exotic picture, which is in marked contrast to Ireland's physical geography. Indeed, the image of heat lends a certain comfort to missionary life not always available at home.

In addition to adventure, the missions suggested heroism, possibly martyrdom. Yvonne admitted to having been influenced in particular by 'the French missionary who said "Cross the seas, save one soul and die. And that's the recipe of a fulfilled life." That remained always in my mind.' Annette's attraction to the missions was based on the lives of martyrs and saints: 'Little Saint Teresa…was held up to us as an example. Fr. Damien [too]. There was all this thing about Damien the Leper and going out and getting leprosy. I think I scared the wits out of my mother!'.

Annette made no distinction between Teresa and Damien. Each were legitimate role models because martyrdom was not gender specific. In fact, the missions might have been regarded as providing a space in which gender roles in *this* life might be re-interpreted. Although women's work on the missions tended to reflect their traditional role as nurturer, the life there was often imagined to be 'topsy-turvy'. The missions were a place where anything could happen, where life might have to be risked, all in the pursuit of others' salvation. These fantasies allowed for, even suggested, daring feats of boldness and bravery, conditions not generally associated with the lives of women.

Annette's ambition to go on the missions was also an act of rebellion against her mother's 'safe' middle-class existence. In fact, it was the perfect antidote. Missionary life was interpreted as more free and less restrictive than motherhood, Catherine making an explicit distinction between the two: 'I felt that if I wanted to go and look after all these babies and children, and wanted to travel and do all these different things, that if I was married and had children of my own, that was the end of it'. Likewise, Geraldine had 'a sense that being married and with children was going to interfere with the plans I had for myself'. In both these cases, the women identified religious life as an alternative path to the limitations, as they saw them, of marriage and motherhood. Nor were these two the only women who drew a binary between motherhood as some-thing that confined women to a particular domestic space and the opportunities of religious life to travel and work. Presented this way, marriage and motherhood signalled the end of something, religious life the beginning. As Josephine put it, not in relation to the missions necessarily: 'If you do have children and...a husband and...a home, although you might have a sense of stability and security, there's a lot of doors closed to you'. Indeed, many of the women took exception to the assumption that women entered religious life due to a lack of eligible bachelors: 'Twasn't that we had to run into the convent because nobody'd marry us. It wasn't anything like that!' (Annette). Many of the women, as young adults, had boyfriends and some came close to becoming engaged to them. A few broke off their relationship only at the point at which they entered religious life. Contrary to popular opinion, the accounts of the women in this study at least show that women did choose to enter religious life over and above marriage, some doing so perhaps consciously to avoid it also.

A life less ordinary: difference, perfection and purity

Another recurrent theme in the narratives, and one which was equally associated with the desire for adventure and heroism, was the attraction to a life that was different, better – perfect even. As Catherine put it: 'There was a real emphasis on ... *doing* something with your life and [religious life] was special. It was different and that sort of thing'. Religious life was regarded by many as a superior life-path to follow. Aisling, for example, described it as 'the highest thing to do ... I mean, serving God and spreading the gospel was very high up on your scale of values'. In explaining why she was drawn to entering, Sarah remarked that 'as a young idealistic woman, you thought, "I'm going to do the very best with my life" ... And the very best that was presented to you at the time was religious life.' Religious life was glorified by the Catholic Church and esteemed in Irish society. To be called to that life meant to be different and special oneself.

One aspect about religious which marked them out as different to other women was their clothes and many of the women gave vivid accounts of the impact the religious habit had on them as young girls, usually in the context of a school classroom. Kate recalled its allure when describing her own attraction to religious life:

> I think I must have been about 15 [when I realised] I wanted to enter religious life...These nuns came [to visit our school]. A postulant and a sister...I liked the postulant's dress. I liked these white cuffs, you see? And the veil and the bit of white around it...that just attracted me.

So arresting in this and other accounts was the colour white. The perfectly pressed dark habit and veil would have contrasted with the whiteness of the cuff or wimple, symbolising the purity and perfection which nuns embodied. In addition, the habit also suggested professionalism, responsibility and power. The calm, controlled demeanour that nuns were supposed to emanate would have added to this professionalism while the habit contrasted sharply with the clothes the women's mothers wore, most of whom worked within the home and on the farm.

Professional advancement, personal achievement

Less exotic than the missions, less high-minded than perfection but hardly less appealing was the opportunity religious life gave women to claim a professional place in society. Religious life was regarded in Ireland as a profession in itself and registered as such in the census. Its professional status was illustrated also in a comment Kate made that 'you either wanted to get married or you didn't and [religious life] was a job, a position, if you like'. Moreover, religious life often involved actual professional training. Eileen situated her vocation precisely in relation to the possibility of further education: 'The opportunities for education [for me] weren't all that great because I came from a big family and my father had died when I was a teenager ...That's how [my vocation] happened...there was no thing [*sic*] about saving souls'.

Training was not available to all women and depended on resources and the support of family. Nor might it have received the same priority a religious vocation would. Eileen suggested as much when describing her family's efforts to assist her entry: 'It was a time when funds wouldn't have been plentiful...but there was nothing spared for...what I needed'. Specific professional training was part of the appeal to other women also. As had been the case for Eileen, Aisling Kate, Sarah, Rebecca and Hannah wanted to be teaching sisters; Angela, Bernadette, Deirdre and Rosemary nursing sisters; and Catherine and Josephine religious social workers.[15] Some desired specifically to become teaching or nursing missionaries. As Eileen had, Margaret described her vocation with respect to other motivations, identifying the opportunities not just for training or travel but career and career advancement. Conceding that 'there was a sacrificial aspect to it' she recognised also that 'maybe unconsciously [entering religious life] did give you an opportunity to be educated, to travel'.

Professional careers were limited for women in Ireland by resources, legislation and social mores. It was especially difficult for women to pursue a career after marriage while considerably negative associations were placed on spinsterhood. Nuns, however, were valued precisely for the work they did. Congregations were often very large international institutions with sophisticated organisational and professional infrastructures, which offered at least the potential of a career and, perhaps, high-powered positions in management. Nuns also had a monopoly over most of the traditional areas of women's paid employment in Ireland. A life-long career distinguished religious from other women, including the women's mothers. It was the prospect of a career over the path followed by her mother and sisters that attracted Teresa to religious life: 'At the time [religious life] was...a way of life that was different to farming...It was one of the paths to choose if you wanted a career...Probably one of my motivations [was to avoid] ending up being the farmer's wife'.

Sacrifice

Both in terms of Irish society during the period and Catholic ideology, sacrifice was a valued quality in women. Thus, it was not surprising that many of the women used discourses of sacrifice to describe their attraction to entering. Among them was Annette, who added also: 'The word sacrifice sounds negative [today] but we were doing something positive by giving up everything to bring a blessing down on those around us and on the world...It was the ideal of doing things for others'. In fact, most acceptable roles for women during the period involved sacrifice of some sort. As Josephine recalled, sacrifice for others was part of her upbringing:

> Looking back now I was imbued with that whole sense of sacrifice and service and doing things for other people. Now, I was brought up that way. I was the eldest girl of seven and so a lot of stuff fell on me by default...So I supposed I saw religious life maybe as an extension of that, [an] extension of service and sacrifice. And I wanted to do things for other people and I felt, you know, that I had talent...Maybe I felt I wasn't entitled to a life of my own...at the time.

Significantly, the kind of sacrifice the women envisaged themselves making in religious life was a particular form of surrender. Theirs was to be more heroic and public than the silent and private sacrifice of, for example, Irish Republican motherhood as explored by Maryann G. Valiulis.[16]

Spirituality and vocation as 'calling'

Many of the women of this study described their vocation in worldly terms. An example of this was Teresa's desire not to become a farmer's wife. Likewise, Eileen commented that her vocation was 'at the more personal level of inspiration and attraction. Nothing...that you'd call, you know, spiritual'. It was, instead, she said, 'on the level of the natural', by which she meant this, the 'real' world. Some of the women, however, did gave more indication of the spirituality which underpinned their attraction to religious life. As Aisling remarked, the women had grown up in an age of faith and it was their faith which ultimately drew them to the religious life, their entry into it an expression of that spirituality. While the spiritual benefits or attraction of religious life could not always be separated from the material, nor should they be overlooked or obscured by them.

Vocations for the religious life in the period the women of this study entered were understood as a calling that was extended to some, though not all, individuals. While not all the women of this study described their vocation in such terms, those who did tended to articulate it in particular ways. Most especially as a personal communication from God and/or a relationship with Him. Elaine remarked that she had 'felt really this call from God', Kate that she had received 'a message from God, [that he was] speaking to me'. Frances 'decided that [entering] was really what God was asking of me' while Irene talked about 'a covenant' made between herself and God, Margaret spoke of being 'romantically...in love with Christ'. When the women talked about committing themselves to religious life, it was directly to God. Annette talked about 'giving' herself to God; Geraldine about wanting to 'dedicate' and 'devote' her life to God; Irene about 'working' for God; and Lillian about 'let[ting] go' to God. Although couched in the language of 'giving oneself up', in relating their calling, the women drew attention to the self, *their* self, and the personal relationship they had with the divine. Although religious tend to be regarded in plural terms, in relation to each other and the congregation to which they belong, this was not how the women chose to present themselves.

When the women spoke of their calling and relationship with God, they invoked ethereality and otherworldliness. Catherine, for example, talked about being 'drawn to something...special, sort of something you can't put into words easily', as though mere language was incapable of adequately defining her experience. Likewise, Lillian summed up her vocation as a 'big spiritual search...[a] feeling that really there was something more that I really wanted to [explore], some kind of transcendence'. Interestingly, there were parallels to be drawn between the way the women talked about their calling to religious life and their religious upbringing – more particularly, the role their fathers had played in their religious education. The women's religious vocation and the mysteries associated with it may have enabled them to identify more with their fathers' deeper spirituality.

Oppositional terms and resistance

Some women, especially those who had a less than positive view of religious either generally or, particularly, the ones they were familiar with, had difficulty reconciling their attraction to religious life. Geraldine 'hated' the nuns at school, while Catherine and Lillian found them 'very strict' and 'quite severe'. These women talked about their difficulties in coming to terms with a religious vocation and relied instead on the language of resistance. Catherine did not want to be seen to be following the well-worn path taken by so many of her relatives ('just joining because of them'), while Lillian was put off by the idealisation of religious life as 'some kind of perfect life', symbolised by the habit, which she regarded as a kind of unconvincing costume. She remembered 'reading books about perfection in religious life and it didn't interest me in the slightest ...There was *no way* I was going down that road, dressed up in a *whatever!*'. All these women 'gave in, in the end', as Catherine put it, by renegotiating the kind of religious they would become. In place of the 'strict' nun (Catherine/Lillian) or 'over-bearing relative' (Geraldine) they would be 'exotic' (Catherine) or 'spiritual' (Lillian). In so doing, these women re-negotiated on a micro-level what religious life could mean by resisting and rejecting particular stereotypical images of religious life for themselves.

PARENTAL RESPONSES

Despite the strong religious faith many of the women's parents held, many of them were ambivalent about their daughter's vocation to enter religious life, and responded to it with mixed, often conflicting, emotions. Parents effectively lost daughters to religious life, as they lost them to marriage and emigration, and there were both practical and emotional deficits to be borne as their daughter's allegiance to family was replaced with that to religious community. Bernadette's mother, a widow, was 'very upset, of course, when I told her first that I wanted to enter' because she relied on Bernadette's help raising her three younger brothers and a younger sister. Though she had long professed an interest in religious life, Kate had not yet entered when she turned 27. Though originally supportive of her vocation, Kate's parents had become accustomed to Kate being available to them. When she finally decided to enter, her mother '...would have preferred if I hadn't at that stage...She said to me, "I always thought you'd be with me when I was dying." And she didn't mean just the actual dying. She meant when I'm old and you'll be able to look after me and so on'.

Kate recalled leaving her father 'in tears' when she left to enter. She was not the only woman to do so. In fact, a recurrent theme in the women's accounts was the emotional impact entry to religious life had on their fathers. Catherine's father, for example, was 'devastated' at the news of her vocation, telling a neighbour 'I never thought she'd leave me'. Likewise, Elaine's father was 'very upset', as was Brenda's because he 'adored me and I think he missed me very much'. May's father was 'very sad' because 'it meant leaving and breaking up the family'. Geraldine, Hannah and Aisling's fathers were against their particular choice of congregation because it involved leaving Ireland. 'England', Geraldine admitted, 'was not what he expected at all' while Aisling's father 'objected strongly' to her desire to enter a congregation with missionary interests.[17] Winnie's father 'nearly died' when he heard the news his daughter wanted to enter before finishing school. Likewise, Margaret's father 'wasn't too pleased [at my decision to enter] because he said I hadn't finished my education, which was true. I went straight in from school and he thought it was too quick and I was too young and all the rest of it... And he probably was right. I should have stayed and done my degree'. In situations like this, the women's mothers provided support, often acting as mediators between daughter and husband. Similarly, fathers could be the supportive party when mothers were less than pleased with a vocation.

Though emotionally at a loss, parents also took pride in their daughter's vocation. Indeed, more often than not, in addition to feeling the pain of separation, parents were pleased. 'Delighted' was the term used by Frances and Elaine to describe their parents' response, while others chose 'happy' or 'very happy'. Some parents had fostered religious ambitions for their daughter while others almost expected a vocation in the family. When Kate first told her family of her vocation, her mother 'was pleased. I think [she] hoped at the bottom of her [heart] that one of us would enter, either my sister or I'. Frances was her mother's 'last hope' given that, with the

exception of a brother who had died, none of her ten siblings had
expressed a desire to enter religious life. While Hannah's parents were
'very happy' with her vocation, they were not entirely surprised by it
either: 'There was [a religious] in nearly every family [at the time]. In
all the families, there was at least one. Either a priest or a nun. Or both
maybe, sometimes'.

Kate's parents were not alone in describing her vocation as a
'privilege', while her sister believed it to be a 'blessing on the whole
family'. It was a blessing that was social as well as religious. Eileen's
parents, for example, thought it a 'great feather in [their] cap' that
their daughter was to become a nun while Margaret's mother was
'very proud that I became a sister. She found that, you know, socially
it was one up on the neighbours'. As a vocation was a direct calling
from God, it served to elevate the individual involved. As a sign of
good parenting, it also conferred status on the family. There was often
an implicit reference to upward class mobility in parents' positive
response. The firmly middle-class congregation that Frances intended
to enter, for example, was 'part of the appeal to my mother because
she was a snob'.

Nonetheless, the women were aware that their vocation was not
responded to as positively as a son's vocation for the priesthood
might have been. As Margaret suggested, priesthood was the ultimate accolade for parents: 'To have a son a priest was ... the height of
whatever, you know, it was wonderful!' Almost all the women
qualified their parents' enthusiastic response to their vocation with
comments similar to Frances' that 'it was second-best to a priest, of
course!'. As Kate put it, 'it was a privilege ... to have a sister [in the
family] but not as great [as a priest]'. The exception was Claire,
though her experience might not disprove the point. Aged 17, Claire's
brother, older than herself by three years, announced his intention to
enter the priesthood.

> Of course, my father was also a good Christian but he really was
> looking forward to [my brother] maybe earning some money or I
> don't know what, but he didn't want this at all. And in a sense, that
> made it difficult enough for [my brother] ... The story was so
> difficult for [him] that I thought, my goodness, when it came to me
> leaving school, I was afraid [to let my father know I had a vocation].
> I was just afraid to say anything. I just couldn't bring myself to say
> anything.

Claire finally did let her parents know of her vocation two years after she left school and was 'quite shocked really' by her father's reaction. Though he was not, as she put it, 'very grateful really', his attitude was 'Ah, sure, if that's what you want, go.'

A useful tool in interpreting the meaning the women's families attached to religious life is Pierre Bourdieu's notion of 'symbolic capital'. Bourdieu was interested in exploring the social aspects of cultural production and understood social relations to be based on the distribution of different forms of capital: economic, cultural and social. Through processes of legitimation, these different forms of capital could be transformed into symbolic capital, conferring strength, power and profit on the holder.[18] The women's parents' responses to their daughter's vocation reflect a recognition that religious life could be translated into symbolic capital due to the status of Catholicism and religious themselves in Irish society. Their correct assessment of the greater social power of priests vis-à-vis nuns in society illustrates the gendered nature of capital.

While daughters might provide a route to accumulating symbolic capital for the family, they might also be the cause of its depletion. In the society in which these women grew up, morality was considered vital to respectability, especially so for women. It is in this context that Elaine's mother responded to her daughter's vocation: 'My mother was delighted!...She said, "Oh, that's fine. She's safe now."' No doubt influenced by the anxieties surrounding women's loss of virtue, Elaine's mother was concerned for her daughter's 'purity', which could be read as virginity.[19] Elaine's mother, and many others like her, regarded the convent as a safe haven which would protect their daughter's virginity, leaving their own social position intact. The status of women religious in Ireland was closely related to their perceived purity and vow of celibacy. Indeed, up until the 1960s, the status of religious as well as married women who were mothers was intimately linked with their sexuality, its control or repression.

Some parents took exception to their daughter's vocation. Winnie's father, for example, knew personally a number of sisters in the congregation she wanted to enter into, but was not fond of them: 'I don't think he particularly liked some of the nuns that I was joining!' Yvonne's father 'was disgusted!', mistrusting what he believed to be religious' beguiling tendencies: 'His idea was that they were reaching out to [us], you know?' Rebecca and Vera came from well-to-do families who distinguished themselves from other Irish Catholics on that basis. Their families did not stand to gain socially from their entry into religious life. In fact, their position might even be threatened by it as religious were generally drawn from the lower middle-classes.[20] On being told of her daughter's vocation, Rebecca's mother refused to be implicated in it at all:

> She said, 'If you've got a vocation, I don't know where it came from. It's not from me and it's certainly not from your father!...You can put it out of your head till you're twenty-one'. So I didn't put it out of my mind but I didn't mention it to her again.

The less than positive response Josephine's parents gave to her vocation was less a defence of class allegiance, more a sign of the changing times. The youngest of the women in this study, she first suggested her vocation to them in the late 1960s, aged 18: 'I threw it out as an idea at home and my parents went ballistic! My father mainly because he didn't want me to leave but my mother because she thought that being a nun was a *total* waste of time'.

Josephine's parents had, as she put it, expected her to do 'the normal thing', which included 'finding a good job, marrying a nice man and having children' ('a lot of my guilt in the early days was that I wasn't giving my parents grandchildren'). Their unenthusiastic response reflected the social changes that had taken place in Irish society, particularly regarding the position of women and the devaluing of religious life. Although still respected and needed for the work they did, the status of nuns had diminished considerably.

Josephine suggested that her parents, as was the case more generally, did not regard nuns as women: 'You see, you didn't see religious as women, as such. You just saw them as this kind of neutered gender, wandering around the place'. This neutrality was echoed by Clear when she commented that nuns were 'ambiguously' positioned in terms of their gender and also in Jenny Beale's reiteration of an 'old saying' that there were 'three sexes – men, women and nuns'.[21] Social mores during the devotional revolution had served to repress women's sexuality in Irish society. This was beginning to change in the 1960s but religious were still regarded as sexually repressed, which served to exclude them from certain readings of womanhood.

As their families had, the women of this study recognised the potential within religious life of accumulating social, cultural and symbolic capital. More than their families did, however, they identified the material and practical advantages of entry for themselves. Terry Lovell has argued that, while Pierre Bourdieu recognised women's ability to accrue symbolic capital, he regarded them generally as 'social objects', mere repositories of value and capital.[22] As such, he failed to explore adequately their potential as 'capital-accumulating subjects' or, indeed, to consider that women might be aware of this potential themselves. The same might be said of the women's parents. By contrast, the meaning the women themselves had of religious life revealed that they were aware both of its ability to confer symbolic capital on them as objects but also of the potential for themselves as capital-accumulating subjects, through education, training, work and so on. The different interpretations of religious life displayed by the women and their parents demonstrate the way women tend to be constructed as objects but present themselves as subjects. The women's understanding of their own situation highlights also their awareness of limitations based on gender and their attempts to work around and within them to achieve personal ambitions.

CHOOSING CONGREGATIONS

Decisions also had to be made concerning which congregation to join. Of the nine congregations the women of this study entered into, six had been established before 1850, one in the second half of the nineteenth century, the remaining two in the second and third decades of the twentieth century.[23] Three of the congregations were Irish,[24] four were French,[25] one was French in origin but had become independent soon after its arrival in England[26] and one was English.[27] Two congregations were specifically missionary congregations, though all had established missions to 'third world' countries by the time the women of this study entered. The charisms of the congregations at the time of their inception focused primarily on education (four) and health (four), one being equally engaged in both.

Despite the importance of the missions in attracting them to religious life, few of the women who had initially professed a desire to become missionaries actually did so. Some 'grew out of the idea', coming to regard the ideas they had of the missions as 'crazy [and] silly' (Vera) in retrospect. Others, like Sarah, were alerted to this by

others ('It was pointed out to me that it was quite a childish idea').
Hannah decided that 'godless' England was as much in need of her
attention than further afield while health fears deterred others from
going overseas.

Eight of the women entered into the congregation they were
educated by, in each case well-respected middle-class institutions
with good teaching reputations. Seven entered missionary congregations or congregations they associated with missionary work. With
the exception of one woman, Irene, whose application to the
congregation she had been taught by was refused (on the basis that
she did not carry the requisite educational qualifications), the rest of
the women made a positive decision not to enter the congregations
they were taught by. For the most part, this meant deciding not to join
the Sisters of Mercy[28] or, for two of them, the Presentation order.[29] The
women gave various, often conflicting, reasons for their decision. For
example, the Mercy Sisters were, according to Annette, 'very aloof
...too formal'. By contrast, Hannah described them as 'generous and
hospitable...You'd be too close to family and there'd be calls and
that'. Elaine decided against the Mercy's because 'at that time, they
were all teachers' while she was training to be a nurse. Later,
however, she entered a teaching congregation. Catherine and
Geraldine, neither of whom had liked the Mercy nuns they had been
taught by, were also discouraged by the fact they had relatives in the
congregation. Perhaps the greatest insight came from Kate, however,
who had the following to say when asked if she had considered
entering the Mercy congregation:

> No, I hadn't. I wouldn't. I don't know what it was...I think it's
> maybe something with me about some place you don't know. Like,
> it's said that the unknown is always more exciting than what you
> know already.

Although Kate could only have been speaking for herself, the
impression was that her comments might be more generally applied.
For many of the women, it seemed the congregations they had been
taught by, especially the large Irish congregations like the Mercy and
Presentation orders, were simply too familiar, not different or exciting
enough. They might also have had negative class associations.
Bernadette, for example, received her education in an industrial
school run by the Mercy order where her mother worked. Though

they had offered her a place in their noviciate. Bernadette chose not to take it, perhaps fearing the association might stick with her. As they had framed their attraction to religious life more generally, the women described their attraction to specific congregations in terms of it being a less obvious or usual pursuit, one that offered them a more exclusive or exotic lifestyle.

The women who entered congregations they were educated by were drawn by a sense of duty to the nuns that had taught them as much as they were attracted to an organisation peopled by women they knew and admired. It was 'something of the spirit of our sisters that interested' Barbara, while Winnie described her vocation specifically to the St Gemma congregation 'more than, I'd say, a general idea of religious life and then finding where would be the best place to go'. It 'never entered [Yvonne's] head' to enter a congregation than the St Helen congregation.

The rest of the women came into contact with congregations they chose to enter through sisters or cousins having joined previously, through family friends, Catholic connections or by meeting members of those congregations canvassing for vocations or donations. These congregations were then described in oppositional terms to the ones they were familiar with, particularly the ones they had been taught by. For example, the sisters of St Louise were 'delightfully simple, compared to the Mercy nuns!' (Annette), while the sisters of St Marie 'just seemed a bit more normal' (Lillian) than the Presentation sisters.

Despite the importance of work to the women's initial attraction to religious life, the specific charism of a congregation was rarely identified as a particular incentive,[30] although this might also have been because specific work opportunities would have been available in more than one congregation. Instead, the women tended to frame their attraction in terms of the particular attitude or atmosphere they could identify within the congregation. For example, May thought that the spirit of the St Mildred congregation was 'wonderful...I was so impressed when I first met them, of their warmth, their welcome, their hospitality, their joy, that it began to work on me'.

All of the women of this study lived part, and some all, of their lives as religious outside Ireland. Only five of them entered religious life believing they would remain in Ireland. Living as religious elsewhere particularly appealed to some. Deirdre, for example, remarked that she 'didn't want to be in an order at home'. 'Fed up' with being compared to an elder sister, also a nun (with the Mercy congregation), Geraldine wanted specifically to enter religious life outside Ireland, in England. Vera followed the same route, considering Irish congregations 'too inward looking, too pinny [i.e. uptight]'. If Hannah was sure of anything it was that she was:

> ...going out of Ireland. That I did know...I didn't want to stay in a parochial [setting] where people knew each other. Where if something went wrong in the family, somebody would be telling you. I mean, that wasn't why I was going to enter religion...In some religious houses in Ireland...there might be two or three [from the one family] or cousins [It's] too much, too close...If something was going wrong in the family, let's say with the marriage, they'd try to get the religious involved. I didn't want that. I knew subconsciously without articulating it.

For these women, either non-Irish congregations or congregations that took them outside Ireland gave them the particular distance they were seeking from the familiarity of home and the obligations associated with it.

In general, the women of this study made up their own minds about the congregations they entered into. Some were influenced by the opinions of others (it was a priest who had introduced May to the St Mildred congregation while Hannah's uncle suggested the same congregation to her) but they claimed their decision as their own. Kate sought the advice of three priests when choosing a congregation. In the drama that was created around her vocation as a result, however, she became more, not less, important to the process. Contradicting the received wisdom that women who entered congregations were dupes, the accounts drawn on here highlight the very discriminating means by which women chose congregations as well as suggesting they regarded neither congregations nor individuals within them in homogeneous terms.

Few of the women could be sure before entering religious life that it was the definitely the right decision to make. As a result, they entered with the attitude that they were, as Josephine put it 'giving it a whirl'. Marriage and motherhood offered no such trial run. Certainly there was a social stigma attached to leaving the convent, of being a 'failed nun', but many of the women of this study entered safe in the belief, if not the knowledge, that their family would support them in such an eventuality: 'There was the real stress [from my parents] on the fact that if I wanted to come back I was to come home

...I was under [no] pressure to stay' (Lillian). If an individual left religious life, their dowry was returned to them. Naturally, they took their training and qualifications with them also. By contrast, few support systems existed to help women who realised they had made the wrong decision in marriage.

CONCLUSION

The women of this study were shaped by the social, economic, cultural and religious context of their times. They articulated their vocation to the religious life with reference to those times also, presenting it as a response to the gendered nature of society and the opportunities open, or closed, to them as women in it. Though often positioned as passive victims of a patriarchal Church and state, the women of this study claimed the decision to enter religious life as their own and had clear ideas of what religious life could offer them as women and as individuals, including the opportunity to be educated, work and travel

Nor could their vocation be separated from the importance of religion either to themselves or in Irish society generally, not least because it ensured that their decision to enter religious life was rarely regarded as controversial. As they were growing up, the women of this study experienced their Catholicism as something innate. This belied, however, the processes of socialisation they underwent and the gendered roles their parents had assumed in passing religion on to them. Catholicism pervaded almost every aspect of their young lives. It's all-encompassing nature meant the women's sense of themselves as Catholic could not easily be separated from their sense of self as Irish, as girls, or as daughters. As will be seen in the Chapter 3, the apparent symmetry between these different identities would, however, be challenged when the women left secular society to enter religious life.

NOTES

1   Josephine.
2   B. Anderson, *Imagined Communities, Reflections on the Origin and Spread of Nationalism* (London: Verso, rev. edn, 1991).

3 The bell rung in Catholic Churches at noon (and broadcast on the Irish national radio station) inviting the faithful to recite a devotional exercise in honour of the Incarnation.

4 Inglis, pp. 60, 90.

5 Inglis, *Moral Monopoly*; Fahey, 'Nuns in the Catholic Church', p. 28.

6 In fact, when asked initially which of their parents was responsible for passing down Catholicism to them, few of the women identified either their mother or father. It was only when they were asked more specifically about who it was that led them in prayer or prepared them for Mass that distinct parental roles were identified.

7 Interestingly, the only woman to describe her mother as 'spiritual' was Catherine.

8 Archbishop of Dublin, 1940–72.

9 1939–1958.

10 This is not to say the women were not also influenced by *women* religious. The impact of religious in society and the missionary sister will be examined presently. In addition, women were influenced by individual religious they knew or met. Both May and Geraldine, for example, considered entering religious life after it was suggested to them by nuns.

11 Prayerful contemplation spent in church before the exposed Blessed Sacrament.

12 See, for example, Inglis, *Moral Monopoly*, pp. 201, 212.

13 Ibid., p. 52.

14 Byrne, 'Single Women in Ireland', p. 415.

15 In articulating their professional desires, the women also high-lighted the limitations of their situation. Rosemary, for example, commented: 'I always wanted to be a nurse. I felt, well, [that] I would be ... a very bad teacher', suggesting these were the only two paths available to her. Likewise, Aisling talked about being either a teacher or a nurse: 'Basically [we] didn't have this huge wide range of [alternatives], to be an accountant or this or that or the other'.

16 Valiulis, 'Power, Gender, and Identity', p. 117. See also Valiulis, 'Neither Feminist nor Flapper'.

17 Some mothers shared the same concerns. Kate's mother 'wouldn't have minded if I'd entered the Mercys because they're diocesan, you see, so ... I wouldn't be far from home and they'd see me and so on'. Irene's mother 'never really accepted' her daughter's vocation: 'I think it was the fact that I was over [in England]. When I first entered we didn't get home ... I didn't go home for the first eight years and then it was only every seven years. I mean, it was a long,

long time. And I think that was what she didn't like. She couldn't see the sense of it.'

18 P. Bourdieu, *Outline of a Theory of Practice* (Cambridge: Cambridge University Press, 1977) (trans. R. Nice); and 'The Forms of Capital', in J. G. Richardson (ed.), *Handbook of Theory and Research for the Sociology of Education* (New York: Greenwood Press, 1983), pp. 241–58. For an application of Bourdieu to Irish Catholicism, see Inglis, *Moral Monopoly*.

19 Under instruction from her mother, Elaine prayed ('three Hail Mary's a day') for her 'purity' although she was never entirely sure what she was praying for. Inglis argues that the Catholic Church in Ireland developed a monopoly on the subject of sex, leaving the laity with 'no communicative competence' to discuss it for themselves (*Moral Monopoly*, pp. 139, 156). The euphemistic language used by Elaine's mother, as well as Elaine's own ignorance concerning the subject of her prayers, would sugggest as much.

20 C. Clear, 'Walls Within Walls, Nuns in Nineteenth Century Ireland' in C. Curtin, P. Jackson, and B. O'Connor (eds), *Gender in Irish Society* (Galway: Galway University Press, 1987), pp. 134–51; Magray, *The Transforming Power of the Nuns*.

21 Clear, 'Walls Within Walls', p. xvii and Beale, *Women in Ireland*, p. 174.

22 T. Lovell, 'Thinking Feminism With and Against Bourdieu', *Feminist Theory*, 1, 1 (2000), pp. 11–32.

23 The nine congregations have been given pseudonyms.

24 Given the names in this study of the Congregation of the Sisters of St Anne (henceforth CSSA), the Congregation of the Sisters of St Brigid (henceforth CSSB) and the Congregation of the Sisters of St Helen (henceforth CSSH)

25 Given the names in this study of the Congregation of the Sisters of St Gemma (henceforth CSSG), the Congregation of the Sisters of St Louise (henceforth CSSL), the Congregation of the Sisters of St Marie (henceforth CSSM) and the Congregation of the Sisters of St Nadine (henceforth CSSN).

26 Given the name in this study of the Congregation of the Sisters of St Cecile (henceforth CSSC)

27 Given the name in this study of the Congregation of the Sisters of St Mildred (henceforth CSSMd).

28 Ireland's largest religious congregation set up in Dublin in 1831 by Catherine McAuley

29 Another Irish congregation, set up in 1775, by Nano Nagle

30 The exceptions were Bernadette's attraction to nursing and Catherine's to working with children.

Part II:

Religious Life, Pre-Vatican II

CHAPTER 3

Religious Life in the Pre-Vatican II Period

'Thus dead to the world and to self, they will live only to Christ our Lord'[1]

INTRODUCTION

It was between 1934 and 1970 that the thirty women who took part in this study joined religious life, entering congregations that were spread across Ireland and England, and extended further beyond these countries also. When they entered, they took with them expectations and ambitions formed growing up in Ireland, influenced undoubtedly by the work of nuns they came into contact with but also by idealised notions of sacrifice and a life of prayer. Whatever expectations they held beforehand, upon entry, the women learned that religious life in the pre-Vatican II period[2] was primarily and fundamentally about 'becoming' a nun through a very scripted process of learning, performance and surveillance, which was itself based on rules, penance and labour.

In this chapter, the organisation of religious life under the pre-Vatican II regime will be explored, not only the technology of government that prevailed but the women's experience and retrospective judgement of it. It will examine the impact of the regime on the women's sense of self as individuals, as family members and as Catholics but, especially, as women. It will also consider how religious life defined womanhood in the period, particularly in the context of its primary motivation to 'transform' women into nuns. Drawing on both collected narratives and pre-Vatican II rule books,[3] this chapter will explore themes of agency and passivity, individuality within community, 'innate' Catholicism and learnt behaviour. Recognising the demands of the pre-Vatican II system, it will consider its rewards as well as the concessions involved. Finally, it will reflect upon the position of religious congregations and religious themselves within the public/private dichotomy and the ways in which that dichotomy is unsettled by the women's accounts.

RELIGIOUS LIFE, PRE-VATICAN II

In entering religious life, women were expected to cut ties with the life they had beforehand, as well as the people who were part of it: '[Sisters] should strip themselves of all merely carnal affection for their relatives...holding [Christ, our Lord] in place of father, mother, brother and all things'.[4] Religious were required to 'cut themselves off' (Frances) or 'deny' (Catherine) their family, contact between them becoming minimal and regulated. Though their families could make supervised visits to the convent, few of the women of this study expected to visit their families more than once or twice after entry, if at all. If they were leaving Ireland to enter elsewhere, their chances of seeing family again were reduced still further. For many, separation from family was the first challenge religious life presented them with. Catherine, for example, recalled being

> heartbroken actually, leaving home...I was absolutely devastated ...I was really, really hurt. I came straight from home, from Ireland [to England]. First time out of Ireland...I remember going into the chapel there and I cried every day for months...I just couldn't stop crying.

Though she had accepted the situation at the time, looking back, Brenda felt 'there were too many things' being asked of religious:

> You know, your relationships with your friends, your relationship with your families. You were very much cut off, in a sense...It was very difficult. Especially, who we were related to, our mother and father and your family. Not being able to go to their funerals. Not being able to visit them when they were sick. All that sort of thing. And very strict hours for visiting and that. I found that very hard.

For those that were able to return to Ireland for visits, staying with family was usually forbidden. As previously noted, religious were not able to go home if a family member fell ill or died: 'My mother had a stroke...she was only a few miles down the road [but] I wasn't allowed to [visit her]' (Annette). Some of the women missed out on seeing family members ever again, among them Hannah: 'In fact, I never saw [my father] again because he died before I went back to Ireland. [He] had a heart attack and died and at that time we didn't go home either, so I didn't go home for the funeral or anything'. Recalling these incidents reflected their impact on the women both at the time and in retrospect.

Separation from family was not the last hardship the women faced in religious life. Although 'active', sisters in the pre-Vatican II period lived under a system which imposed monastic restrictions upon them, limiting their movement outside the convent as well as their lives and relationships within it: 'We were extremely strict and, I mean, we were allowed very little latitude' (Brenda). Presided over by the absolute authority of the superior, religious life was organised according to an elaborate set of rules, strictly enforced, which governed every aspect of a sister's life from appearance and deportment to behaviour and thought. Heavily laden timetables of work and prayer placed further demands on them, both physically and psychologically.

The roots of the pre-Vatican II system lay in the suspicion surrounding women who chose to eschew marriage and motherhood for life in all-female communities and attempts by the Catholic Church to exert control over them. By the time the women of this study entered, however, the rule had become the faith and remained so until the changes introduced under Vatican II: 'The sacred collection of rules...was the be all and end all. The black book was what was keeping you...You had this kind of idea, "Keep the rule and the rule will keep you". [There was] no [other] judgement of how you were doing' (Frances).

Known as 'the rule', rule books prescribed, often in the greatest detail, the particular self-identity and subject position religious were expected to inhabit, or strive to inhabit, completely and absolutely and at the expense of all other identities. Religion, previously experienced as 'innate' and 'natural' (though it was not, of course) became something to be learned, constantly performed and upon which the women would be judged (as successful sisters) by their superiors, fellow religious and themselves. This was essentially an identity project involving the breakdown of the individual and its replacement with the congregational identity as set out in the rule book.

There is no doubting the severity of the pre-Vatican II regime. Almost without exception, the women of this study described it in terms of hardship, for example, Irene: 'It was very, very difficult. *Very hard*. I'm not making it sound easy because it wasn't'. 'Looking back on it,' Norah wondered 'how we survived really'. Beyond separation from family, particularly difficult aspects of the life the women focused on included the rules of enclosure and silence ('At that time, there was a rule of silence. You never talked. I found that very hard, as you can imagine!' – Winnie), the harsh conditions under which religious lived ('When the children went home, the heating used to go down and we used to have this real cold [we] had to endure' – Elaine) and the lack of independence ('You had to get permission [for all sorts of] crazy things' – Catherine). Of course, religious life was meant to be difficult and this formed part of its heroic and martyrological appeal: arduousness was both a discourse of the regime and intrinsic to the experience of it.

GENDERED PROCESSES OF TRANSFORMATION

When describing their moment of entry into religious life, some of the women presented it as a step away from femininity. Annette, for example, remembered being 'tormented with anxiety' arriving at the convent with a handbag full of makeup, hidden there from the eyes of a disapproving mother. In the grounds of the convent, she 'went into the woods with the handbag and threw away the last vestiges of my adolescence and my material freedom'. Clothes were a recurring theme in Kate's narrative. Initially drawn to the postulant's habit, she had reservations about the full garb, which contrasted starkly with the outfit she remembered wearing the day she entered: 'A red dress and …heels as high as that! (*motioning very high heels*) Red shoes [too]!'.

Moving into the convent, wearing a habit and replacing one's baptismal name with that of a saint's name were all metaphorical symbols by which the secular self was put to death and the women were 're-born' into religious life. As a process, however, it was thoroughly gendered. It demanded that the women strive to become, through repression and denial, a particular *kind* of woman based on very particular notions of what women were like 'in essence' and the necessity of controlling them. Or, more correctly, of putting in place a system by which they controlled themselves. Women's bodies were central to the process of transformation.

One of the ways the system controlled women was through the

habit. The pre-Vatican II habit was unwieldy, restrictive and uncomfortable. Difficult to maintain, it covered the female body from head to foot, concealing the shape of its wearer and forbidding any investment in femininity. Teresa recalled having to 'strap [her]self into this thing, this terrible thing, everyday', remarking: 'It was terrible!...We were all bound up and tied up!...Any bit of femininity was completely squashed!'. Symbolically covering the women, the habit also physically repressed the female form by keeping the breasts not only hidden, but flattened: 'There was this denial of ...your womanly body...In the very early days, you weren't allowed to wear a bra...I mean, your breasts didn't exist. You didn't *have* breasts so there were no bras. [They] were bound' (Margaret). Clearly, there was a tension between the divine spiritual calling of a vocation and the 'inferior' female body in which it was housed. The discomfort of the habit represented the uneasy relationship between the spiritual and the corporeal, accentuating the female body as 'wrong' and other to its vocation.

Investing in physical appearance was regarded as vanity, a 'natural' female fault which the pre-Vatican II regime aimed to contain. As Catherine put it:

> You were taught – conditioned – not to [like yourself]. Anything to do with yourself was considered to be pride. How you looked, how you dressed, how you walked, how you talked. If you had a rib of hair showing. When I was a postulant I had very curly hair. And when I washed it, it used to fall into all waves...I remember [once, my] veil [was] hanging off the back of my head and getting *slated* for being proud, showing off my hair, you know?

There were no mirrors in convents, hair was cut short and hidden (as were bodily curves). Though expected to be well turned out, religious were not supposed to be concerned with their appearance.

Religious life also controlled the body by keeping it busy, especially through prayer and work. Rule books stated this quite clearly. For example: 'In order to avoid the innumerable faults of which idleness is a pernicious source, each [sister] shall always be occupied at some work [or] spiritual exercise.'[5]

Before they entered, the women adhered to the obligations of lay Catholicism through frequent rituals that were carried out even daily. The routine expected of them in religious life, however, was far more onerous. Typically, prayers and spiritual duties – all prescribed and mostly in common – took up about five hours of the day.[6] In addition, the women had their professional commitments as teachers, nurses and so on to attend to as well as domestic duties. Recreation and mealtimes were also scheduled. Many of the women were able to recall their daily routine in striking detail and, in so doing, drew attention to the physical demands it made upon them:

> I'd get up in the morning at half five. A quarter to six, you'd be down in the chapel. You had to say your prayers first and then you made a meditation. Then you had a gap, you had five or ten minutes. Now during that time you could get out and make your bed but I had charge of opening and shutting the [school] gates and all the shutters on the ground floor. Then, I'd rush upstairs and get the big mop and mop the corridor before the Blessed Sacrament would come up to the old sisters, the sick sisters. And then, make your bed and [go] down then and get mass. [After breakfast] we had a twenty minutes walk down to school and then when you got down there it was helter-skelter again. [Annette]

> There was Office [liturgical prayers] in the evening from say five-thirty to six and then there was adoration from six to six-thirty and then there was spiritual reading from six-thirty to seven ... And I can remember kneeling in church just falling asleep after having done a heavy days teaching and no outlet, you know? We had an hour's recreation, together, in the middle of the day. If you were free. But you might have duties in the school. And the same thing then from eight till nine at night, sitting around a table sewing ... You were under *terrible* strain, trying to live like this. [Frances]

Timetables, which tended to be the same throughout one congregation, were not easily changed: 'The horarium ... must be the same in all houses, and it must not be changed for light reason or without real necessity'.[7]

Considered essential to formation, religious life was specifically designed to be full in order to avoid the 'dangers' of indolence. As one rule book put it: 'Work, together with obedience and prayer will be the surest safeguard of the mind, while idleness ... begets every vice'.[8] The work of active nuns was considered particularly dangerous, putting them at risk of 'temptation'. According to Frances, active religious life was deemed inferior to contemplative ('the ideal really'). As a result, sisters were expected to fit their working lives into the superior model of contemplative life.

From the moment the women rose until going to bed at night, nearly every moment of their day was accounted for. As Annette put it:

> It was a fairly busy, full life... [We were] teaching full-time. And we were chars, we were gardeners, we were cooks, we were door-keepers, we were everything!... You hadn't time [to think], you'd so much work to do.

The demands of their timetable was something most of the women commented upon, whether only in passing, to describe their daily activities or, more pointedly, to make a judgement about the regime.

Detailed instructions were also given on deportment. For example: 'The head...should be kept straight and bent a little forward...The eyes should usually be cast down...The lips should be neither compressed nor too much open...The hands...should be kept still and placed modestly'.[9] If the body was taught to behave in a controlled and disciplined manner, the mind would follow suit.

The body was also controlled by keeping in check how it was nourished, both mentally and physically. In the Christian tradition, women were regarded as mentally weaker and less rational than men. This was reflected in religious life. As Frances put it:

> The attitude to women religious was that they were not capable. Their minds were so limited they couldn't appreciate the full Office so...because we were women...we had what was called a 'Little Office of Our Lady' which was a *tiny* group of songs [and] little bits of scripture in Latin'.

Access to reading material was closely monitored and restricted. Indeed, nuns' whole intellectual diet was rationed, partly because they were not deemed capable of digesting it but also, perhaps, to keep them weak. While religious were given 'adequate' (Aisling) food to sustain them for the work they did they were expected to limit their intake. As Annette recalled: 'After Mass, you'd go down to breakfast. Now, at that time, if you had porridge, you couldn't have bread and butter and if you had an egg, you couldn't have marmalade. You know, 'twas very, very rationed'.

In addition, the women were encouraged to fast regularly and were expected, as an act of humility, to eat food they did not like over food they preferred. In this, as in all cases, care needs to be taken distinguishing between the rhetoric of the rule book and the reality of sisters' lives. Annette herself remarked that, 'if you said you liked something, you got the opposite [but] you could work the system if you wanted to'. Moreover, given the position and status of religious in Irish society and, crucially, the power they had over those in their charge, it would be wrong to describe all nuns as 'weak', either in their manner, their actions, their physical appearance or their mental state. Be that as it may, the purpose of rationing was, as one rule book put it, to 'guard against the natural inclination to satisfy sensuality'[10] and women were more intimately associated with the body and the senses than the mind and its intellect.

Margaret described being a woman as 'something to be ashamed of in religious life', not only its exterior appearance but its interior functions too. She pointed out that 'in the early days', the sisters 'didn't even have proper sanitary protection' because 'it was a shameful thing to have periods...to need things for your body'. Once again, the tension between good and bad female is being reproduced. Women were capable of being good by striving for perfection but they were potentially, because they were intrinsically, bad. Their female bodies were a constant reminder of this. Before Vatican II, female religious were not allowed to touch the vessel that held the Blessed Sacrament if they were menstruating. This represents the central tension of religious life for women: despite their vocation, their earthly female bodies were difficult to overcome. The menstrual cycle served to reduce religious to this essential 'impurity'.

Of feeble mind, women's bodies were regarded as potentially powerful and dangerous and were especially connected with sexuality and reproduction. Despite official Church teaching that religious were asexual, some pre-Vatican II religious rule books displayed an almost obsessive preoccupation with sexuality. Elaine euphemistically connected the physical demands of religious life with the purpose of those demands:

> You were regulated: the way you talked, the way you walked, and your eyes cast down and not searching and looking around, you know?...Religious life was terribly guarded. You were secured all the time. Even if you wanted to, you couldn't commit it! You couldn't do anything.

Although in this instance, Elaine offered no explanation, in other comments she made about the importance of the rule in protecting women from developing or acting upon attractions to others, it was clear she was talking about sexual behaviour.

Whole chapters of rule books were dedicated to the correct behaviour of nuns in the presence of men. Although the convent and its enclosure provided a degree of protection, active religious came into contact with men through work, administration and convent management, during which times they were urged to 'take all precaution'.[11] Another rule book read:

> To preserve [their] virtue in all its integrity, the sisters will, with the help of grace, exercise the greatest vigilance over all their senses interior and exterior alike. They will never speak without witnesses with those of the other sex, except when and where they are allowed to do so...And as idleness leads to the loss of all the virtues but especially of chastity, they will never remain without some useful occupation.[12]

Religious had to cover their faces in public, avoid eye contact with men and control their thoughts through prayer. Catherine recalled the repercussions if these rules were not properly adhered to: 'If you were caught talking to a man or a priest, oh, sure!...It mattered a lot to other people. You'd be seen talking and then they'd stop [you]...I think they thought they were safe-guarding you, you know? [So] you wouldn't run off with them or something like that'. Rule books made clear the dangers of sexuality but tended to construct the women themselves as the problem – potential temptresses – and to locate danger within women themselves, rather than the men they met.

Religious life was not only concerned to protect against heterosexual relations but also to control relations between women. 'Particular friendships', as rule books termed them, were forbidden 'since nothing is more contrary to the chastity and union which must reign in a religious house'.[13] Several of the women in this study mentioned the rules governing relations between sisters. Frances remarked that 'getting together in twos or threes...was *absolutely* frowned upon' while Annette recalled that 'if anyone got very great [i.e. close] with another sister in the community, I think she'd have been put out [or] changed to another house'. Suspicion could be easily aroused: '[If] you talk[ed] to *anybody*...they'd think you had a particular friendship with them and they'd be separating you' (Catherine).

Religious also had to control the relationship they had with their own body. It was as they dressed, undressed and in bed that the women were least protected by surveillance and clothes, and many rule books instructed the women on correct behaviour to avoid seeing or touching their own naked body. Some directed women on how to position their bodies – hands crossed across the chest – and what to think of as they fell asleep. One instructed its members when going to sleep to 'occupy themselves with the thought of God, and of the subject of their meditation for the morrow'.[14] Despite the Church's official teaching that nuns were asexual, according to the rule books at least, the women would have had to think, though not speak, about controlling their sexuality daily. In this way, rule books offered a discourse of sexuality in which the existence, albeit repressed, of heterosexuality, lesbian sexuality and autoeroticism were referred to in veiled or less-veiled terminology.

Religious life continued to sex and gender those within in particular ways. Everything about religious' lives – the clothes they wore, the work they did, their living arrangements, reading and prayer material – was organised according to sex. The Catholic Church's theology prior to Vatican II regarded human nature as inherently dangerous and evil.[15] Hence, reformation of the individual was central to the aim of religious life. Importantly, however, the Church's interpretation of human nature was also gendered, based not only on preconceived notions concerning the essential characteristics of humans but the essential characteristics of men and women. Consequently, religious life was organised precisely to mitigate against women religious succumbing to their female nature and, especially, its bodily desires.

AUTHORITY AND OBEDIENCE

Authority and obedience to authority underpinned the pre-Vatican II system. Religious were expected to obey their superior 'completely, promptly, courageously...and without resistance'[16] 'even if it be difficult and repugnant to nature'.[17] Unsurprisingly, obedience was an overarching theme in the women's accounts also. Frances, for example, described it as 'spelled out' in religious life, while many of the women repeated rules specific to obedience in the interviews, often verbatim. Most, indeed, recalled their response to the pre-Vatican II regime in terms of their own obedience to it. For example, Pauline commented that 'We did what we were told to do, we were very obedient', while Annette remarked in retrospect that she was 'quite obedient. I'm that kind of person'.

Religious were expected to recognise their own worthlessness in the face of God and their superior, learn not to trust themselves and submit, instead, to the authority of others. As the St Mildred rule book put it, sisters were to be 'internally resigned... to renounce their own will and judgement'.[18] Much was made of the authority of the superior. As God's representative in the congregation, superiors were held to be endowed with a special knowledge mere sisters did not have. It was they, for example, who decided upon training paths for individual sisters and, with their council, the most suitable direction for the congregation as a whole. Vitally, superiors decided whom of the novices 'genuinely' had a vocation.

The power of the superior to expel individuals was great indeed and informed the relational dynamics within the congregation. Most sisters would not have wanted to displease their superior or question her authority, fearing the consequences for themselves. This was evidenced in several comments made by the women which revealed their anxieties about being asked to leave the convent and 'failing' as a sister. Geraldine, reprimanded by her superior for not 'keeping custody of the eye' (it was noticed that she had looked around the room during meal time), spoke of her 'sheer relief' at finding she was not to be sent home for this misdemeanour. When Annette remarked that her 'big worry from the day I entered – oh! For years! Until I came over here – was that they'd send me home. I was *terrified!*', she was talking about a period of time that amounted to eighteen years. While rule books offered specific guidelines on behaviour, they did not give much practical advice for recognising when the state of perfection had been achieved, if, indeed, it could be. Individual religious were not qualified to judge their own vocation. This was the job of the superior. Annette and others' uncertainty about what constituted a vocation and led them to question if they really had one at all and many feared exposure as a 'fraud'.

Referring to the preordinance of religious life before Vatican II, Elaine remarked 'Our lives were so laid out for us and we had everything really: our prayer life, ...our work life'. Others were more critical. Geraldine, for instance, described pre-Vatican II life as 'institutional', Teresa referred to it 'a restricted regime'. Catherine likened it to 'a strait-jacket' while Margaret talked of women religious having 'absolutely no freedom'. These were, of course, retrospective judgements. At the time, the women had, as Deirdre and so many others put it, 'accepted it'. Such was the frequency of this phrase, in fact, it was an important and recurring theme running throughout their accounts. For Brenda it was 'part of the deal ... If God had called you and this was your life, then this was the price'. In many of the women's accounts, however, was the recognition of another time, not easily understood from this distance. Frances thought it *'extraordinary* when you look back on it now'. Similarly, Aisling remarked: 'How we did it, I don't know. People don't do that kind of thing now! But that was what you did.' As if in response, Brenda pointed to the safety of numbers: 'It was just part of [it], and everybody else was with you. We were good numbers in those days'.

The women accepted the regime because 'when canon law says [something], you kind of accept it' (Frances) as 'the way to holiness and the way to God and the way to everything' (Lilian) but equally because 'you never questioned *anything*' (Frances). Obedience was both the cornerstone of religious life and the mechanism on which it depended. Obedience was also something that had been developed in the women as they were growing up: in school, at home and in society. Only Vera suggested any equivocation when she remarked that she had 'accepted things [but] accepted them reluctantly'.

Some of the women talked also about bending or breaking the rules, drawing attention to their disobedience.[19] Irene and Catherine mentioned the sign-language developed to aid clandestine communication, while Joan recalled her own attempts to 'break the rules left, right and centre'. Certainly, it seems unlikely that Annette (see p. 84) was alone in recognising the situation could be manipulated. If caught breaking the rule, however, there were penalties to be faced. Catherine, for example, was 'always getting into trouble. *Always.'* Publicly questioning the rule was also severely disciplined. Vera's time in the noviciate was extended for this very reason: 'I kept saying "this is contrary to reason!" [and] got six months extra for my disobedience.' Of course, if women were found to be breaking the rule frequently enough or if they seemed to truly disagree with the pre-Vatican II regime, they could be expelled. In acts of resistance such as these, however, the women challenged, albeit subtly, the scripted identity[20] they were expected to perform in religious life.

Although not a rejection of religious life, in a small way their resistance represented a renegotiation of its terms.

AGENCY AND PASSIVITY

The women's expectations of religious life as set out in Chapter 2 need to be reconciled with the realities of its repressive structure. Elaine described the position of women religious during this period, not unfavourably, as 'guarded by authority, as somebody who had no mind [or] will of your own'. Religious life required 'docile bodies',[21] women who were capable of submitting to its strict regime. This was made clear in the rule books, all of which profiled the ideal temperament and characteristics required of aspiring religious. The St Marie congregation, for example, prized 'moral qualities such as judgement, piety, strength of will [and] docility'[22] while the St Nadine rule book noted that 'those in whom a taste for singularity is noticed will be carefully excluded'.[23] Most rule books also identified an ideal age for aspirants, based on an assumed compliance of younger women: 'The age most suitable for admission into the [congregation] is about eighteen. Those who have reached an age at which formed habits would make it difficult to mould them to religious life should not easily be received'.[24]

The 'passivity' demanded by absolute obedience sits uneasily with the way the women framed their attraction to religious life, especially with respect to their claims to subjectivity and agency. In fact, theirs was an 'active' passivity. The women chose to enter religious life (an act of agency in itself) and, in so doing, actively produced their own obedience. As Frances put it, 'As I say, it was all part of what you took on. You went in with your eyes open'. Although several of the women spoke of responsibility being taken away from them ('You just passed the buck. You just went and asked the Reverend Mother and she had to make the decisions' – Rebecca), at the same time, they were accountable for themselves literally every moment of the day. Their stories of accepting, consciously, the rule suggests as much.

The very existence of convents depended upon individuals choosing to enter and remain within them voluntarily. The technology of government, which was based on authority and surveillance, could succeed only if individuals were willing to submit themselves to it. It was a government of the self, by the self. Although religious life was expressly concerned with the 'death' of the secular self, the self was vital to its aims, and challenges any simplistic reduction of religious life as a passive existence. That said, the opportunity in which to exercise agency within convent life was limited, if not distorted. While the women were actively involved in submitting themselves to the pre-Vatican II regime, there was precious little space for them to exercise agency not dictated by it.

REWARDS

Religious life was not, of course, without its rewards. For some, spiritual rewards were found in the structure of the regime itself, one they not only accepted but invested in. Physical and psychological hardship was a discourse appropriate to the ideology of religious life which was, according to one of the rule books, 'a life of penance and privation'.[25] For Elaine, reward lay in the hardship:

> The novice mistress used to say…'don't think you're giving Our Lord a full service if you're not so tired that you have to drag yourself up to bed at night'. And you felt like that. You felt very eager to do as much as you possibly could…There was something in that hard and suffering life that cleaned you interiorly…and drew you to…a greater light,…a knowledge of God [and] of yourself. I thought, if I stick this then really I've been called to heaven.

For others, recompense came almost in spite of the regime:

> You never questioned *anything*. And you were never given any encouragement to. Discussion was *out*. It was a kind of military discipline. But all the time, you have to balance it with [the] real spiritual richness [that was there also]. And although prayer in a sense was kind of mechanical, just giving time to prayer, I think, does do something to spiritualise your outlook on life…So, we made it work somehow or other' [Frances].

For some, the simple fact of being in their chosen religious congregation was enough. Ruminating on the difficulty of the pre-Vatican II regime, May remarked:

> I expected things to be [hard]. [But] I didn't mind what they asked me to do. If I was to walk on my head, I didn't mind, I'd do it…I

loved [the congregation] so much. And I think I've loved [it] ever since. Ever since. I've never, ever not loved it. *Never.*

Work was an important source of fulfilment for many of the women, one not easily separable from religious life itself. Not only was work fundamental to being an active nun, religious during this period worked only within their own institutions, which were very often close, if not attached, to the convents in which they lived. When asked if religious life had lived up to her expectations, Hannah replied that it had because 'I always... really did enjoy teaching', revealing that for her at least, there was an inextricable relationship between religious life and work.

Work also provided, for some, an outlet for energy that might not have found expression in the convent itself. In the following quote from Yvonne, the sense of fun is palpable, something she associated directly with teaching and the extra-curricular activities:

> I enjoyed very much my few years here in Ireland [before leaving for the missions in 1949]. I spent three years [teaching]. And liked it very, very much. Very much. They were boarding schools, you know? And I was kind of pretty good at organising games and things. And I was always getting into trouble because I'd... make a terrific [racket]. Whether it was outside or inside, [the girls would] be shouting their heads off and there'd be nuns above going to bed early or something and I'd be getting into trouble!... But I loved it, I must say. I loved it. I suppose I loved teaching, really, you know?

In fact, Yvonne resisted the suggestion that pre-Vatican II religious life was over-regulated. For her, that description 'doesn't ring a bell at all'. Later, however, she described some of the religious she had met in the years after her profession as 'sad wrecks of women... [Not] normal, balanced women', which she believed was 'possibly the result of that strict enclosure'. In commenting thus, she recognised the existence of such a regime, even if it was not how she claimed to experience life herself.

Many of the women commented on the sororal rewards of religious and community life. Margaret, for example, found a 'real joy in being together' while Irene found a 'great peace' knowing herself and her co-religious were 'all focusing in the one direction... all in it together'. Given the intensity of the rule, small gestures of friendship might have seemed more significant such that whether the women broke the rules or not, close friendships could be formed. At any rate, friendship was identified by several of the women as one of the most rewarding aspects of religious life. For Joan, the regime actually facilitated strong ties of friendship:

> You went home twice in a lifetime...You [knew you'd have] your rough days, your rough weeks...You [knew you'd] get news of a death in the family. But [the congregation would] always be there, you know?...There was that tremendous bonding...It wasn't found in any books, it wasn't written into any rule but it was a real human, loving, supportive thing that was very, very powerful.

The exception to this experience was Annette, who remarked that communal living was for her 'the real trial...of religious life', illustrating that community could be constraining also.

Religious life also had much to offer women as *women*. The societies in which these religious congregations existed and, more especially, the society in which the women grew up, placed particular and sometimes elaborate restrictions upon women's lives that were guarded by Church and society, including by other women. Interestingly, although religious life exerted control over nuns' bodies, it gave women religious a degree of autonomy over their bodies, at least with respect to preventing others from touching or harming it. This was something marriage, for instance, could not guarantee. In addition, institutional channels were in place for religious to complain if they were being mistreated and one of the few private correspondences they were allowed was with a priest or bishop (how seriously complaints would have been taken is, of course, another matter).

Although remarkably structured and regulated, religious life did present women with opportunities not always available to them outside. It gave them the opportunity to pursue a respectable alternative path to marriage and motherhood, to be educated, receive training, work and travel. It did not, however, provide them with an opportunity to transcend the limits of their gender. In fact, there was little space under the pre-Vatican II regime to negotiate or question the form of womanhood the women were expected to take on, which is not to say all of them would have done so. Many religious, the women of this study included, accepted the Church's teaching on women. Elaine, for example, talked about the protection women religious needed from 'human frailty', while Margaret admitted in retrospect that she had 'took on the prevailing attitude of the inferiority of women'.

IDENTITY RECONFIGURED

Entering religious life fundamentally altered the relationship women had with their families, so crucial to their sense of self prior to entering. Harder for some than others, there is no doubt that relations with family entered a period of arrested development under the pre-Vatican II regime. Elaine remarked that the censorship of letters limited their content to 'the weather and the land', while Catherine opined that there could be 'no real communication' with family after entering. For Aisling, even when she heard news from home, it was always one step removed: 'My mother, especially, wrote. My father would write two or three lines, to keep up all the news. But you never remembered it in the same way. You know, that somebody died or somebody got married. You didn't remember it as well as you would have if you were there, you know?'

The religious identity prescribed by religious life was significantly different to the one the women had held prior to entering, rooted as it had been in family, home and Irishness. In reconfiguring their religious identity, the women changed the terms and references used to describe it. For many, community life became important, communal identity being one of the few identities sanctioned by religious life. On entering, women ceased to be individuals and became 'one heart and one soul'.[26] The women dressed alike, had no personal possessions and a large part of their daily activities were carried out in common:

> In the old regime you had your Office at the same time [every day]. You got up in the morning, you were all in chapel [together and] said your morning prayer together. You did your half an hour meditation [together], all sitting in the chapel. Then, I think we had a Mass together. You'd tea-time together, you'd supper together, dinner together... recreation together... All at certain times. [Kate]

Moving immediately from their natal family into religious life as so many of the women in this study did, it was not surprising that for many the community replaced the family. Some women adopted congregational histories as their own. For example, May enquired if I 'kn[ew] about our life?', referring to the history of the St Mildred congregation. When Bernadette, a member of a nursing community that had originally made home-visits, remarked 'that part of nursing closed down for us so we started having our own hospitals', she was referring to a practice that ended before she was born. Irene also admitted that ties to her community had replaced those she had felt for her family.[27]

PRIVATE OR PUBLIC?

Religious life took women out of the home, but could it be said to take them out of the domestic sphere? Was the convent an extension of the home, in which submissive women were confined and silenced? Or did religious life provide an entry point to the public arena? And, if so, at what cost? As previous chapters have illustrated, in terms of the expectations they had of religious life prior to entering, the women of this study conceived of religious life primarily in terms of the public sphere. Nor was this surprising. Providing health, education and other services, religious were 'of' the state and there is no denying their influence in forming that state and its people.[28] But their position was complicated by rules which limited them, individually and collectively, in interacting personally with the public, expressing or voicing opinions, challenging Church or state policy. Though there is much evidence to the contrary,[29] religious were expected to be seen without, necessarily, being heard. Theirs was a particular kind of 'public', made possible because female religious were generally regarded as adjuncts, be that of the state, the Church or the divine.

As professed religious, the women were instantly recognisable as nuns and became, as they saw it, 'ambassadors', representing, variously, all religious, the Catholic Church, Ireland itself. Their public persona was qualified, however, by the regulations religious life imposed upon them:

> It was really strict and they wouldn't *allow* us to talk to the boarders. You just didn't. And then we weren't allowed talk to the parents. And you'd walk up and down the street and you never spoke to anybody. I found it very difficult. Awful difficult! [Annette]

Despite this, for some women, Annette included, it was in the public aspect of their persona that the essence of religious life lay: 'I used to go out and you'd see poor people and they'd salute you and you'd think, "I must deserve the salute!", you know? I must be able to put up with things that are difficult and hard'. Such were the rules governing the convent and its cloister, women in religious life in the pre-Vatican II period lived in all-female communities, their 'private' sphere almost entirely gendered. However, the rules and hierarchy that underpinned the system prevented congregations from being, automatically at least, havens in which positive femaleness dominated.

CONCLUSION

Religious life during the pre-Vatican II era was an apparatus, a structure designed to transform those who entered into it. Although the state of perfection which the women were striving to achieve might have been out of their reach, they were undoubtedly influenced by the pressure placed on them, as well as their own attempts to conform to it. Appropriating a congregational identity involved personal modification, adaptation and reformation, if not complete transformation. For Catherine, this was most obvious during her first visit to her family in Ireland,[30] by which time she had been a religious for seven years:

> Everything was strange. My house was strange. My family were strange ...I was moulded by then into ...saying my prayers at a certain time and keeping aloof...Going to bed at a certain time ...I wouldn't spend any money ..., wouldn't be late for anything or put up with anything ...I thought to myself I had to do all these things because that was important ...[My family] thought I'd lost a lot of my fun and my naturalness. They said they noticed it very strongly. You know, that I used to be very, well, hearty and full of life and all that sort of thing. And I'd lost a lot of it. I got more 'nunny'.

Catherine's personality had in effect been re-shaped such that the rules and obligations had become, while not second nature, a defining part of her personality.

In contrast to how the women (mis-)remembered the early socialisation processes by which they had 'become' Catholics in early life, religious life under the pre-Vatican II regime was experienced as a scripted and learned performance: a difficult, conscious, but ultimately rewarding adherence to rules and regulations which governed the women's form and behaviour for almost every moment of the day. The process by which they became nuns was thoroughly gendered, rooted in particular notions of women and womanhood which far pre-dated the lives of the women in this study. As mentally inferior and latently sexual, a certain shame was attached to womanhood within religious life. Although there was little space during this period to question or negotiate gendered identity, this is not to suggest the women of this study were unfulfilled by religious life or, indeed, that they rejected the particular prescription of womanhood they were presented with within it. While few thought to question it, most derived meaning and value from it.

NOTES

1 *Constitution and Rule Book of the CSSMd* (1954), p. 74.
2 Only one woman, Josephine, entered religious life after Vatican II. However, because change was introduced piecemeal and over time, all of the women were familiar with the pre-Vatican II style of religious life, and many, indeed, had been formed by it.
3 In order to be approved by Rome, religious congregations were required to have a written constitution which outlined not only the internal structure of the congregation, the work it was set up to do (its 'charism') and the dress or habit which would distinguish its members from others but also, often in great detail, how its members should behave, think and act. Known as 'the rule', these books instructed women religious on every aspect of their day including work, prayer, appearance and deportment and were literally a blue-print for religious life. Although each rule book was particular to its own congregation, they generally followed a set pattern based on the writings of either St Augustine (AD 354–430) or St Ignatius (AD 1491–1556). The pre-Vatican II rule books consulted for this study had between fifteen and forty-nine chapters, with as many as 416 specific directions to be followed.
4 *Constitution and Rule CSSMd*, p. 74.
5 *Constitution and Rule Book of the CSSN* (1934), p. 50.
6 This estimate is based on the women's accounts and with reference to their pre-Vatican II rule books.

7   *Constitution and Rule CSSMd*, p. 58.
8   *Constitution and Rule of the CSSL* (1927), p. 125.
9   *Constitution and Rule CSSMd*, pp. 59–60.
10 *Constitution and Rule CSSN*, p. 87.
11 *Constitution and Rule CSSMd*, p. 35.
12 *Constitution and Rule CSSM* (1925), pp. 41–2.
13 *Constitution and Rule CSSMd*, p. 50.
14 *Constitution and Rule CSSL*, p. 145.
15 L. Fuller, *Irish Catholicism Since 1950: The Undoing of a Culture* (Dublin: Gill and Macmillan, 2002), p. 119.
16 *Constitution and Rule CSSN*, p. 53.
17 *Constitution and Rule CSSMd*, p. 20.
18 Ibid.
19 The women who mentioned breaking the rules did so safe in the knowledge that Vatican II had since judged the rules they broke as archaic and unnecessary.
20 E. Goffman, *The Presentation of Self in Everyday Life* (New York: Doubleday, 1959).
21 M. Foucault, *Discipline and Punish The Birth of the Prison* (Harmondsworth: Penguin, 1975), pp. 135–69.
22 *Constitution and Rule CSSM*, p. 17.
23 *Constitution and Rule CSSN*, p. 20.
24 *Constitution and Rule CSSMd*, pp. 257–7.
25 *Constitution and Rule CSSL*, p. 115.
26 Ibid, p. 118.
27 After Irene's parents had passed away in the early 1980s, she ceased to visit Ireland with any regularity. Such was the strength of her connection to other members of her congregation who had died, however, that she continued to visit the town where they were buried every year 'just to pray with them and be with them in spirit'. For Irene at least, the connection between herself and her community seemed to transcend the physicality of mortality in a way that was not the case for her family.
28 Inglis, *Moral Monopoly*.
29 MacCurtain, 'Late in the Field'.
30 During which she had a constant chaperone, an elderly nun, and stayed not at her family home but in a local convent.

CHAPTER 4

Irish Women Religious: England and the Missions

'Of course I was emigrating. But you didn't call it emigrating if you were entering a religious order...It was a different kind of emigration, you see?'[1]

INTRODUCTION

The pre-Vatican II regime demanded that religious, as part of the process of becoming a nun, shed as much of their secular self as was possible, including national, regional and familial identity. The women were 'not encouraged', as Irene put it,[2] to talk about where they were from, a regulation made clear in the rule books. The St Louise rule book stated, for example, that 'the sisters...will strip themselves of their self-will, as well as of all natural attachment to their country, parents [and] friends'.[3] The ability to move away from such affiliations was considered a sign of progress towards becoming a nun, evidenced in the superior tone Joan, who entered a congregation in England in 1949, assumed over another Irish postulant more recent than herself: 'I remember well, Eilish must have been in for a week. We had recreation in the middle of the day and she said to me, "Where are you from?" And I said – only six months down the road ahead of her, mind! – "Oh! We don't talk about these things!"'

One aspect of their lives common to all the women of this study was the fact that they each lived some, some all, of their lives as religious outside Ireland. Twenty-two of the thirty had or still lived in England, while fourteen of them had lived, for varying periods of time, on the mission fields of Africa, Asia and Latin America, each of these places providing a very different setting for religious life. This chapter does not set itself the task of comparing those experiences – to do so would be impossible. Rather, it will explore how the women's experiences of religious life in the pre-Vatican II period could be, and was, shaped by the specificity of their situation as white, Irish women in religious congregations outside Ireland.

ENGLAND

More than half of the women in this study left Ireland to enter religious life in England or left Ireland for England having already recently entered religious life.[4] Between them, they entered five different congregations. Although the rule was designed to eliminate, often through repression, personal identities or histories, religious life in general and congregations in particular continued to position the women within them in specific ways with respect to ethnicity, as it did in relation to class and gender. Under the pre-Vatican II regime and from the moment of entry, novices were schooled to replace their self identity with a communal congregational one. In reality, however, this corporate 'personality' tended to have an ethnic basis. For the women of this study who lived in England, their experiences were influenced significantly by their choice of congregation, most especially by whether that congregation had a majority-Irish population, as four in this study had, or not.

The majority-Irish congregations (the Sisters of St Louise; the Sisters of St Nadine; the Sisters of St Cecile; and the Sisters of St Marie)

Though none of the congregations the women of this study who lived in England entered were Irish in origin, four had majority-Irish populations. For the women in these congregations, 'Irish' proved a popular adjective used to describe the congregations, not only their populations but the institutions themselves. Catherine, for example, described her congregation as 'a very Irish community' while Margaret remarked that, 'in fact, there was a very Irish feel to the [community] in this country... *All* the vocations came from Ireland... Irish culture was just transposed'.[5]

Culture is a nebulous concept. When referring to a country, a nation and a nationality, it would be difficult, if not impossible, to pin down in any specific or non-contradictory way what its culture is. In this instance, Margaret was referring to certain 'badges' of Irishness that were maintained within religious life but which befitted the refined, regulated and strict nature of religious life in the period, as well as its class identity. Thus, she meant a particularly middle-class Catholic Irish identity, one selected and sanctioned by the congregations themselves. Irish feast days, for example, were given greater recognition, pictures representing Ireland hung on convent walls, conversations during recreation focused on Ireland and the limited news the women received often related to what was happening 'back home'.[6] Positions of authority within the congregation were also for the most part held by Irish women, a reflection of demographics certainly but also, perhaps, of nepotism.

That these congregations had 'Irish' populations, and personalities, made the transition – from Ireland to England, as well as from secular to nun – easier for the women of this study and gave rise to feelings of belonging in what were essentially alien environments, both of the congregation and English society. This was something most of the women commented on. For example, Kate said she 'felt more at home ...our spirit is a very family spirit anyway'. Feeling 'at home' conveys a sense of belonging. For Kate, the intimacy of her own family was being recreated in religious life. That the congregations were 'Irish' gave the women a sense that they were still 'at home', despite, for the most part, having left Ireland for the first time. For Margaret, living with other Irish women in a congregation in which an expression of Irish culture predominated allowed her to imagine that she had never left Ireland at all: 'It didn't seem like England ... just seemed [like] a little bit of Ireland stuck in Manchester.'

The predominance of Irish culture, and however that was defined by the congregations,[7] was maintained at the expense of other ethnicities and cultures, especially Englishness. By the nineteenth century, Catholicism had been established as a vital component of Irish national identity, in opposition to English Protestantism. Intrinsic in the discourse of innate Irish Catholicism was a degree of Irish superiority and anti-English/Protestant bias. This was reflected in the congregations themselves. For example, the Irish way of doing things was considered to be the 'right' way: Catherine was told as a young novice to 'follow what the Irish sisters are doing' while another woman overheard one sister being told she was 'doing fine for an English nun'. Clearly, some Irish women took attitudes of Irish Catholic superiority and English inferiority with them to England: 'There was a judgemental attitude towards [English] people ... Their faith wasn't as strong as ours ... England was not as Catholic and as faithful as Ireland. [We were] closer to God!' (Margaret).

The binary in which Irishness was constructed as superior to Englishness, based on the assumption that it was more intrinsically Catholic, affected English sisters within the congregations.[8] Lillian, for example, observed that 'sometimes sisters would become more Irish than the Irish themselves...to do that when there's a couple of other English sisters in the community can be quite insensitive'. Some of Kate's Irish co-religious would make verbal reference to the positive character traits of Irishness at the expense, she felt, of English sisters:

> Some sisters, they're very 'the Irish' this and 'the Irish' that and 'the Irish' this that and the other. It's too much when you're...living in a different culture and that can put people's backs up. See, the English were very much in the minority in our congregation and I think sometimes they got a bit too much of the Irish. They did. *Some* of them said [so]. Some of them wouldn't let you know. [Kate]

Processes of 'othering' such as these served to mark the English sisters out as 'not quite as good as' the Irish sisters. Interestingly, this was occurring in the broader context of England where Irish people tended to be positioned as inferior to the native population. In reality, the two were interconnected. While an element of innate Irish Catholicism, and religious superiority, was evident in the Irish missionary project, in England this existed in response to a society which positioned Ireland, the Irish and especially Irish Catholics as an unruly and suspect minority. The construction of Irish Catholic superiority cannot be separated from constructions of Irishness by or in Britain. In asserting an identity from a marginal position, the Irish women were entering into an othering project themselves (against English sisters) based on established discourses of Irishness formed in the nineteenth and twentieth centuries.

Useful to making sense of these dynamics is Avtar Brah's notion of 'diaspora space', which problematises the notion of places and nations being made up of majorities and minorities, or dominant and dominated groups. For Avtar Brah, diaspora space is a 'conceptual category inhabited not only by those who have migrated and their descendants, but equally by those who are constructed or represented as indigenous'.[9] This more fluid approach to subjectivity, and it is one Bronwen Walter uses to explore the experiences of Irish women in Britain,[10] allows us to move away from colour-based notions of who is 'inside' and 'outside' and think instead of people inhabiting dominant and dominated spaces simultaneously or in sequence, depending on the particular 'dimension of differentiation'.[11] The women of this study occupied both dominant and dominated subject positions simultaneously: in the context of English society, where they were othered as Irish, as Catholic and as women, and within the religious communities in which they lived, where they formed the dominant group. Although Brah did not use diaspora space to explore these particular dynamics,[12] her more fluid approach to place allows for the women's membership of a dominant group in one respect, them being othered in another.

Organisationally, congregations were religious communities, and also communities of women, but they could be internally divided along ethnic lines,[13] creating a situation in which, in the same religious community, some members were more 'in' than others.[14] Religious congregations maintained clear and distinct boundaries between themselves and the 'outside' which allowed for different dynamics to operate within them. Despite the high ideals of the pre-Vatican II regime, it is obvious that ethnicity remained important within these congregations. Religious communities were still social institutions – modalities of social relations – and, as such, were riddled with hierarchies and exclusionary practices. They were also sites of power. Power is not generally associated with minority or excluded groups but religious congregations are 'discursive formations' in which constructions on the basis of ethnicity gave power to some of the women over others.[15] The experiences of the women of this study bring out the complexities of othering projects, including the possibility of one person or group being simultaneously involved in othering projects as they are othered themselves.[16]

Othering could also occur on the basis of ethnicity within the same ethnic group. In contrast to the experiences recounted above, Annette felt distinct in a majority-Irish congregation in England precisely on account of her Irishness, or form of it. Due to travel restrictions imposed between England and Ireland during the Second World War, the St Louise congregation created a provisional noviciate in Ireland for Elaine and two other postulants. Elaine remained in Ireland following her profession for eighteen years before being moved, in 1957, to England. In England, she felt dislocated: classed and 'raced' differently to those around her: 'I found it very tough. [The congregation] was very British. And very upper class. [I] began to feel this inferiority complex...They kind of looked down on me. I was from the bogs and knew nothing'.

Annette felt positioned as rural, working-class (though this was not her background) and inferior, which conforms to stereotypical assumptions made about Irish people in England generally. She often used the terms 'British' and 'Irish' to distinguish between 'them' and 'us/me', relying on historical constructions of Irish as *not* British and vice versa. Interestingly, however, Annette was referring primarily to other Irish women, who, for her, had 'become British', thus suggesting a fluidity around ethnicity. By contrast, Kate described the same congregation (St Louise) as 'very Irish'. Clearly, however, whatever way it was Irish for Kate conflicted with Annette's notion of Irishness, which included using the Irish language: 'Irish culture is so different...I did everything through Irish all my life: I was trained through Irish, everything was through Gaelic and...Gaelic culture was [not] appreciated [in England]'.

The women of this study entered non-Irish congregations which, outside Ireland, certainly would not have worked through the medium of Irish. In addition, English might have seemed more appropriate to their class position.[17] For Elaine, however, the language medium created a division between herself and her Irish co-religious. By providing an alternative reading to Kate's of the ethnic identity of the St Louise congregation, her account also illustrates how differently ethnic 'personalities' could be read, interpreted and experienced by individuals. It is worth noting, however, that moving to England following a considerable period in religious life in Ireland did not automatically produce this response. Bernadette, who had been a religious for twelve years before moving to England during the Second World War, found the transition to be almost seamless, remarking: 'well, once we were with the sisters, we were at home'.

The English congregation (the Sisters of St Mildred)

Looking back, 'the thing [Eileen] remember[ed] most [about moving to England] was a sense of inferiority'. The nine other women who, during the pre-Vatican II period, lived in religious communities in England without a majority-Irish population had entered the same English congregation as Eileen did, which, from its inception in the nineteenth century, maintained a middle-class English ethos. Prospective candidates were expected to be able to reflect this ethos themselves. For Irish women, this meant 'becoming' English and, if they were not already, middle-class. To this end, Irish choir sisters were offered elocution lessons to get rid of their 'brogue'.[18] According to its dictionary definition,[19] 'brogue' refers not only to an Irish accent but a speech impediment. Interpreting Irish accents or speech patterns as defective epitomises one of the most commanding stereotypes of the Irish in England: as people of low intelligence. As a negative judgement on their ability to speak properly is certainly how the women of the St Mildred congregation who mentioned the elocution lessons interpreted them. Aisling, for example, commented that 'within the community, I must say, we did suffer over our accents ... We did have speech training ... to learn to read properly'. Mary Kells describes speech as central to a person's sense of identity[20] and this is, arguably, especially the case for Irish people in England, for whom accent is a key form of identification as Irish.

While the women interpreted speech lessons in the same way, they responded differently to them. Aisling politely declined, Hannah refused to take part.[21] Pauline, though she regarded them as part of a project of Anglicisation ('Really, you had to become Anglo-Irish'), agreed to attend because they appealed to her interest in drama and role play. While Pauline did not feel that she was 'badly affected' by the lessons, all three women recognised they could be psychologically damaging to women less self-assured than themselves. Hannah remarked, for example, that she:

> never felt any inferior[ity] complex [but] I think some people did ... They had elocution lessons so they'd speak correctly. Some of them had to [learn] to talk [again] ... They laugh about them [now] but I think they found it very difficult.

Aisling felt that those who had changed their accents 'became kind of affected sounding', which suggested also that she, at least, was not convinced by their attempts to 'pass'. As noted by Mary J. Hickman, Bronwen Walter and others,[22] many Irish people living in Britain have elected to change their accents so as not to be recognised as Irish. In the case of the St Mildred congregation, however, the pressure was internally applied.

Irish women were not the only women in the St Mildred congregation to be offered voice training. Women with strong regional English accents were also given the opportunity to take the edge off their accents, although for them this would not necessarily have represented de-nationalisation. Regional accents were associated with the working classes and elocution helped conceal working-class roots. The implied message for Irish sisters, however, was that they were *all* working class. Irish migrants in Britain had traditionally been homogenised as working class (and potentially contaminant).[23] In fact, class and ethnicity could not easily be separated. Regional accents might have betrayed not only class but ethnic backgrounds. The majority of working class Catholics in Britain were Irish migrants themselves or descendants of them.[24] As such, the Catholic Church in England was eager to accent its patriotic *English* character in order to counterbalance the Protestant claim that it was a 'mysterious, threatening and unEnglish force'.[25] To this end, it made great efforts to obscure the numerical importance of its Irish members.[25]

The respect and prestige of the St Mildred congregation was built upon its ties to a specifically English, middle-class church and it might not have wanted to emphasise its Irish element (generally about one-third of accepted vocations came from Ireland, although the majority of lay sisters were Irish). In fact, there had been some debate within the community concerning the wisdom of opening a recruitment house in Ireland: 'There was quite a bit of fear in the English province that the standards would go down with this influx of the Irish' (Pauline).

In addition to the formal distinction between choir and lay nuns, the St Mildred congregation was internally organised according to a complex hierarchy based on ethnicity and social background, one not lost on entrants. For example, Frances was aware that 'nationality[-wise] the Irish were...fairly low' while Pauline recognised that ethnicity and social background combined to position her in a particular way with respect to her fellow postulants:

> I wasn't the only Irish but I must say, we were very few...and the others [had] been to a St Mildred school. Muggins had not!... Everything I did was wrong: my accent was wrong, what I said was wrong. Even the understanding of religion...Irish religion was very devotional and this was considered very ignorant and low-class.

This othering of the Irish sisters on the basis of ethnicity, religion and class was the inverse of the situation in the majority-Irish congregations where 'Irish' Catholicism was categorised as superior.

Post-noviciate, the women in the St Mildred congregation learned, 'how to behave', as Pauline put it, and being Irish became less of a problem for them, externally at least. Internally, however, the women continued to feel Irish and be aware of it as a distinguishing feature about themselves. Pauline, for example, felt 'sick' when she heard her superior comment: 'of course, with an Irish priest, you never know their background'. Similarly, Hannah would 'get so mad [but] couldn't say *anything*' when her 'very, very British' co-religious made ill-informed or racist comments concerning Ireland and its history. Given the strict nature of the convent, there was no space for these women to articulate their feelings other than by continuing to be conscious of and claiming a sense of themselves as Irish. By reacting to these sorts of situations, albeit silently, they were both holding on to their ethnicity and resisting de-nationalisation projects.

Concerning their life in England, questions about Irishness within religious life in the pre-Vatican II period tended to yield more detailed and lengthier responses from women in the St Mildred congregation than was the case for the rest of the women who had or still lived there. Unlike the women from the majority-Irish congregations who were able only retrospectively to recognise the importance of ethnicity in the pre-Vatican II regime (Catherine, for example, remarked that she 'didn't know any different, to be honest ... for many, many years'), the women in the St Mildred congregation had a 'double knowledge' of what was occurring. They recognised simultaneously the different treatment themselves and other sisters were receiving.

Despite the importance of ethnicity, focusing solely on it serves to highlight ethnic communities or differences while temporarily erasing other forms of collective identity formation, including those based on gender, religion or congregation. It may also mask the gains of religious life for the Irish women in the St Mildred congregation, as it would those of English and other sisters in the majority-Irish congregations. While the hierarchical structure of the congregation positioned Irish women in a particular way, the prestige of the organisation was part of the appeal to the women. Moreover, many achieved for the most part what they had hoped to in religious life: Eileen, for example, continued her education and became a teacher, while Pauline and Aisling both worked on the missions. Personal ambitions could be met without rising through the ranks of the organisation. Frances, for example, remarked that she 'was given the best education and...was teaching [so] life was just great and I didn't really think very much about the government of the [community]'. In any case, some of the women held what were considered to be very prestigious positions in the St Mildred congregation in the pre-Vatican II period. Rebecca, May and Hannah each taught in St Mildred's independent schools in England and Ireland, May and Hannah also becoming headmistresses of them.

Beyond the convent walls

Under the pre-Vatican II regime, religious had very little contact with the wider society and that which existed was regulated by strict rules of conduct and behaviour. With the exception of letters to and from family, contact with the wider society was often confined to work situations. None of the women in England felt that the hospital ward or classroom was 'Irish' in the way they spoke of their congregations being so, despite, for example, the number of first or later generations of Irish children that attended their institutions. Indeed, the security or assumed sense of belonging an 'Irish' convent provided could be challenged in the work place. Margaret, who had taught in Ireland for four years, doubted her abilities when she entered a classroom in England and remembered 'feeling shy in front of English students, [wondering] "am I up to this?"'.

After some time spent teaching in England, Lillian finally began to 'realise that it was okay. I was me and it was alright to be me and it was alright to be Irish'. Within a week of her arrival in England, on her first day at work in school, she met the parish priest. An Englishman, the priest enquired, in what Lillian took to be a condescending manner, if she had 'come up from the bogs in Ireland', which was an example of the stereotypical construction of Irish people as rural and suggested also that he at least considered Irish migration to England in terms of automatic upward mobility. It took Lillian two years to recover from the priests comments.

As members of majority-Irish congregations, women religious occupied dominant and dominated subject positions simultaneously, traversing invisible boundaries as they left their institutions and returned to their congregations. Interestingly, it was only women from majority-Irish congregations who felt aware of their Irishness in their work situation. Presumably, the women from the St Mildred congregation had already 'confronted' their Irishness within community.

The stated aim of the pre-Vatican II regime was to strip religious of ethnic and other affiliations. Far from it withering away, as the rule required, however, ethnicity was actively inhabited, continued to be vested with meaning and was used as a marker by other religious as well as by those in wider society. The particular form of ethnic identity that religious unconsciously inhabited, or were more consciously expected to take on, was not formed in a vacuum but was underpinned by deeply political histories. In attempting to draw attention to the different types of othering revealed in the women's narratives, the intention has not been to suggest that forms of othering are equivalent in scale or consequence, or that the experience of being an English sister in a majority-Irish congregation was equivalent to the experience of being an Irish migrant (religious or not) in English society. Rather, the point has been to explore the complex dynamics of othering as experienced by a group of women previously overlooked in studies of Irish people in England.

THE MISSIONS

The significant elsewhere the women of this study spent time was the missions. In total, fourteen of the women became missionaries. Four of them (Angela, Yvonne, Aisling and Pauline) left for the missions prior to Vatican II, three (Brenda, Winnie and Rosemary) while it was still in process, two more (Frances and Claire) before the end of the 1960s. Margaret, Deirdre and Barbara followed in the 1970s, Geraldine in the late 1980s and Joan in 1993. As their accounts focused more on the post-Vatican II period, they will be explored in greater detail in a subsequent chapter. It is worth noting even briefly, however, the pre-Vatican II missionary experiences of those who had them and the significance of being white, Irish women to those experiences.

It was not the missions that had originally attracted Winnie, Frances or Brenda to enter religious life and they were each shocked to find themselves being sent out after, respectively, sixteen, eighteen and twenty-five years in religious life. The manner in which the women were told of their imminent departure, as well as their reaction to that news, reveals much about the relational dynamics between sisters and their superiors within pre-Vatican II religious life. Winnie was asked by her superior if she would like to go on the missions. Though aware other sisters would be delighted to find themselves being considered for missionary work, she was not 'all that attracted to going'. More to the point, she did not want to go. Winnie kept these feelings to herself, however, remarking to her superior only that she 'hadn't thought of it but feel that if I *was* to go, I would like to be sent'. Not only was Winnie unwilling to express her true feelings, she would not express an opinion either way. Abdicating responsibility for the decision highlighted the faith she put in her superior's better knowledge of God's will as it applied to her, as well as her own commitment to obedience: 'I really felt very strongly that this was God's will and obedience in that sense was very [important], was something strong'.

If Winnie chose not to reveal her true feelings, neither Frances nor Brenda were asked for theirs in the first place. Like Winnie, however, they did not think to question the decision of their superior. Frances, for example, was aware of:

> a kind of rumour going round that I was going to be moved. We were never told of course ... Then the superior said to me one day 'You're going to be moved'. And I said, 'I know that'. And she said, 'Do you know where you'll be going? Have you any idea?' I said, 'No'. She said, 'Africa'. Well, I nearly fell off the chair! To teach French! Not having opened a French book hardly for twelve years! 'Go to Africa and teach French!' So anyhow, I did what I was told. Never even crossed my mind not to.

Aged 42, Brenda learnt of her removal to the missions. By then, she had been a religious for twenty-four years and had lived in various communities throughout Ireland and in Britain where she held a variety of different posts, including that of local superior. One day, she received a phone call from her mother superior summoning her to meet. Her first response was to ask not why but how, the practicalities of organising a journey herself seeming somewhat beyond her. With some assistance, she made the journey and the two women met:

> She just looked at me and she said to me, 'This day next week, you will be in Uganda'. And I looked at her and said, 'Where is Uganda?' And she said, 'You'd better get an atlas and look it up because you're going to be there for the rest of your life'.

While she professed 'no particular' attraction to the missions, Brenda thought it a 'wonderful opportunity'.

Angela, Pauline, Aisling, Rosemary and Claire had each entered religious life with the expressed desire to go on the missions, Yvonne volunteering herself for them a few years after entering. They were delighted, though not necessarily better prepared, to find they were to be sent on the missions after, respectively, two, eight, thirteen, six, seven and six years in religious life. The news was delivered to the women in a similar manner as it had been to Winnie.

The women were sent to different countries (with one exception, all in Africa), to areas that were in various stages of development, some not at all, to missions that were more and less established. Some of the places they travelled to were colonial outposts of the British Empire, others had already gained independence from it. The people they went to serve, be it the offspring or descendants of colonials or the indigenous population varied by race, religion and ethnicity. Any kind of generalised overview of life on the missions presented here has been garnered from varied, not uniform, experience.

The adventure began with the journey out, which was for most women, with the exception of Britain, their first trip abroad and, for all the women, their first trip outside Europe. The voyage was by turns long, exhausting and exciting. It was also, of course, a complete change from convent routine. Exotic-sounding places, previously familiar only through mission literature and classroom geography, were experienced firsthand. Whatever restrictions they lived under in transit, and these varied, making the journey made the women more worldly, separated them from religious who had not and gave them entry to a new community with missionaries who preceded them.

Although the women's basic job description as nurses or teachers remained the same, the missions were for all intents and purposes a different world, a world apart and, in some respects, the world turned upside down. One of the over-arching themes in their accounts of the missions was how entirely different they were to home, be that Ireland, England or both those places. As Winnie and Brenda put it, 'everything was different', Rosemary remarking that 'the missions are always different. Course, they have to be'. Knowledge gleaned either from mission literature or missionaries themselves proved ineffective in preparing them: 'No matter what people told you about the place, and they were always telling us what it was like and what the people were like, you have to really experience it for yourself' (Angela).

Acclimatising to the heat and getting used to unusual food was as much a theme in the women's accounts, as it had been in the mission literature they were reared on. Culturally, of course, the missions were very different to home. Though some of the women moved into large buildings modelled on European architecture, certainly not all did and living conditions for most declined considerably as basic amenities either were not in place or could not be relied upon. As Angela pointed out, however, the living conditions they endured were not always entirely unfamiliar to them: 'When I was there first, we didn't have running water, we didn't have electricity. But ... I grew up in the Ireland where there was no electricity'.

Another significant difference between the missions and home was that congregations and the institutions they ran, however long they had been in existence on the missions, did not have the same history or tradition as they had in western Europe. In addition, communities tended to be smaller, sometimes greatly so, and were proportionately smaller also in relation to the population they served. Generally speaking, they were also more international, taking their number not only from the Irish or English province but the American and Australian ones too.

The most common, as to be almost universal, contrast the women made between life 'out there' and home, especially in reference to the pre-Vatican II period, was the greater freedoms enjoyed on the missions. This needs to be unpacked. Certainly, it did not mean either freedom from work or for recreation. In fact, due to the small size of communities and the large populations religious were there to serve, the workload on the missions was usually greater than elsewhere. This tended to be regarded by the women as a positive feature. Hard work was, of course, fundamental to the discourse of religious life in general and missionary work in particular as representing the ultimate sacrifice. In addition, however, demand opened up opportunities for religious to take over positions of importance, responsibility and power more swiftly than might have been the case elsewhere. Several of the women quickly found themselves in positions not commensurate to their experience, among them Claire: 'I was never a staff nurse even here and yet [there], I was a ward sister overnight ... I arrived on a Thursday and I was a ward sister on the Monday'. This baptism of fire was for the most part enthusiastically embraced. Yvonne, for example, particularly welcomed being called upon to get involved in extra-curricular activities she felt sure would have been reserved for 'specialists' at home:

> We'd produce plays, little operettas ... various things like that. It was great fun when you had time for it. But then you had to stay up at night to correct your copies! ... [But those opportunities] wouldn't even have surfaced in [Ireland]. I got scope for it [on the missions] because there was nobody else to do it. But I was only very small fry in Ireland.

The missions were certainly more free of routine. For a host of reasons which included the demands of work, the remoteness or otherwise undeveloped nature of their location and the often less than stable social, economic, political or climatic circumstances in which they lived, it was less easy on the missions to institute strict adherence to set timetables, so much the feature of religious life elsewhere. Simply put, life on the missions was less predictable. Without exception, this was regarded as a positive, if sometimes frustrating, feature of missionary life. Angela described it as 'great. Because nothing is the same. There's so much routine here, you know? I hate routine ... There's nothing in it, you know? I love to go in and find something different'.

Accounts varied regarding the commitment to recreating the pre-Vatican II system on the missions. While Frances remarked that in her congregation, they tried to 'stick to the rules. Absolutely', she conceded at the same time that 'you can't have lock, stock and barrel, everything brought over. So, of necessity, there was more freedom'. Winnie was less convinced her congregation even attempted to replicate the set up: 'We wouldn't even try ... I mean, you couldn't. It would have been ridiculous. There were more important things to be done'. Of course, in order for the mission to survive, the practical demands of establishing missions and running schools and hospitals would have to take precedence over rigid timetables. Not only the notion that there were more pressing issues to deal with, however (a theme common to many of the accounts), but the very language Winnie uses to express this point highlights the significance attached to missionary work, which the Church regarded as no less serious than saving souls from eternal damnation.

Perhaps the strongest theme to emerge from the accounts of the missions, and it is one which served to distinguish the missions from elsewhere as well as draw attention to the greater freedoms that existed there, were the less formal relations missionary sisters enjoyed within the community, with other Catholic religious congregations and, most especially, with the wider society. Obviously, smaller communities could not maintain the formal structure of religious life as it pertained elsewhere. Significant in this regard too was the internationalism of communities whose tradition of religious life might not have been as formal as was the case in Europe. Aisling, for example, remarked that: 'We did acknowledge...that when we lived with the Americans, the American sisters had more, I suppose you'd call it humanity than the English sisters[26]...[They] were less reserved. Yes. And [none] friendly and hospitable'.

In terms of relations enjoyed between congregations, many of the accounts suggested a community beyond community. The reality of the missions was such that formality and protocol were often abandoned in the pursuit of self-preservation. On the journey over, on journeys between and within mission countries and with respect to work, congregations co-operated and mixed more than they would have at home, a feature of missionary religious life nearly all the women reflected upon, usually in purely positive terms: For Yvonne, for example, 'it was just wonderful, all the linking up that is done'. Equally, Angela spoke of the co-operation that existed between communities: 'We helped each other out, put it that way. There were great relations between ourselves and the other missionaries.' The missions were, she suggested, 'much less formal...we're all one big happy family'. Many of the women recalled particular incidences of hospitality extended or received, some of them referring to this specifically as 'mission hospitality'. Angela first travelled to Africa in 1944, having entered religious life two years previously. Shortly after arriving, whilst making a trip from one mission house to another, a storm broke out which prevented her party travelling further.

[The bishop] said, 'Well, I don't think we can go any further. You'd better get on to [another congregation] and [the sisters there will] put you up for the night'. So, we went [to them]. There were two of us. And their Reverend Mother and her assistant were [out]. So we were put in their beds. To me, this was awful! Using their beds, you know? [...] So, the middle of the night [came], two o'clock. We heard the dogs barking...The [Reverend Mother and her assistant] had come back and we were in their beds! And I thought this was *terrible!* But it was the usual thing. I came to know it afterwards. [That] was my first experience of mission hospitality.

In particular, the women talked about the less formal relations they enjoyed with the wider population. Indeed, what 'the people there' were like and how close to them the missionaries became was a theme in all their accounts and dominated some. 'The people' tended to be spoken about in glowing terms, described, for example, as 'so friendly' (Aisling), 'very friendly' (Angela), 'lovely' (Claire), 'great' (Rosemary) and 'so good and so nice [and] kind-hearted' (Yvonne). Despite how different the missions were in many respects, it did not take long for the women of this study, at least, to adapt. Yvonne, for example, settled in 'very quickly', Aisling 'in no time [because] the girls were so friendly, you felt so much at home with them... They were your real friends'. Likewise, it was other people that helped Angela adjust: 'Everybody made it so easy... We were very, very close'. Of course, presenting their experiences in terms of close community and fraternity with indigenous populations required the women to gloss over obvious differences between them of culture, language, race or religion – sometimes all of these things. Though the 'happy family' motif will be interrogated further in a subsequent chapter, suffice to say at this point that the central message of the accounts of missionary life was the extent to which the women embraced an identity as missionary sisters and the positive associations they made around that identity. Through their stories, they sketched a picture of a place that was both apart – and upside down. Difficult, chaotic and even dangerous, the missions were also, for some, an idyllic place, far surpassing whatever idealised expectations they had of them.

CONCLUSION

Vocations, believed to be a calling from the divine, separated religious from the laity. Likewise, their convents existed in an almost supernatural dimension, not entirely of this world. As such, exactly where those convents were placed or where the individuals within them were from was not supposed to be of relevance to the broader aims of those institutes to protect and save souls through the provision of health, education and other services. As this chapter has illustrated, however, both where the women were from, and where they lived within religious life affected their experience of it. The accounts of the women of this study who lived in England differed considerably from those who were missionaries. Some of the women in England drew on their Irishness in describing their experience of community, others of alienation. Missionaries, on the other hand, tended to ignored their Irishness and other facts of their biography to enable a more coherent story of community to emerge. Despite important differences in their accounts, collectively, however, they served to highlight the continued significance of context to the women's experience and understanding of religious life, as well as the distinct identities it provided them as Irish sisters in England or missionaries abroad.

NOTES

1 Kate.
2 Similar comments were made by several of the women.
3 *Constitution and Rule of the CSSL* (1927), p. 113.
4 Only two (Annette and Bernadette) did so as professed nuns. Ten of the women left Ireland to enter congregations in England while five left after a short period of (between six months and two years) spent in noviciates in Ireland. The remaining four women had left Ireland for England prior to entering religious life: Frances and Rebecca to attend school, Elaine and Kate in search of work. These four experienced their ethnicity in new ways in England. For Frances, Elaine and Kate, a sense of belonging and national community was replaced by a recognition of themselves as different. Elaine immersed herself in an Irish Catholic community and would always refer to members of this community as 'us', her English colleagues at work as 'them'. Fearful of losing her faith, she went to great lengths to ensure against this (including organising a special daily Mass to be said for herself and her cousin in a local church). Kate formed communal ties with non-Irish Catholics. Though she was aware of anti-Irish sentiment in England, she did not feel 'personally' affected by it as she had plans to enter religious life and did not, therefore, consider herself to be part of the wider migration of Irish people to Britain. In fact, Kate enjoyed the challenge of being a Catholic in England, especially because it forced her to separate her 'real' faith from her 'cradle Catholicism'. In Catholic boarding

schools, Frances and Rebecca noticed little change in the way that religion was practised, though Frances adopted a regional accent (later lost) in an attempt to fit in with those around her. Rebecca, from an upper middle-class background, felt at home in her middle-class boarding school in England.

5 Each of the four majority-Irish congregations were described as 'Irish'. Although no exact figures were available to explore, the women's testimonies suggested that while the majority of vocations were from Ireland, England, Scotland and Wales were also represented. There were, in addition, a 'smattering' of French sisters as well as individual sisters from elsewhere.

6 The majority-Irish congregations that the women of this study were members of were probably not all 'Irish' to the same degree (the impression given was that the St Marie congregation was the most Irish). The women's accounts, however, suggest that an Irish culture, (variously defined) dominated in each of these four institutions.

7 There was no space for the women to express a personal ethnicity based, for example, on their particular regional or family background.

8 Scottish, Welsh and even French seemed to exist somewhere in between Ireland and Britain on the continuum.

9 A. Brah, *Cartographies of Diaspora: Contesting Identities* (London: Routledge, 1996), p. 209.

10 Walter, *Outsiders Inside*.

11 Brah, *Cartographies of Diaspora*, p. 189.

12 I am talking about occupying dominant/dominated positions simultaneously, not based on alternative or varying dimensions of differentiation but the same dimensions i.e. ethnicity, religion (and class).

13 As well as class lines. Many congregations maintained formal distinctions between 'choir' and 'lay' sisters, at least until the 1950s. Even where formal distinctions did not exist, congregations could operate less official distinctions.

14 Here, I refer to Zymunt Bauman's use of 'in-group' and 'out-group' (*Thinking Sociologically* (Oxford: Blackwell, 1990), pp. 41–4).

15 Brah, *Cartographies of Diaspora*, p. 125.

16 E. W. Said, *Orientalism, Western Conceptions of the Orient* (London: Penguin, 1978).

17 Thus highlighting how particular the 'Irishness' of religious congregations was, in fact.

18 In her research on English congregations between 1840 and 1910,

Susan O'Brien noted that Irish accents were problematic in English congregations: 'Although all English congregations readily accepted Irish born sisters as lay sisters, the brogue was not always felt to be suitable in a choir nun' (O'Brien, S, 'Lay-Sisters and Good Mothers: Working-Class Women in English Convents, 1840–1910', in W. J. Sheils and D. Woods (eds), *Women in the Church, Studies in Church History* (Oxford: Basil Blackwell, 1990, pp. 453–65, p. 455.). Only three of the St Mildred sisters interviewed mentioned the elocution lessons: Pauline, Hannah and Aisling. None of the women who was a member of majority-Irish congregations mentioned elocution lessons, which is not to say they definitely did not occur. Even if they did, however, they might not have been interpreted in the same way as they were by the Irish women in the St Mildred congregation.

In the notes made following the interviews, some of which were made before finding out about the elocution lessons, I noted that three of the St Mildred women (Rebecca, Vera and May), spoke with barely-detectable Irish accents. Indeed, when I first met Vera (who was also the first of the St Mildred women interviewed) I wondered if she had misunderstood my research project because I was unsure that she was Irish. This reflects my own subconscious notions of Irishness, which seemed to include an inability to conceive of an Irishness that tolerated particularly middle-class English traits. If Vera had spoken with a strong Liverpool accent, I probably would have presumed that she was second-generation Irish, still 'Irish' in my books. The rest of the women spoke with slight regional Irish accents with the exception of Elaine, who had maintained a strong Munster accent. As a lay sister, she would not have been required to take elocution lessons.

19   *The Chambers Dictionary* 1993, this edition (1998).

20   M. Kells, '"I'm Myself and Nobody Else": Gender and Ethnicity among Young Middle-Class Irish Women in London', in P. O'Sullivan (ed.), *Irish Women and Irish Migration* (London: Leicester University Press, 1995), pp. 201–34.

21   Hannah was confident in her Irishness to the point of believing that she was 'doing God a favour' by coming to England.

22   Walter, *Outsiders Inside*, p. 165. See, also, Hickman and Walter, *Discrimination*.

23   See J. MacLaughlin, '"Pestilence on their Backs, Famine in their Stomachs": The Racial Construction of Irishness and the Irish in Victorian Britain', in C. Graham and R. Kirkland (eds), *Ireland and Cultural Theory, The Mechanics of Authenticity* (London: Macmillan,

1999), pp. 50–76. Also, B. Walter, 'Gendered Irishness in Britain: Changing Constructions', in Graham and Kirkland (eds), *Ireland and Cultural Theory*, pp. 77–98 and *Outsiders Inside*.

24 S. Fielding, *Class and Ethnicity, Irish Catholics in England, 1880–1939* (Buckingham: Open University Press 1993).

25 Ibid., pp. 40–1.

26 By which she meant sisters from the English province, which would have included Irish sisters. In fact, a higher proportion of the St Mildred sisters on the missions were Irish than was the case for the congregation in England.

Part III:

Religious Life, Post-Vatican II

CHAPTER 5

Vatican II – A United Response?

'We suddenly discovered freedom and responsibility and that we shouldn't just be saying "yes" all the time'[1]

INTRODUCTION

In November 1958, Angelo Roncalli was consecrated Pope John XXIII and quickly made public his plans to convoke an Ecumenical Council of the Church. By the time his pontificate ended in June 1963, the first of the Second Vatican Council sessions had taken place. The fourth and final session ended on 8 December 1965. The aim of Vatican II, as it became known, was to consider and clarify the Church's position with respect to a changed and changing world and it did so through sixteen documents which, footnotes aside, ran to over 103,000 words.

The central participants of Vatican II were Catholic bishops, of whom there were over 2,500, and a number of male leaders of religious orders, all of whom had voting rights. In addition, there were, without voting rights, 450 priests, a small number of Protestant observers and representatives also of the main non-Christian religions. All of these were men. By the time the council ended its debates, twelve lay women and ten religious women were admitted to the sessions. They did not have a vote and were forbidden to speak. As a result, during the entire deliberations of Vatican II no woman's voice was ever heard.[2]

The Vatican Council issued its decree on religious life late in October 1965. *Perfectae Caritatis* (1965) aimed specifically at the appropriate renewal of religious life. Given that religious life prior to Vatican II was a structured life, not only pre-ordained but divinely so, its impact could not but be immense. *Perfectae Caritatis* called upon religious congregations to renew themselves by jettisoning rules and rituals deemed archaic and irrelevant, while maintaining the 'essentials' of religious life.[3] Religious life had changed little in the 150 years prior to Vatican II, a revision of canon law in 1917 serving only to further entrench the monastic restrictions under which nuns lived. Though some change had been introduced prior to Vatican II (for example, many congregations dispensed with the formal distinction between lay and choir sisters), the life was, as one of the women of this study, Elaine, described it, 'very constant'. Indeed, the notion of change was anathema to the principle of religious life as fixed and divine. Suddenly, religious were being asked directly to question, and consider altering, what had become the fundamentals of religious life: rule and adherence to rule; abidance and obedience; rigidity, inflexibility and permanence. What is more, religious congregations were being asked to do this themselves in consultation with their members, though any changes made would eventually have to be ratified by Rome.

Changes instituted as a result of Vatican II included the introduction of more simple habit, many congregations later giving the option of discarding it altogether, and greater access to scripture and theology. Congregational charisms were reinterpreted, expanding the work of individual congregations and the work opportunities for women within them. Regulation and controls on relations between women in religious life and between them and the secular world, including with their families, were lessened. At the same time, alterations in the living arrangements of religious enabled sisters to move out of large convents into smaller communities, often in residential housing. Generally speaking, religious were given greater freedom of expression as the strict hierarchical and authoritarian regime of the pre-Vatican II period began to be challenged. Through a convoluted process that was faster or slower depending on responses from congregations as well as individuals within them, religious life became less 'scripted'. If not change itself, then the prospect of change began to replace decades of divine custom.

Despite its impact, little attention has been paid to the subjective experience of Vatican II by women religious. The same and more can be said in relation to Irish women religious.[4] Though it took place in the 1960s, the reverberations of Vatican II continue to be felt today and religious life has been left utterly altered by it. Remarking on Vatican II, Angela suggested there could never be a Vatican III because 'Vatican II will never end'. This chapter considers the women's response and interpretation of Vatican II both at the time and also over time. In particular, it looks at the impact of Vatican II on the women's sense of religious identity and spirituality as well as their sense of self as women. It then turns its attention to explore the tension and contestation that naturally arose from the women's varied interpretation of Vatican II, what these differences of opinion might be said to represent and how they have been accommodated within religious life.

RELIGIOUS COME OF AGE

Many of the women of this study described Vatican II as a sort of rite of passage, a process which allowed but also forced them to mature into adulthood. Sarah suggested that religious under the pre-Vatican II system had 'maybe become a bit infantile [because] everything was decided for them'. Likewise, Irene described religious pre-Vatican II as 'almost childlike...we had a kind of infantile mentality, if you like'. This was set in contrast to the contemporary period: '[we're] much more grown up [now]'. Similarly, Hannah remarked that the changes 'made you grow up' while Frances commented that 'once the lids were off, you know, [we] suddenly realise[d], gracious! We've been living like infants!'. At first, Aisling was unsure of the value of some of the proposed changes, until a member of the general council arrived 'and explained the *reasons* for lots of these things. How we were meant to be mature women and make our own decisions'. By way of comparison, she described the situation prior to Vatican II:

> Before that, you see, you never had a penny in your pocket. Never ...I remember the surprise...going out [on the missions] the first time, Mother General said to me, 'Now, there may be emergencies on the way so you should have some money'. Which I hadn't thought of...And it was a very wise thing to do. But you didn't think that way before...Somebody else did it for you, I suppose [you] didn't *have* to.

A related outcome of Vatican II, and a recurrent theme to emerge from the accounts, was that women religious had to take much greater responsibility for themselves. As Hannah put it: 'You have to be more responsible for yourself. For your prayer life. For a whole lot of things...We started having personal budgets and [became] more responsible [for] finance'. Responsibility for self was reflected in changing work and living arrangements, the women having to organise their own days and lives to a much greater extent than ever before. Kate observed a 'certain freedom...you find time for your own prayer. We pray in the evenings together but, apart from that, you're totally free'.

Modern constitutions of religious congregations reflect these changes. In many ways, they are not rule books at all, more often guides for women pursuing a life as religious. They are generally shorter and lighter documents, less prescriptive and place far less emphasis on surveillance. The language used in modern rule books is also different: it is less authoritative and there is more emphasis on 'dialogue', 'freedom' and 'responsibility'.[5] There is also less focus than was the case in pre-Vatican II rule books on the inherent weaknesses of women and the dangers they present to themselves.[6] Though religious are still required to take vows of poverty, chastity and obedience, the way these vows are written about and practised has changed. Chastity is constructed as choice, poverty in the context of the times and obedience is to 'the spirit' rather than the superior. As Kate put it, 'you still have obedience but you carry it in a different way'.

Unsurprisingly, the relational dynamics within communities have been affected, tending more towards the democratic than the oligarchic. Yvonne, for example, noted that superiors could no longer:

> ...just make decisions on their own. They have to get the votes of the people who they are looking after, I mean, which is very good. You know, it sort of guarantees a certain [freedom from tyranny] because if the head man goes off the top, well, you know, somebody might be out of control or something.

Certainly, the status of the superior within the congregation has been modified, her power over other members of the community reduced. Religious are no longer required to kneel before their superior nor ask permission from her for every act. Some congregations, including some of the ones the women of this study are members of, have replaced the title 'superior' with a more democratic-sounding address such as 'team leader'.

More than was ever the case before, women in religious have since Vatican II been given more and more opportunity to express their own opinions.[7] Indeed, they are often encouraged to do so. The modern rule book of the St Louise congregation, for example, affirms that 'because we respect each sister and the gifts she brings to the community, we encourage one another to express opinions, insights, and aspirations'.[8] Previously regarded as a vanity against the principle of humility, individual work or training preferences are now taken into account to a much greater extent and many religious are able to suggest their own personal ministries, though these have to be approved by the community. Some communities are, of course, more lenient in this respect than others.

Also in contrast to the pre-Vatican II regime, there is a recognition that religious need space and privacy within their own lives. Unsurprisingly, this came as a shock to some of the women of this study, albeit not an entirely unwelcome one:

> I remember [in the wake of Vatican II] some of the nuns in the [United] States were writing what they wanted and so on and they wanted 'unscheduled free time'. I couldn't think what on earth they were on about!... You see, [before] you never had free time really, it was all organised. I know now! And I make good use of it! [Rebecca]

These changes are significant because they strike at the heart of pre-Vatican II religious organisation and identity. Responsibility for self is indicative of a theology that puts greater value on the individual, indeed makes an *investment* in the individual. In terms of its approach to the human form, it is certainly a more optimistic theology than existed previously. For Deirdre, religious life 'became more human and more normal' after Vatican II, in particular, 'the fact that you could be yourself'. As was noted in previous chapters, the pre-Vatican II regime was precisely organised to repress, deny and erase the individual. Post-conciliar thinking represented a monumental shift in ideas, one not lost on religious themselves. Irene, for example, opined that Vatican II allowed for religious to: 'become a lot more caring for one another. We ourselves are given …much more consideration …We're much more valued, I would say, as human beings … An individual now really matters. Long ago, you were one of a number'. Likewise, Winnie talked of having previously 'seen ourselves as all the same. [Whereas] now, we see people, I think I do anyway, as individuals'.

The respect accorded the individual might, in fact, be the most radical and far-reaching element of *Perfectae Caritatis*. It is also the aspect of it which mirrored modernisation projects more generally. While not exactly representative of a shift from self-denial to self-indulgence,[9] *Perfectae Caritatis* at least opened up the space for the individual to exist within the religious community. As it had in western European society more generally and within Irish society more recently, a new philosophy of liberal individualism began to emerge within religious life in the wake of Vatican II, albeit one still consistent with the ideals and ideology of the Catholic Church.

The less scripted form of religious life that Vatican II allowed for has given women religious the opportunity to renegotiate their sense of themselves as religious and to consider individual identity projects of their own. Some of the women in this study welcomed the opportunity to rethink, question, discuss and ultimately transform their own religious identity. For Frances, Vatican II was almost a call to arms: 'We suddenly discovered freedom...That we were responsible and that we shouldn't just be saying "yes" all the time, but that we should be questioning...Oh!...it was like...a new dawn for me...The benefits were incalculable'.

RESPONDING TO VATICAN II

The women of this study did not unanimously support Vatican II. Nor, indeed, did they interpret renewal in the same way. While the majority of the women were supportive of some change, they varied significantly in terms of the extent to which they felt religious life needed to be altered as well as the manner in which this should be done. Those women who were unreserved in their support of Vatican II and the potential of *Perfectae Caritatis* to effect change included Vera, Frances, Geraldine, Josephine, Lillian, Margaret, Eileen, Pauline, Sarah, Teresa, Joan and Barbara, whose enthusiasm was demonstrated in comments such as those made by Frances (see above).

Catherine, Norah, Rebecca, Winnie, Yvonne, Rosemary, Angela, Claire and Deirdre were also supportive of Vatican II but more so in terms of the changes it did bring about than the extent to which it might be regarded as a stepping stone to more radical change. These women tended to show their support for Vatican II with respect to material changes actually and already introduced. Deirdre, for example, thought Vatican II was 'great...Because at that time, we never went home. It was part of the rules and you accepted it. And after the Vatican II, we celebrated our silver jubilee...and for that, the gift we all got was a week at home.' Likewise, Claire welcomed the less regimented system allowed for in the wake of Vatican II, though this was not something she had questioned previously: 'We were really tied up in rules and regulations and all of that. And that side of things, there was no harm in getting rid of a lot of those rules. And I'd say a lot of them were man-made too, but that was the way it was'.

A significant number of the women were, however, ambivalent about Vatican II. Annette, Hannah, Kate, May, Aisling and Brenda each expressed reservations about changes that were introduced, though, naturally, there were differences in opinion over which changes in particular they had reservations about. Many of the women were uneasy about what they regarded as modernisation at any cost and feared losing elements of convent life they deemed vital and sacred. As Kate put it 'I thought it was a bit stupid. Some of [the changes] were not for the best...I think sometimes you can throw out the baby with the bath water'. Practices, beliefs and customs which for decades, if not centuries, religious had invested in, derived meaning from and were considered to be divine were suddenly open to question and possible discardment, eliciting a less than enthusiastic response from some. May, for example, felt 'the sense of mystery' of both Catholicism and religipous life was being eroded while Brenda felt part of its beauty was being lost:

At the Vatican II time, the changes came about [and] that for me was a very difficult time...Initially, I didn't know what to think...I had a special love for Gregorian music. There's a Gregorian style of music. The Liturgy to me was sacrosanct. And I loved it, and I taught it to the students and they really could sing beautifully, the Gregorian music. And then to find, when people came back from the council that everything was, or I felt, bitty-piecy. I felt there was a lack of reverence or something. And I found that very hard to take. Because I was one of these people who had been very obedient and kept things as they were.

The contrast Aisling drew between the pre- and post-Vatican II system highlighted the drastic effects of Vatican II within the context of religious life as well as her personal response to the prospect of those change:

Up till then, everything was regulated: what you wore, the length of your habit, the number of buttons you had and everything like that. And we had to have a Special Chapter [on account of Vatican II]...[And then] it was [all] experimental, you see? Experiment with lifestyle and the hours, what time of the day you prayed. Everything you did before that, you did at a certain time. It was all fixed. So well, with changes like that, people go at a different rate, people are different. Some people had wanted it ten years ahead. Well, I didn't because I was happy with the way I was doing things.

Some women were positively traumatised by Vatican II and tried as much as was possible to hold on to a sense of religious life that was familiar to them. As Elaine put it, 'I have remained very much what I was [with no] need to ... strike out for a different type of life.' Of all the women in this study, Elaine seemed least comfortable about Vatican II. In many of the comments she made, it was clear she was struggling with the practical implications and realities of change, as well as the fact that Vatican II itself had been instigated from within the Church itself. Her hesitancy in the following remark, for example, gave the impression she was trying to convince herself, more than she was anyone else, of the benefits of change: 'I wonder is [change] a good thing, you know? You just ... but I think it is. "All things worse to good"... if you've heard it ... if you love God.'

In fact, Elaine employed interesting tactics to deal with Vatican II which included telling herself that she must, by her vow of obedience, now adapt to change. An example of this was her attitude to home visits. According to the rule of her congregation, Elaine had been forbidden to visit home after she entered religious life in 1945. This rule was changed in the 1960s but Elaine was reluctant to 'break the promise I had made'. Eventually, in the late 1970s, she felt compelled to relent: 'You felt the odd one out and you were sort of saying, now you *must* go home. This is the regulation. And you feel this was obedience too and you *have* to'. Bernadette, though aware that Vatican II had taken place, appeared not to have let it affect the way she lived her life to any great extent. She remained throughout reluctant to talk about her feelings or offer her opinions. Consistently, she used language that emphasised a collective, communal identity, describing events in her life as objectively as possible.[10]

Despite their varied responses, however, the women of this study chose to remain within religious life. Many of their co-religious did not. While the changes brought about by Vatican II were neither introduced in the same way or at the same time, it sent an immediate psychological shock wave throughout religious life and precipitated a haemorrhage from it.[11] The exodus consisted of those who found in change the freedom to realise they did not have a vocation, as well as those who 'were lost...couldn't cope [when] the structures were removed' (Kate). Consequently, and regardless of their own personal opinion of it, Vatican II was experienced by most of the women in this study as a difficult time in their lives. The fact that it precipitated the departure of so many naturally had an impact on those who stayed. As Irene remarked: 'That was a hard period because that was when a lot of our friends left and you'd wonder...should I do the same?...It was very, very tough'. Even those who ever doubted their own vocation nor their support for Vatican II found transition difficult. Frances, for example, believed in hindsight that the 'constraints [of the pre-Vatican II regime were] really burdensome,...reform absolutely necessary', yet she still experienced Vatican II and its aftermath as 'a very painful process. Because it's extremely difficult to undo something that has been so sacred'.

RELIGIOUS IDENTITY RECONFIGURED, ONCE MORE

As entering religious life had, Vatican II necessitated a renegotiation of religious identity. Reflecting their varied responses to it, the women of this study reconfigured their religious identity in the wake of Vatican II to a greater and lesser degree, some focusing on one primarily theological aspect of it, others finding through it the means to reconsider their whole spirituality. Though initially unsure of its benefits, both Aisling and Brenda came to appreciate Vatican II following sabbaticals spent studying the documents in detail.[12] Aisling was particularly supportive of its commitment to ecumenism:

[In religious life] we did learn that through every man, is open the way. But we did also learn outside the Church, there was no salvation. But [during a sabbatical spent] in Maynooth certainly, I mean we threw that out altogether and there was good in every religion and I thought that was wonderful...A lot of [Vatican II] was made clear. You know, the reasons for it. You didn't go along with everything but...I remember feeling extremely happy that year...The Vatican documents, there's an awful lot of lovely stuff in it, I must say.

Similarly, Brenda, was 'greatly helped by all that I learned' during her year of study: 'This obedience of the rule, well, I couldn't understand

why that didn't hold anymore but now I had another understanding
and that's where it had helped me... The different ways that you can
serve God and that... it doesn't have to be this [one] way'.

Some of the women, among them Frances, went further, experi-
menting with the way they prayed and incorporating their own
feelings into their expression of religious identity:

> We said we'll have shared prayer, we'll use the scripture and ... get
> a passage of scripture and read it and reflect on it. Maybe [each of
> us] say a few words about it, what has struck you and then read it
> again and then reflect for a little bit longer and share. And of course
> the depth of the sharing automatically, you know, changed our
> community.

Reflecting the more positive rendering of the individual, some of the
women began to define their vocation and sense of religious self more
on their own terms. Catherine was a case in point: 'I'm guided more
by instinct...what my conscience tells me rather than...rules and
regulations and 'do's' and 'don'ts'. One time I could quote all the
rules and regulations off by heart...I wouldn't even know where
they are now!'

Catherine talked a great deal about the need to be 'free' to follow
God and described her previous convictions as 'crazy' and 'tortuous'
in retrospect. Vatican II gave her the opportunity not only to create a
new religious identity for herself but to redefine her former beliefs and
practices. Her life was no longer dictated, she said, by a 'false' set of
rules but was instead guided by a developed sense of her 'spirituality'
(akin to that of her mother, in fact). Catherine described her religious
identity as 'my own personal relationship with God, whoever he or
she may be'. Others (among them Frances, Josephine, Margaret and
Lillian) also spoke of a more 'adult' relationship with God, one they
had a personal input in. Both God and the self were discernible in
Barbara's account also, who chose to describe her religious identity at
a distance from organised religion also:

> I used to say to people, I'm 'un-Churched' [...] in that, you know,
> I belong to the people of God. And therefore, the way in which I
> worship is first and foremost to be true to my own self and my own
> belief in God and God's part in my life...Therefore, whether I
> worship with the Catholics or the Presbyterians or [whatever
> religion], it's just a matter of chance [and of] geography.

Considering herself 'unusual' in her thinking, Barbara felt that her views were influenced both by her experiences as a missionary and also the preparation she had received for Vatican II. In fact, many of the women chose to define their spirituality without reference to the formal organisation of religious life itself. In so doing, they created a distance between themselves and the institutionalisation that had been the backbone of the pre-Vatican II regime.

One of the most significant ways the women separated themselves was in choosing to live or work outside their congregations. Congregations and the institutions they ran were often housed in large, imposing buildings that physically and metaphorically created a barrier between religious and seculars. As Vera put it: 'We [had] to get down to true religion ... And I welcome it. I think it's very good. I think it's very good for religious orders to shed the habit, shed the buildings and do what we're there to do. What we came into religious life to do'.

Moving out of convents enabled religious to establish a closer relationship with the laity and be less distinct from it as a result. At the time of the interviews, less than half the women lived in convents in the traditional sense of the word,[13] while the majority of them had been in the past or were presently engaged in work outside of their congregation. In reconfiguring their religious identity and taking a more active role in defining it, the women were effectively relocating it: it became part of them rather than they a part of it.

GENDERED PROCESSES OF RENEWAL

Given the structure of religious life for sisters prior to Vatican II, the reinterpretation that occurred in its wake particularly affected women in religious life. Many of the women in this study described Vatican II as a 'revolution'. For some, the revolution was gendered. Frances, for example, defined Vatican II as the means by which she 'became a woman'. As such, Vatican II was not just a rite of passage but a *gendered* one. Significantly, and in contrast to what had held previously, Vatican II gave the women an opportunity to claim a more positive identity as women, something Margaret had, as she put it, 'denied for so long'. For her, this was the 'most important' thing about Vatican II 'and [now] that's what I value most, is my womanhood'. For those that wanted to and could, there were various ways to negotiate and reclaim – or, indeed, claim – a more positive identity as women.

Re-Naming

One significant way in which women redefined themselves in terms of gender in the wake of Vatican II was in the apparently simple gesture of re-naming. After Vatican II, many congregations gave women the opportunity to revert to their baptismal name. Of the thirty women in this study, most reverted to their secular name, a small number chose to keep their religious name while two were obliged by their congregation to do so. Reverting to their baptismal name reconnected the women with their birth family and their secular selves, the gendered person they had been expected to repress. Moreover, it required them to think fundamentally about their self identity and who they were.

Equally, in the title or form of address they chose to use for themselves, some of the women claimed a gendered identity for themselves. During the course of the interviews, each of the women were asked what badges or labels of identity they might use to define themselves, which ones they would privilege above others and which ones they would choose not to be used. The terms 'sister', 'nun' and 'woman' were proffered, along with others which related to work, congregation, ethnicity, age and so on. For some of the women (among them Frances, Josephine, Lillian, Joan, and Irene), the titles 'religious' and 'woman' were of equal importance: 'being a woman, being a religious ... would [both] be very high...sort of a level pegging' (Joan). Claiming an identity as a woman alongside that of a religious demonstrated a re-negotiation of 'nun/sister' as a complete or total identity in itself.

Some women (including Geraldine, Teresa, Sarah, Vera, Margaret, Catherine and Barbara) chose to privilege their identity as women above that of sister. Barbara remarked that being a woman was her most important identity, adding that she would 'omit' both the fact of her Irishness and her status as a religious from any description she gave of herself: 'I don't see myself as kind of specifically religious or specifically Irish'.. Some women who privileged their identity as women above others felt this was not a subjectivity others tended to associate them with. For example, Geraldine said: 'The "sister" comes out on top. That's the way people perceive me principally...and then

"Irish" and then a "woman"! [But] I put "woman" first... "Irish" second and "sister" *third*!'.

Clothing

Dress was another significant means by which the women claimed an identity as women. The more simple habit was less cumbersome and less likely to completely hide the female form than its predecessor. Hair protruded from the smaller veil, while the shorter dress revealed that nuns did, indeed, have legs. Of course, habits continued to distinguish religious from secular women and emphasised their identity as religious. When the opportunity arose, many of the women chose to abandon their habit altogether. The predominant reason given for this was the desire to 'fit in' but it also gave religious space in which to express a female self identity. Teresa was 'absolutely delighted' about changing into secular dress because 'it made me feel [like] a woman'.

The female body and femininity

Vatican II enabled women religious to think about themselves and their bodies in new ways, a fact reflected in modern rule books which make far fewer references to the shame surrounding the female body and the need to cover it. Several of the women commented on their appearance during the interviews. Irene remarked on the size of her hips (getting bigger, a bad thing), while Margaret talked about the possibility of getting a perm. Lillian apologised for wearing jeans and jumper when we met[14] and mentioned it again during the interview, remarking 'The state of me now! I mean, I'm not even respectable!'. Although these comments were made casually during the course of conversation, they revealed an investment in femininity not possible, or perhaps necessary, previously. The opportunity to make such an investment was something many of the women valued as a means of positively repositioning themselves as women. For example, Teresa:

> I was aware of some liberation around myself as a woman, you know? I [had] missed the things... like clothes, like perfume, like hair-dos. All of that [was] part of the sacrifice... But there has been, over the last X number of years, [the opportunity] to re-claim that sense of care for myself as a woman and ... the femininity bit of me.

Collective Gendered Identities

Vatican II gave many of the women the opportunity to work in new areas of employment and some chose to work specifically with other women.[15] The desire to work with women often reflected a gender-based collective identity. Josephine referred to herself and the other members of a local women's group she was involved with as 'us' or 'we', making no distinction between herself as a religious and them as seculars. Margaret found working as a therapist with women 'very satisfying' because 'I understand women better, obviously, [because] I'm a woman myself'. For her, a collective gendered identity was based on a shared experience of patriarchy and she defined her work in terms of women's empowerment:

> I particularly want to work with women and for women...I think women get an awfully raw deal, [they're] discriminated against, they're set aside. And I know what that feels like because I feel that, as a woman, I've been discriminated against in the Church...I can get angry about that...it's something I know about. So I suppose from that point of view, that's why I want to work with women. Even though [therapy] isn't consciousness raising, not overtly anyway, it is helping women to get some insight into their own situation and take some control over it.

Sarah expressed similar sentiments when describing her work in female adult education classes as advancing the 'liberation' and 'empowerment' of women.

Josephine formed gender-based communities with other Irish women she knew in England (not religious, some not Catholic) while Margaret echoed Virginia Woolf's statement that 'As a woman, I have no country',[16] when she made the following remark:

> We have an awful lot in common...especially women...it's like belonging to the woman family!...Because I associate with women naturally, it's like belonging to this human, feminine group. And we all have the same difficulties and struggles. It's kind of universal.

Sexual identities

Since Vatican II, the Church's teaching on sexuality and religious life has changed and it now recognises that religious are not asexual, thus enabling women religious to claim a sexual identity for themselves.

Some of the women did so in the interviews. Margaret called religious 'sexual beings, like everyone else' while Lillian described herself as a 'perfectly normal heterosexual woman'. These women presented their celibacy as a sexuality of choice, not denial, a position again reflected in a number of the modern rule books, which tend to place much less emphasis on the 'dangers' of sexuality. Some congregations highlighted the importance of religious discussing sexuality, including any difficulties they might be experiencing with their vow of celibacy. A number of the women had attended workshops or courses on sexuality and seemed quite comfortable speaking about it with someone who was a relative stranger. Indeed, the language they used and their purchase on sexuality generally seemed unusual for Irish women of their generation.

Though it was changes in the Church's teaching that had given the women an opportunity to claim a sexual identity, some of the women expressed views about sexuality that were at odds with the Church's official line. Lillian, for example, described a friend's lesbian relationship as 'perfectly natural' while Rebecca disagreed strongly with the Church's attitude to contraception, remarking 'I feel the church needs to move on [but] I think if I said all I feel, I would be excommunicated!'

Feminist identities

The desire to renegotiate their identity as women and occupy the category 'woman' differently, as some of the women of this study clearly have, suggests a consciousness as women, if not feminists. Only two of the women claimed this title themselves: Margaret called herself a feminist, while Pauline defined herself as a Christian feminist.[16] It was clear, however, that the women were aware of feminist ideology and used terms popularised by feminism, such as 'patriarchy' (Lillian), 'female subservience' (Frances) and 'women's liberation' (Frances, Teresa and Sarah) to talk about their own experiences. This was not surprising. Vatican II coincided with the second-wave feminist movement. Congregations and individual sisters were influenced by it and some incorporated elements of feminism into their redefinition of religious life, even if the term remained anathema to some of them. Many of the women, for example, drew attention to the pioneering work of women's religious congregations in the areas of education, health and social work. Some were of the opinion, retrospectively at least, that the strict pre-Vatican II regime was stood in opposition to the original ideals of active female religious congregations. As Pauline put it, 'By the time I entered [in 1948]...we were very obedient [but] religious aren't meant to be that kind of person at all'.

Though Annette did not describe herself as a feminist, she was 'very proud' that nuns had been responsible for the education of 'very feminist' women such as Germaine Greer and Benazir Bhutto. Nor, by her own admission, could Yvonne claim to be 'terribly feminist'. However, she 'rejoice[d] to see women taking their place', though for her, it was ever thus within religious life:

> In a sense, we have been doing it all the time, do you know what I mean? Like, our Mother General now is a woman now. We run our show ourselves. We've always done it...I mean, we don't feel any kind of inferiority complex about [being women]!

A woman-centred consciousness, if not a feminist consciousness, was sometimes discernible at an institutional level too. A publication by the St Mildred congregation, based on a Chapter held in the mid-1990s, for example, made several references to the commitment of the congregation to women's issues and the empowerment of women.

Certain tenets of feminism, such as the valuing of the female experience and notions of gender equality, have impacted upon religious life in the post-Vatican period and have given women in religious life, perhaps no matter the extent to which they agreed with Vatican II, the opportunity to see their femaleness in more positive terms. In giving them greater freedom to be women, and greater responsibilities for themselves as women ('to make choices...as a woman rather than just being subservient' – Teresa), Vatican II has effectively recognised and acknowledged the capabilities of women more, enabling them to 'craft', to borrow Dorinne Kondo's phrase,[17] their gendered self in its wake.

Relocating religious identity on gendered terms

In reformulating their religious identity, some of the women were keen to establish a distance between themselves and the Roman Catholic Church, an institution they felt was not representative of them as individuals, as members of their congregation or as women religious. For example, Margaret opined that:

> We, as a group of women, [have] crept out from [the Church's] influence and we run our own affairs. And that's the good thing of being a congregation of women...Even though we're in a male-dominated Church, I think we're very much in charge of our own lives and our own affairs...People...*associate* us with the Church, they *identify* us with the Church [but] we're *not* [of the Church].

In particular, the desire to claim some distance from the Church appeared to be related to that institution's reluctance to modernise, especially in terms of its gender politics. Frances, for instance, was frustrated by the attitude expressed by the Church and its priests towards inclusive language, which she interpreted as a reluctance on their part to concede power: 'You find priests go on "men, men, men, men, men". You find a few who don't and it's very arresting because it's so rare...There are very few ones that really have gone into it properly and let it affect themselves...It's about power'.

Vatican II was experienced for some of the women of this study as a project of, if not an opportunity for, self-renewal and self-actualisation. Through it, and by constructing a narrative about their own experience of it, they re-invented the self, noteworthy given the very notion of the individual self was in conflict with pre-Vatican II thinking. How some of the women chose to talk about Vatican II, how some constructed themselves in response to it, inhered to, if it did not embody, the way theorists have discussed individualisation.[18] While not all the women who were enthusiastic supporters of Vatican II regarded it or their re-negotiation of self in its wake as necessarily *gendered* projects of renewal, some certainly did. In addition, those who might not have described it specifically in such terms often articulated their interpretation of the renewal of religious life with reference to womanhood, femininity and gendered subjectivity.

DIFFERING RESPONSES

Women who were more ambiguous about Vatican II and the changes that were introduced in its wake tended to respond to Vatican II in less totalising ways. For example, they might have been in favour of the opportunity to establish closer relations with family but less supportive of religious wearing secular clothes; they might have welcomed the opportunity to retrain, but not for religious to live alone. Some of the women of this study were against the wearing of secular clothes and chose to wear the habit or an approximation of it. For them, the habit was not an unnecessary encumbrance associated with religious life but a fundamental element of it, one that fulfilled an important dual function: publicly affirming their decision to follow the path of religious life over others and making them instantly recognisable as religious to others who might be in need of them. Though it exposed her to possible abuse, verbal and otherwise, Annette felt it was important to wear the habit in public because 'it's a kind of mission going out with the habit on ... it makes you feel what the blacks feel...the people who are persecuted feel'. Moreover, she believed that by abandoning the habit in favour of 'civvies', religious were allowing themselves to be silenced by the spread of secularism, acquiescing in the 'banish[ment] of God from the streets'.

Perfectae Caritatis was open to both conservative and creative interpretation and those whose interpretation of it veered towards a more conservative slant tended to identify themselves first and foremost as religious, subsuming all other possible identities within it, including their identity as women. Annette, for example, identified 'sister' as her 'proudest, proudest title' while Kate seemed unable to countenance the idea of an alternative identity at all. When asked if she felt people in England positioned her any differently because she was Irish, Kate remarked, almost in exasperation, 'but I was a sister', suggesting that, for her at least, religious identity negated all others.[19] Aisling identified herself particularly as a missionary sister, as did Deirdre: 'Automatically, off the top of my head ... I'm a religious sister [of the St Brigid congregation] and that's number one'. Brenda described herself simply as 'child of God'.

Not only did these women privilege their identity as religious above others but they tended to ignore the option of identifying themselves as 'woman'. This was the case with Annette, Bernadette, Elaine, Hannah, Irene, May, Rebecca, Winnie and Brenda. Others seemed not to take the term seriously at all. Deirdre, for example, having been proffered 'woman' as a possible badge of identity and having described herself first in terms of her status as a missionary religious then added, laughing: 'And, yes, I'm proud of being a woman. I am, you know? There's no doubt about that!' She continued 'but I would describe myself first as being a [sister of St Brigid] and being a religious', the expression 'but seriously' suggesting itself as a conjunction. While Yvonne was 'very happy to be a woman. I was very happy to be myself! [laughter] I hope the Lord is equally happy about me! [more laughter]', she admitted that she 'never had any words about that', meaning she had not thought about it. Likewise, Aisling did not 'think too much about that. A woman is a woman and that's it', adding 'but I understand your interest, and especially in your field'.

This is not to suggest, of course, that these women did not regard themselves as women. Of course, they did. However, their sense of self as women was subsumed within their identity as religious to the extent that it negated any assertion of their womanhood independently of religious life. In addition, implicit, if not explicit, in their accounts was a certain resistance to claiming an identity as women because of the tacit associations they made around it with feminism. Those women who did assert an identity as women tended, by contrast, to be more self-consciously aware of gendered subjectivity and expressed a desire to identity themselves in terms of their gender. The women's use of the terms 'woman' and 'sister/nun' conformed to this pattern also. Those who claimed an identity as women tended either to use this term exclusively when referring to themselves and others in religious life or use it interchangeably with 'sister/nun'. Those who did not claim an identity as women tended to use the term 'nun' or 'sister' but not 'woman'.[20]

TENSIONS

Tensions naturally arose between, on the one hand, those sisters who desired change and, on the other, those who regarded communal conformity as the essence of religious life and relied upon it to define themselves as religious. Humorous but dismissive remarks were made, for example, about 'modern' nuns to the effect that they had 'no faith' (Bernadette) or took 'no vows' (Annette). Others choosing not to wear the habit also created problems:

> I preferred people to know I was religious...I think it's important ...I mean, I laugh at some. We had some [sisters] who didn't want to wear a veil at any cost. As soon as they could, [they] gave it up.

And then they got all dressed up to be scout mistresses or whatever
you are at Brownies,[21]...in their hats and their uniform. I said, "Why
do you wear that if you're not prepared to wear a veil?" "Well, you
have to be recognised". I said, "That's why I'm wearing this!"...Yes,
I think there was a certain amount of unease and tension. [Hannah]

Religious who chose to remain in habit tended to dismiss those who
wore secular dress as cowardly or less brave than themselves,
interpreting it as a refusal to take on the demands and responsibilities
of religious life, especially in the more trying circumstances of the
present times. Also for them, it was important that religious present
a united front.

   Likewise, tensions arose because some religious were claiming
greater independence within community life, thinking in terms of 'I'
rather than 'we'. One way this manifested itself was with respect to
personal possessions. Prior to Vatican II, religious owned nothing and
held all goods in common (a point beautifully highlighted in a poem
by Eiléan Ní Chuilleanáin which recalled an incident in which her
aunt, a member of a French congregation, told her dentist that she
had a pain in 'our teeth').[22] Hannah in particular took exception to
what she regarded as the rise of proprietorship within community:

   Possibly because of the rapid changes after Vatican II, people said,
   well, they [can] have their own cars and their own things. What they
   don't realise is that [it's] *not* your own car. It's for the use of the
   community. Or for the use of your work...I was sick of people
   talking about 'my, my, my, my'.

The communal, congregational identity that Hannah and others were
trying to hold on to was undermined by other sisters' claims to
individuality. It was impossible to be 'one' in religious life with
differing and apparently incompatible notions of what religious life
meant. Simply put, communal identity relied upon the community
defining it similarly.

   The incidences related here point to a wider tension amongst
religious over the extent to which women religious wished, remained
or could claim to be intrinsically 'distinct' from seculars in the post-
Vatican II period. Equally at issue was gender: the 'kind' of women
religious were and the extent to which they could claim to be different
from other women. The desire to renegotiate their identity as women
and to occupy the category woman differently reflected a desire to be

seen to be 'just like' other women (whatever that might mean) and, in turn, to be treated as such. In essence, the women were demystifying and demythologising religious life in favour of a more realistic notion of themselves as women. These women embraced the opportunity to be 'normal' women and to be regarded as such. Retrospectively, they considered the distinction made between themselves as religious and other women as seculars to be negative. For them, the habit marked religious as different from women generally, highlighted their inferior status vis-à-vis male religious and prohibited them acceptance as normal women: 'The habit made you stand out like a sore thumb ... I'd love to have said, "Look, in spite of the way I look ... I'm *not* a freak!"' (Margaret). Others, however, did not want to distinguish themselves from women who did not have a vocation, had not entered religious life and had not take holy orders. For these women, difference remained the very essence of religious life.

In addition to individual religious asserting an identity which served to undermine the notion of a collective religious identity, the extent to which women religious embraced 'modern' womanhood was also an issue around which conflict emerged. In as much as some women were frustrated by the Catholic Church's hesitancy to take progressive gender politics on board, the same could also be said for the women's individual congregation and co-religious. Likewise, some women were uncomfortable with the way their co-religious embraced feminism and women's issue within the Church. May, for example, was 'irritated' by other religious 'going to town with inclusive language', no doubt a reference to the decision which had recently been taken by the St Mildred congregation to convert to inclusive language in documents and prayer, a change other St Mildred sisters expressed support for, among them Frances. While female ordination did not 'appeal' to Aisling ('not yet anyway'), she was clearly unimpressed with the stance certain members of her congregation took on the issue: 'Some of our sisters protest the place of women in the Church. I haven't done it, but they do do it. It embarrasses me a little bit.'

While the women of this study expressed different opinions on how it should be expressed and practised, the notion at least of a communal, congregational identity remained important to them all. Some of them subscribed to a communal religious identity that was not congregation-specific, usually in response to negative attitudes levied against religious generally and to emphasise the importance and positive influence of religious historically. The women also tended to emphasise various distinctive, and positive, characteristics about their own congregation. For example, individual congregations were described as more democratic, less strict, quicker to modernise or more in touch with tradition than others. Attention also tended to be drawn to the reputation of individual institutions in the areas of teaching or health. For all the women, community was a vital source of belonging and support which could be experienced materially or psychologically. Elaine, for example, felt 'naked' when outside her congregation and was always in a hurry to return to its secure fold. Vera, by contrast, lived alone so her sense of belonging (to the same congregation) was necessarily more abstract than Elaine's. She did, however, keep a database of contact details for all the members of her congregation across the globe and felt able to call upon any one of them for support or assistance. Although, post-Vatican II, the less regimented structure of religious life has allowed religious to pursue individual identity projects beyond their congregation, many of the women of this study still considered themselves to be 'at one' within it.

CONCLUSION

The aim of Vatican II was to identify and clarify the position of the Catholic Church with respect to the changed and changing realities of the modern world. *Perfectae Caritatis*, the document aimed at religious life, was not expressly designed to elicit a gendered revolution although, for many women religious, this was how it was experienced. For these women, Vatican II liberated them from the strictures of a gendered subjectivity based on denial and repression and allowed them to claim a more positive identity as individuals and as women in its wake. For those less enthusiastic about change, the response of others within religious life challenged their own notions of what it meant to be a religious. Unsurprisingly, tensions arose. While Vatican II gave those women who were able and who chose to do so greater latitude to renegotiate their identity as religious and as women, their freedom to do so was contested by others, a theme that will be returned to in subsequent chapters. In fact, however, conflict could emerge within individual religious also. Though fully supportive of Vatican II, Vera was frustrated by the lingering influence of the pre-Vatican II system:

Even though I say I kicked against the regime for a quite a long time, it's amazing the impact it's had on me and how in certain respects, even though I seem to be free of it, I am *not* free. I'm *not* free of the yoke of religious life that was imposed.

Women religious have tended to be ignored as women, though religious life both before and after Vatican II has continued to sex and gender them in particular ways. This chapter has explored the significance of Vatican II in the lives of Irish women religious in terms of how they lived and interpreted it but most especially the impact it had on their sense of self as women. It so doing, it has drawn attention to the contested and contingent nature of gender identity and subjectivity, as well as pointing to some of the negotiations that occur around it.

NOTES

1   Frances.
2   R. A. Wallace, 'New Roles for Women in the Catholic Church' in H. R. Ebaugh (ed.), *Religion and the Social Order, New Developments in Theory and Practice, Volume II* (Greenwich, Connecticut, USA: JAI Press Inc., 1991), pp. 123–36, pp. 123–4.
3   W. M. Abbott, *The Documents of Vatican II* (London: Geoffrey Chapman, 1965), pp. 466–82.
4   Although there are a selection of books on Vatican II itself, see, for example, G. Bull, *Vatican Politics at the Second Vatican Council, 1962–5* (Oxford: Oxford University Press, 1966); and A. Stacpoole, *Vatican II By Those Who Were There* (London: Geoffrey Chapman, 1986); and a number of books which explore the consequences of Vatican II on lay Catholicism, see, for example, A. H. Hastings, *Modern Catholicism, Vatican II and After* (London: SPCK, 1991), few focus on the impact of Vatican II within religious life itself – an exception is L. M. Örsy, *Open to the Spirit: Religious Life after Vatican II* (London: Geoffrey Chapman, 1968) – while none at all on its impact on women religious. This is remarkable given the significance of Vatican II in the lives of religious. With respect to Ireland, in addition to articles in journal periodicals, J. Beale explores the impact of Vatican II on sisters, but only among women who were enthusiastic supporters of it (*Women in Ireland*). Helena O'Donoghue's 'Women's Congregations 25 Years After Vatican II', *Religious Life Review*, 30, 3 (1991), pp. 115–123 is more insightful

5 Actual quotes from modern rule books of the congregations of which the women of this study are members.

6 Not all the congregations had 'modernised' to the same extent. Of the congregations the women were members of, the St Celia congregation remained the most traditional, a fact reflected in its rule book.

7 Of course, congregations vary as to the freedom they give religious.

8 *Constitution and Rule of the CSSL* (1984), p. 78.

9 T. Inglis, *Truth, Power and Lies, Irish Society and the Case of the Kerry Babies* (Dublin: University College Dublin Press, 2003), p. 129.

10 An example of this was the several attempts made to find out how Bernadette felt leaving Ireland. Having entered religious life twelve years previously, Bernadette had no expectation of being moved to England in 1943, nor was she given any prior warning. Although I asked her many times how she *felt* about leaving Ireland, her answers detailed instead the boat trip to Wales and the train journey from Wales into London, including the refreshments she had consumed along the way.

11 See, for example, Inglis, *Moral Monopoly* and Whyte, *Church and State*.

12 Sabbaticals themselves would not have been common prior to Vatican II. Aisling had not requested her sabbatical: 'now, sabbatical[s] weren't in our heads, we just went and did it'. Likewise, it was an unusual departure for Brenda, though it was she who requested it: 'at that stage, I wrote to our Mother General and asked her if I might take a sabbatical year and go and study the theology of religious life'. So disconcerting had the experience of Vatican II been for her that she believed this new departure to be a drastic but necessary step to help her come to terms with it.

13 Of the women in this study Winnie, Aisling, Yvonne, Rosemary, Angela, Brenda, Deirdre, Irene, Frances, Elaine, Bernadette, Geraldine and Catherine lived in communities of over five women. The rest lived in smaller communities, with the exception of Vera and Annette, who lived alone.

14 I was wearing a dress at the time.

15 Sarah, Josephine, Eileen, Pauline, Claire and Margaret each worked on gender-based projects while Lillian, Norah, Barbara and Teresa expressed a desire to do so.

16 However, as the women were not asked specifically if they would identify themselves as feminists, it is impossible to know how many of them would do so.

17 D. K. Kondo, *Crafting Selves: Power, Gender, and Discourses of Identity in a Japanese Workplace* (Chicago, IL: Chicago University Press, 1990).

18　See, for example, A. Gittens, *Modernity and Self-Identity, Self and Society in the Late Modern Age* (Cambridge: Polity, 1991) and U. Beck and E. Beck-Gernsheim, *Individualization* (London: Sage, 2002).

19　This was Kate's initial response. In fact, as has been seen in a previous chapter and will be seen again later, Kate talked at length about her experiences of being an Irish sister in England.

20　It was less easy to adjudge broader generalisations based on this pattern. For instance, it was not necessarily the case that younger religious were more likely to claim an identity as women or to have undergone a consciousness-raising experience of their own womanhood. Women who had spent a large, perhaps the majority, of their life as religious on the missions, however, tended not to identify themselves in terms of their womanhood. Though these women were also generally older, given the similar age of many of the women who did assert an identity as women, the fact that they lived in areas and conditions perhaps less influenced by second-wave feminism might have been more pertinent to their sense of self than age was.

21　The junior Girl Guides.

22　E. Ní Chuilleanáin, *The Magdalene Sermon* (Dublin: Gallery Press, 1989), p. 29.

CHAPTER 6

Vatican II:
England and the Missions

'As the tenor of the times indicates'[1]...and place also?

INTRODUCTION

As was suggested in Chapter 4, religious institutions, while distinct from the wider society in which they were placed, could not be divorced from it. One of the aims of Vatican II was to define the Church's position with respect to the modern world and, in so doing, make it more relevant to that world. In this chapter, the themes of Chapter 4 are revisited to consider more specifically the significance of place when the boundary that separated religious life from the wider society was knowingly and intentionally eroded. If one of the objectives of Vatican II was to 'open up the shutters, and let the outside in' (Kate) then the socio-cultural and socio-geographic co-ordinates of religious communities were intrinsic to the experience of Vatican II and would inform its legacy. Religious, individually and collectively, reconstructed, redefined and resisted reconstruction in relation to their circumstances, not only where they lived but how others around them lived. The settings in which those deliberations took place also proved vital to their outcome.

ENGLAND

Within religious life

Vatican II allowed for a gradual relaxation of the strict convent rules which governed the way religious lived. The wider society entered the congregation through the media of newspapers, television and radio and, for the first time, religious began to talk more freely about occurrences 'outside'. In England, initially at least, this allowed for a further entrenchment of divisions within the congregations of which the women of this study were members. There was *more* opportunity within the majority-Irish congregations to assert an Irish identity while the women in the St Mildred congregation became *more* aware of being Irish in an English congregation. A significant contributing factor to this was the period in which the changes of Vatican II filtered down into religious life, coinciding as it did with the outbreak of violence in Northern Ireland, a renewed IRA campaign in Britain and increased anti-Irish hostility there also.

The majority-Irish congregations

In the majority-Irish congregations, that the women of this study living in England were members of, relaxation of the convent rule gave rise to a more vigorous expression of Irishness. It was *Irish* media and music that entered the congregation ('we got Irish newspapers, Irish magazines...there was Irish dancing, Irish singing' – Margaret) and it was Irish feast days that were celebrated even more vociferously ('St Patrick's Day was just *mega*' – Joan). Given that the majority of the women in these congregations were Irish, as they began to be allowed to visit home more regularly, a stronger connection with the island of Ireland also began to be formed. Stories about what was happening there and the experiences of the women when they returned could dominate conversations in the convent.

As before, but to a greater extent, this was at the expense of other, especially English, sisters. Lillian remarked, 'It was quite strong, Irish songs or an Irish programme...and sometimes the English sisters, they wouldn't say anything but they might not come [to join us], you know?' The reaction to the preponderance of Irishness by English sisters was often to retreat to other areas in the convent, including their own rooms. Community life was transformed by Vatican II, which allowed for less regulated communal gatherings and conversations to take place. As this was happening, however, the communal space was also becoming, for some, more exclusive.[2] An incident Josephine recalled served to illustrate this, revealing how certain viewpoints, or at least their articulation, might come to dominate the communal space:

> I remember Bloody Sunday[3] *very* well. [It was on] the news. I [sank] into the chair saying 'oh my God', with my hands in my head...I was so devastated by this...and when I lifted my head, the English

sisters had left the room...That was a terrible time, but we didn't really discuss it...The English, to my knowledge, unless they spoke amongst themselves, never discussed it.

In this example, while the congregation becomes a space in which ethnicity might be experienced and played out openly, the communal religious identity is ruptured by the circumstances of the time in which it was occurring. The English sisters, clearly made aware of the ethnic divide, withdraw elsewhere. Ironically, they are silenced at a time when there is more freedom for speech within religious life.

At the same time, the convents were themselves gaining significance as a place of refuge for Irish sisters given increased levels of anti-Irish hostility outside it. Teresa felt that 'no comparison, really' could be made between Irish religious and other Irish emigrants in England because 'anybody coming over wouldn't have had any of the security that we would have had. And [would have] suffered incredibly in terms of trying to get jobs or work or money or social welfare or whatever'. Josephine admitted that she felt:

> ...very secure in that I lived with Irish people, Okay, I lived with English people as well but the majority would have been Irish [so] on a home front, you were kind of secure [because] you went home to that at night. You could sit down and say, 'God, these people are a soulless bloody bunch.' And so I think, yeah, we were very secure.

So protected, in fact, was Josephine that she did not feel the need, as she judged other Irish people in England might, to lose her accent in an effort to 'pass' in English society. As she put it, 'we weren't coming over here and working in a hospital or a factory or something where you were "the Irish", you know?'. The reference to speech is of course poignant given the silencing of the English women's voices in the same congregation.

Hostilities clearly affected the dynamics of convent life, although not always in the same way. In Josephine's congregation it was the English sisters who were silenced. However, as the number, frequency and fear of terrorist attacks escalated in Britain, it was Irish women who began to feel less at ease, as was suggested by Kate: 'It was fairly uncomfortable when the news was on and they were talking about the IRA... because [the IRA] were Irish and you were coming over to another country with bombs and you were killing innocent people and destroying buildings'. In this case it is the minority who are questioning the legitimacy of the majority to hold onto the dominant position they had assumed. Kate uses the terms 'them' and 'us' interchangeably to refer to members of the IRA and Irish people in England. While it might not have been her intention to suggest that all Irish people in England were members of the IRA, her comment does reflect the collective criminalisation of Irish people in England.[4] In these comments, Kate also seems, as an Irish person, to accept some responsibility for the activities of the IRA, a tendency noted also amongst Irish people living in Britain more generally.[5]

The English congregation

Though Aisling had commented that she and other Irish sisters in the St Mildred congregation 'suffered' because of their Irishness, she qualified this statement with reference to the strictures of the pre-Vatican II system: 'But within the... constraints or restraints of religious life, it wouldn't matter that much'. Though Aisling had left for the missions by the time the effects of Vatican II were felt, Elaine noted that being Irish in the St Mildred congregation became more problematic after it, especially, again, because of the escalation of violence that coincided with it:

> But now [in the wake of Vatican II, we] can talk to each other and ...I would feel that the English nuns... get very upset about the [activities of the IRA and] because we're Irish, we're [made to feel] in some way responsible... And you feel that they are very English. And we are very Irish.

Elaine's awareness of herself as Irish and others as English is in direct contrast to her experience of pre-Vatican II religious life about which she commented 'we were all the same'. In replacing the communal 'we' with 'them' and 'us', the protection and security of the congregation is undermined. Although the communal 'we' was very obviously cross-cut in the pre-Vatican II period by the categories of lay and choir sisters (Elaine herself having entered as a lay sister), class may have seemed a more 'natural' or acceptable distinction to make.

As was the case in the majority-Irish congregations, greater access to current affairs and media highlighted ethnic differences in the community in specific ways. When asked if she was aware of being Irish within the community at this time, Frances replied: 'I did really, though it was something you wouldn't discuss. And I often felt the reporting on the TV and media was entirely biased. You *never* got the Irish side at all. We just kept quiet about it' (Frances). Although Frances would, because of Vatican II, have been able to voice opinions, she did not feel able to. Similarly, Geraldine remarked:

> I was...conscious of an anti-Irish atmosphere [when] listening to the news. My policy when anything about the North of Ireland is on the news [is that] I don't join the community to listen to it because I don't want to hear people tut-tutting. It makes me angry and makes me say and think things that are not really me. They're just contrary to what's the general feel[ing]... Irish people [are] dismissed as not quite up to English standards. [It's] 'the Irish Celt', fighting as usual.

For Geraldine, the attitude that was expressed in the media and in the congregation understood IRA violence as a product of Irishness rather than the political situation. This interpretation was based on essentialist readings of Irishness and age-old stereotyping of the Irish as inferior and violent. It was not a point of view Geraldine shared but, though she wanted to challenge the stereotyping, she did not feel the space existed for her to do so, without her views being misinterpreted. In trying to defend being Irish, she might have been seen to be defending the activities of a group she was not in sympathy with. Her solution was to leave the room and avoid the situation entirely.

As in the pre-Vatican II period, by maintaining a sense of themselves as Irish, the women created the space in which to hold on to two identities: both as St Mildred sisters *and* Irish women. The latter was an identity also projected on to them by English sisters, at least in terms of how they experienced life within the congregation. As Elaine put it: 'They make you feel bad for [IRA activities]'. The women felt they were made to feel Irish, thus suggesting that despite the St Mildred policies of de-nationalisation, Irish sisters were never actually regarded as *non*-Irish.

Elaine, Frances and Geraldine each qualified the statements they made about the dynamics around Irishness within their congregation by back-tracking slightly. Frances' and Elaine's comments were modified with the use of more ambiguous language (Frances: 'But I didn't feel it very strongly'; Elaine: 'we're getting a little bit of that)'. Geraldine also seemed reluctant to allow her statements to stand without further qualification ('But I don't know that I'm really aware of [anti-Irish hostility] myself . . . I have never experienced . . . anything that went against me because I was Irish)'. It appeared the women did not want to come across as having strong opinions on the issue of anti-Irish hostility or admit to having personally experienced it. This could reflect a reluctance on their part to claim a strong opinion, either as women or religious sisters, or a reluctance to give the impression that divisions existed within their own religious community. This was certainly on Frances' mind when asked, at the conclusion of our second interview, if there was anything else she would like to add, to which she replied: 'I'd just like to say about the [community] here in general. Even though... there are all these difficulties and it isn't all that easy to be Irish...the goal of the [community] at large is racial acceptance, racial tolerance and I think that's terrific'.

One St Mildred sister described a contrasting subjective experience of ethnicity to those explored above. During the interviews, Vera had consistently drawn distinctions between herself and other Irish Catholics, refusing categorisation as a traditional Irish Catholic.[6] On entering religious life, she had embraced a St Mildred identity at the expense of her Irish identity in a way the other women did not ('I suppose I have become more English than the English'). When asked about her experience of 'the troubles' within the congregation, Vera replied 'Well, we were all shocked', and continued to speak in communal terms, suggesting a shared community experience amongst all the St Mildred women. Vera made no distinction between herself as Irish and others as English, as some other women had. In fact, in contrast to what sometimes occurred outside the congregation, she appreciated the fact that within it she was given the space to adopt, by association, an English identity. It was religious community that allowed Vera to transcend her Irishness and assume the ethnic identity of the congregation.[7] Her individual experience 'collides'[8] with that of the other women, highlighting the multiplicity of experiences within the diaspora space and illustrating also how diasporas can be the sites of new beginnings.

Vatican II gave women religious more freedom but, for some, it also served to emphasise divisions between them, including ethnic divisions. Although the women experienced their ethnicity in different ways, for the most part they described it in relation to feeling a sense of belonging or exclusion: a more conscious awareness of an 'us' and 'them' and the processes of othering that produced it. The women were not, and could not be, removed from the social and political period in which they lived and their subjective experiences of ethnicity reflects competing discourses surroundings what it meant to be Irish, to be English and to be Irish in England during the period.

Outside the congregation

As the wider society began to permeate religious life, so the women who chose to avail themselves of the opportunities presented by Vatican II began to move into it to a greater extent than ever before. The women could pass more freely between the convent and the outside, and, in time, were able to take up employment independent of their congregations, although only with its consent. Some women began to move out of congregations altogether, into residential properties with smaller numbers of sisters or, in some cases, alone. Those women who chose to wear 'civilian' clothes were also less conspicuous as religious.

For the women of this study, entry into the wider society occurred at the same time as the renewed IRA campaign and increased anti-Irish hostility in Britain. Throughout the 1970s, 1980s and into the 1990s, the women were aware of their Irishness in the context of a society where to be Irish was to be suspect and where circulating discourses allowed for few positive interpretations of their ethnicity. The subjective experience of ethnicity explored below demonstrates the othering of Irish people in Britain generally, although this occurred simultaneously with whatever processes of othering existed within the congregations themselves.

Several of the women mentioned becoming aware of their Irishness directly in relation to anti-Irish hostility and admitted having negative feelings about their ethnicity. Hannah remarked that she was 'aware of my nationality and ashamed of it!', although in fact several of the women expressed similar sentiments to this. Some of these women took on prevailing attitudes concerning the collective guilt of the Irish in Britain, whereby the activities of the IRA were reduced to ethnic essentialism. For example, Lillian commented that 'there's a shame attached to that kind of violence... and there's a sense of being associated with that group, you know?... If they're Irish and you're Irish'.

As Irish, the women were racialised in a particular way, usually as violent, although this tended to co-exist alongside a host of other negative stereotypes. Bernadette, a be-habited octogenarian, suggested two such associations when she said: 'Bombs and alcohol. Sometimes you'd be afraid to open your mouth'. On occasion, racialisation was experienced directly. Lillian, for example, was asked by one of her students during class if she was a bomb-maker. On hearing that an Irish woman (who was also a nun) was to begin working in the same social welfare organisation as himself, a colleague of Teresa's moved his desk to a different office. Neither of these women made any complaint about what had happened to them, suggesting once more the acceptance of anti-Irish comment or hostility as an integral part of the experience of being Irish in England.

Josephine was also the victim of racist comment, not at work but in the public domain. In the early 1970s a woman standing at a bus stop, on hearing her Irish accent, drew her umbrella in the air, hit Josephine across the arm and remarked 'Bloody Irish, why don't you go home?'. In a separate incident, Josephine was on a bus in Knightsbridge when the IRA bombed 'Harrod's:[9]

> The buses were stopped when we got to Knightsbridge and nobody knew what was going on and this [police] inspector got on our bus [and said], 'F****** Irish, they're at it again'. And like that [flicks her fingers] the bus went up and everybody started saying they'd like to string up the Irish and what they wouldn't do to them if they could get them. And I was *sick*... I didn't know what to do. I hopped off and I sank down onto these steps of a house... This woman sat down beside me and she said 'Are you Irish?' And I looked at her. She said, 'It's alright, I am too'. She said, 'What are we going to do?' and I said, 'I don't know'.

Hickman and Walter argue that anti-Irish attitudes are ingrained in the British police force, which they consider 'particularly serious because the police are in a position of authority and have the power to enforce their prejudices, including the apparently legitimate use of violence'.[10] The comments made by the police inspector on the bus might be seen to legitimate anti-Irish hostility. In both instances, the alleged violence of 'the Irish' is, however, reversed.

The comments Josephine hears on the bus suggest a collective assertion by an 'us' over who belongs and is excluded from English society, one that highlights the instability of belonging in England for Irish people. At the bus stop, Josephine is recognised as Irish by her accent. In the bus, she is 'invisible' as Irish because of her silence. This reflects the ambiguous, but none the less insecure, position of Irish people in England ('no one knows you're black till you open your mouth' – Josephine). As members of the white majority, Irish people tend to be located within the dominant group. However, they also continue to be simultaneously constructed as outsiders on the basis of their ethnicity, and, often their religion.[11] The experiences recounted here show the lived reality of this precarious position. Irish people might be commonly regarded as belonging in England but member-ship can be and is revoked suddenly. While the physical appearance of Irish people may not mark them immediately as outsiders, their accent has the potential to do so. As the woman with the umbrella reminds Josephine, England *cannot* be her home. Josephine's departure from the bus is likewise symbolic of her exclusion.

Vera, who had abandoned her Irishness within the congregation, found this was less easily achieved outside it, where others continued to categorise her as Irish. Working in the public sector when the IRA detonated a bomb in Birmingham,[12] she unintentionally arrived into work in a green suit:

> Whether that's significant to you or not, it was significant to everybody else. I stood out as an Irish woman in a green suit in Birmingham. And yes I did, when I got home that evening, I got rid of my green suit. I never wore it again. And I became aware of my accent as well. And I switched duties with people to do other work. To do field work...Oh, it was a very uncomfortable place to be.

The tension between how Vera chose to categorise herself and how she felt others categorised is illustrative of the dynamic that exists between subjective and objective identity formations.

The women of this study reacted to anti-Irish hostility in various ways. Kate's strategy was to avoid talking about Ireland or issues related to the situation in Northern Ireland and, in so doing, 'to let people know... that you weren't of this' (i.e. supportive of the IRA). As has already been noted, other women avoided drawing attention to their Irishness, often by choosing not to talk in public. Teresa 'acquired', as she put it, an English accent to avoid being marked out as Irish. Walter has described this strategy as 'drastic....available only at considerable personal cost'.[13] This was not, however, how Teresa presented it. Rather, her nonchalance might reflect instead a casual acceptance of anti-Irish sentiment in Britain and the 'common sense' approach adopted by many Irish people to it.

Other women refused to hide their Irishness and tried, instead, to create a space in which to assert a more positive Irish identity. Hannah, for example, made simple but bold declarations such as the following: 'I used to say "*I'm* Irish"'. Following her experience on the bus, Josephine decided it was time to 'fight back. [Those] people aren't doing these things in my name and I'm *not* ashamed to be Irish'. She began to work as a counsellor for Irish migrants and also campaigned for the release of the Birmingham Six.[14] Later, she began to direct her counselling work more directly towards Irish women migrants. This represented a re-working of her own identity over time: first in relation to her ethnicity, later with respect to her gender. Starting in 1970, Annette devoted herself to working for Irish prisoners in British gaols. Each of these acts may be seen to represent a form of resistance by the women: both a refusal to be silenced themselves or to acquiesce in the silencing or 'active unseeing' of the Irish in England.[15]

Although religious have not traditionally been regarded as a migrant group, the women's accounts of Irishness and the strategies they employed to deal with, overcome or resist social constructions of themselves as Irish resonate very much with research by Hickman and Walter[16] on the experiences of Irish people in Britain generally. While their stories contribute to the collective history of the diasporic experience of Irish people, the women did not see themselves as part of the second great wave of Irish migration to Britain. When asked if they regarded themselves as Irish emigrants in England, the interesting and almost universal response was in the negative. Their movement was undertaken, for the most part, as religious or to enter religious life. As such, their movement was not regarded by themselves nor by others as emigration, which, for the period in which the women of this study were leaving, had chiefly negative connotations and was discursively constructed in terms of enforced exile for men[17] and selfish opportunism by women.[18]

Despite the experiences outlined above, the women of this study continued to draw distinctions between themselves and 'the Irish' in England. Rarely did they consider themselves to be part of an Irish migrant or ethnic community,[19] which they tended to associate with forced economic migration from Ireland and discrimination in Britain. Josephine and Joan believed that they were there to 'serve' this group without necessarily being part of it. Two women actively excluded themselves from Irish communities they came into contact with through their work: Pauline on the basis that it was exclusively white, Josephine because it was, for her, a 'ghetto' of nationalist politics and exclusively male. She did, however, feel informally connected to other Irish women in England, be they from a different or no religious background at all. Although a number of the women of this study occupied the same space as other Irish people in England, some even working directly with or for them, they did not see themselves as occupying this space either exclusively or at all. For them, membership of a religious congregation separated them from other Irish people in England. None of the women ever considered their own religious congregation to be an 'Irish community' in England, though some of them clearly were.

Defining Irishness and forms of expression

Two of the women in this study, Vera and Margaret, were reluctant to claim an Irish identity for themselves and, instead, drew upon gender and religious identity to transcent ethnic boundaries. Vera abandoned the title 'Irish' in preference for 'cosmopolitan... professional woman' while Margaret preferred to think of herself as belonging to the 'human family' rather than being 'just' Irish. The rest of the women who had or continued to live in England, however, continued to claiman Irish identity, though the importance they attached to it and the degree to which they emphasised it varied, as did the ways in which they chose a display or express it. For these women, being Irish continued to be a significant part of their identity, both as a reference to the place they came from, the past tense, as well as part of who they continued to be, the present tense. Many of the women used the term Irish to describe themselves. For example, Frances remarked 'I very definitely see myself as Irish', Kate that she was '*very* Irish!'.

When asked how important being Irish was to them, most of the women living in England replied that it was second only to their identity as nuns or as women. For these women, being Irish was something natural and unquestioned, a fact of having been born and raised in Ireland, as well as something that referred to an essential truth about themselves. Annette remarked, for example, that she 'couldn't help being [Irish], that's what I *was*', while Lillian described herself as 'just Irish... It's just how I am. It's a fact of life... I am Irish and my parents are Irish'.

As was the case with Lillian, family was a recurrent theme in many of the women's accounts of themselves as Irish, as was a shared sense of national community with other Irish people. Elaine talked about feeling 'still... very attached to your own', meaning other Irish people, while Catherine remarked that she felt Irish people, wherever they were in the world, were connected, 'tuned in [to a] Celtic spirituality'. Although necessarily imagined, this had material consequences for Catherine: she found it easier to build up a rapport with strangers who were Irish than of other nationalities, especially English people. Catherine stressed that the inter/national community of Irish people she imagined was not based on Catholicism but it was not surprising, given the close relationship between Irishness and Catholicism as they were growing up, that many women continued to make a connection between Ireland/Irish and Catholicism/Catholics. For example, Elaine was 'proud [to be Irish] because I got my faith from my Irish inheritance'. Other women talked about a shared linguistic (Hannah) or cultural (May) heritage. Josephine formed gender-based communities with other Irish women she knew in England, women who were not religious, some not Catholic.

The women demonstrated their Irishness in different ways. Some felt they physically embodied Irishness and could be easily recognised as such: through accent principally, but also by 'looking' Irish. Catherine, for example, talked about having 'that real Irish hair'. Other forms of expression included an interest in Irish current affairs, exercised by reading Irish newspapers and other forms of Irish media. Irish literature and music was also referred to to illustrate one's Irishness. Annette and Josephine's work with Irish people in Britain might be regarded as an expression of their Irish identity.[20] Catherine's work since the mid-1990s in a homeless shelter, where the majority of users were Irish, had also given rise to a greater sense within herself of being Irish in England. Some of the women who had experienced living in majority-Irish congregations did not feel their Irishness was something they needed to display externally. This perhaps represented a re-formulated ethnic identity distinct from the one that previously existed within their congregation. As Lillian put it: 'I am Irish [but] on St Patrick's Day, I don't need to go out with a mound of shamrock... Whether I wear it or [not], I'm Irish ... but I don't have to push it down people's throats'.

Visits to Ireland represented an expression of Irish identity also, though they should not be considered a litmus test of Irishness. Elaine and Bernadette did not visit Ireland although they both considered themselves very much as Irish. As Elaine put it 'I would never feel that I was anything else *but* Irish'. By their own admission, they were too old and frail to make the trip. By contrast, Vera and Margaret visited Ireland, albeit irregularly, but did not privilege their Irish identity.[21] As Margaret remarked: 'It doesn't matter to me if I'm Irish, English, Scottish or Welsh... I couldn't care less what nationality I am.' For these women, being Irish was a fact about who they were – a statement on their passport – though neither felt it a relevant or appropriate description of their identity.

For those women living in England, claims to an Irish identity was one that was at a geographical distance from Ireland and expressed in terms of a conscious sense of being other. Moreover, it was influenced by the specific circumstances of the relationship between Britain and Ireland and the experiences of living as an Irish woman in England, what might be termed an 'Irish-in-England' identity. The women talked about being 'so' (Catherine), 'very' (Kate) and 'real[ly]' (Annette) Irish precisely in relation to what they were not, i.e. English and/or British. As Lillian, echoing an earlier quote from Elaine (see above) put it, 'I'm not anything else', adding, 'I mean, I would *never* see myself as British'. Both Geraldine and Josephine talked about being 'very conscious of being Irish', a consciousness likely to be felt more acutely outside Ireland. Within Ireland, as part of the ethnic majority, ethnicity can seem to fade, a fact reflected in the tendency to speak only of ethnic minorities, not majorities. Significantly, as Lillian suggested (above), although the form their Irishness took might change, the simple fact of being Irish was not something many of the women felt was negotiable or, indeed, replaceable. As Annette said of being Irish: 'I didn't have a choice.'

Changes within religious life

Both within and outside community, the fact of their being Irish has affected the women of this study who lived or continue to live in England. Initially, Vatican II served to expose and reinforce ethnic cleavages. More recently, however, several factors have combined to diffuse the situation. A fundamental part of this has been the oppor-tunity for individual women to speak out to their congregations about their experiences of exclusion and marginalisation and, in so doing, make others aware of power dynamics with community.[22] As vocations from Britain and Ireland have declined substantially, and as those from the 'third world' have increased, the ethnic configuration of religious congregations has also begun to change, forcing communities to face up to internal problems of racism and ethno-centrism. Two of the congregations involved in this study had committed themselves to issues of discrimination and racism, not only in the wider society but within their own communities. This has been achieved by recognising that problems exist and actively dealing with them through the organisation of workshops, employment of facilitators and so on. It has not been easy to undo the hierarchies that have built up within religious congregations (sometimes over centuries) and it is clear from the testimonies of the women that individual members of communities remain reluctant to change. However, attempts to dismantle internal structures have been fruitful and have directly and positively affected the women's sense of being Irish, a fact illustrated in their accounts.

With respect to the community at large, the position of Irish people in England has also been much improved by the Northern Irish peace process, which became public in 1994, and the repositioning of Ireland, in the 1990s, as a modern, economically successful European country. Irene talked about it being 'easier' to be Irish since the IRA cease-fire, a sentiment echoed by many. Josephine observed also that the position of Irish people in relation to other ethnic minorities had improved over time: 'I think we're a bit fashionable at the minute, [the] perception has changed. That we're not a nation of "ignorant Paddies" ... We ain't at the bottom anymore.'

Although 'easier' to be Irish in England, the women's experiences before, throughout and since the period known as 'the troubles' has illustrated to them the precarious position of migrant ethnic minorities in England and the speed with which acceptance by the host nation can be revoked. Residual insecurities tended to remain and often rose to the surface. Lillian, for example, continued to worry about how she might seem to others as an Irish person, especially in the context of her professional position as provincial in a large organisation: 'If I come up against people who are "terribly" English and I'm obviously Irish... there's a sense of do I fit in here? Do I belong? Am I accepted?' By 'terribly' Lillian was referring to people with upper-class accents who, in her estimation, were confident of

their own position and questioning of her's. Once again, accent is key
to revealing ethnicity (and, perhaps, class) and also to precipitating
exclusion because it is through speech that Lillian becomes obviously
or recognisably Irish. Margaret, who did not privilege her Irish
identity, found nonetheless that it 'sneaks up on me every now and
then'. One example she gave was feeling 'less intelligent' than other
students on a post-graduate course she was then registered on:
'inferior to all these clever English people'. Remarking on this, she
commented on 'Irish people', whom she called 'we', feeling 'inferior
as a race'.

Whatever the shifting experiences of Irishness in England, the
women continued to experience their Irishness in terms of being
different, of not being indigenous and, in certain circumstances, of
not being welcome. By their own admission, few claimed to have
assimilated into English society, at least at the expense of their Irish
identity. Although, many of the women found a sense of belonging in
England, none of them expressed this with reference to an English or,
indeed, hybrid Irish-English identity. Linguistically, a traditional
incompatibility between Irish and British or English exists which is
not the case for other binaries based on nationality. For example,
although 'Irish-American' and 'Irish-Australian' are acceptable
terms, 'Irish-British' or 'Irish-English' are not generally used. This
was reflected in the way the women talked about being Irish as a
statement of what they were not or could not be, meaning
English/British. Even Vera's claim to be 'more English than the
English' (see p. 151) suggested a kind of hyper-identity, one that
lacked authenticity.

THE MISSIONS

Because religious life operated differently on the missions, Vatican II
was experienced differently by the missionary religious in this study.
In some respects, its immediate impact was less radical than
elsewhere. Indeed, at first, Brenda was unsure of the point of Vatican
II. When asked to describe her reaction to it, she replied: 'Well... we
were out in Uganda where there were very few, as it were, of the
restrictions that we had [in Ireland]. It was a much freer country
...and I found very few of what other people would have considered
hindrances in the way we lived'.

This is not to suggest, however, that Vatican II was less immediately appreciated by some of the other missionaries. Many, in fact, embraced it, both for the opportunity it provided to jettison further rules and regulations but also to be liberated from the notion of a more superior and authentic form of religious life existing elsewhere, to which they should ultimately aspire. For Angela, Vatican II was 'fantastic' and particularly suited to the missions: 'Maybe it was too rushed for a country like Ireland. But for people like us out in the missions, it was great. It helped you to mix, made you freer to mix around with other people'.

Implicit in this remark was the suggestion that the missions and missionaries themselves were better equipped to deal with change. In the same vein, Frances remarked that being on the missions when Vatican II occurred was 'a great blessing in the sense that we were away from the main burden of religious observance'. These women saw the missions not so much as a step removed from religious life as it was lived elsewhere but as a step ahead. In fact, most of the missionaries regarded themselves as living in a manner that was more in tune with post- than pre-conciliar thinking and regarded Vatican II as a vindication of that life.

Angela talked about Vatican II almost exclusively in terms of the greater opportunities it provided for religious to mix both among themselves and beyond community. In fact, this was a fundamental aim of *Ad Gentes*, the Vatican II document which dealt specifically with missionary activity. Pre-Vatican II theology held that *extra ecclesia nulla salus* ('outside the Church there is no salvation'). This uncomplicated, largely pessimistic doctrine reflected the Catholic Church's dualistic outlook which pitted good against evil, mind against body, itself against the rest of the world.[23] It was also a theology which lent importance and urgency to the missionary project itself and proved hugely successful in generating support for that project, both in terms of finance and personnel, from lay and religious alike. *Ad Gentes* represented a softening of the Church's position. Though baptism into the Catholic Church remained the ultimate goal, the Church began to take a less fatalistic view of other Christian and non-Christian faiths, to recognise them as 'authentic spiritual impulses' and to call, in the sprit of ecumenicism and inclusivity, for greater dialogue, communication and co-operation between peoples of different religions. *Ad Gentes* also stressed the importance of establishing native churches, best achieved through communication and understanding of native populations and their culture. To this end, it called upon missionaries to adapt to local conditions through greater participation in community and national affairs.[24]

None of the women of this study mentioned *Ad Gentes* specifically However, their narratives of missionary life post-Vatican II served to illustrate its significance in their experiences, especially with respect to the breakdown of barriers between religious and those to whom they ministered. Already an important theme in the accounts of pre-Vatican II, missionary life, intimacy with 'the people' took on even greater significance with respect to the post-Vatican II period. Several of the women talked about the closeness they enjoyed with others to the extent that they felt 'at one' with the local population. This tended to be achieved through active immersion, living among and like the general populace, which many of the women experienced through outreach work, a practice which became more prevalent after Vatican II. Angela recalled the stages of accession:

> The hard part, I suppose, would be getting used to the food and things like that that you weren't used to. But at the same time … that's how people accepted you. If you eat their food. Like, if you go out to a village and they hand you food in a banana leaf, that's their plate. And you have no knife or fork? Well, you just eat it like they do, you know?… That's when they really accept you.

Likewise, sharing events, especially difficult or dangerous episodes, helped to engender a sense of solidarity, and served to distinguish missionaries from other white visitors:

> You [used to be] considered a colonial person. All colonials were the same people: took their land and their property and used it and made money out of it and all the rest of it, you know? That was their idea. But then when [times got hard] and the missionaries stayed, 'twas only then they realised that the missionaries were there to help them. [Angela]

As Barbara suggested, a sense of community could develop around sufferance: '[During war] the people were very impressed that we stayed with them, that we didn't move away. That we were willing to endure what they were enduring'.

'The people' was neither a flippant nor hollow theme in the

accounts but one that represented for many the very meaning, the essence and the reward of missionary life. Warmly received and accepted, the women felt appreciated and valued. When thanked by local people for remaining in Uganda during civil unrest, Winnie remarked that it was 'one of the greatest things I [ever heard]. It was an affirmation. It was what it was all about'. Likewise, the 'best compliment' Brenda ever received came from the 'poor boys' she taught in Africa:

> And that was, 'Sr, we never think of you as white. You're one of us'. I mean, that to me was the essence of what it meant to be a mission[ary]. Because I loved them so much.

Relations between religious missionaries of different congregations and faiths was aided by Vatican II. With respect to other faiths, Angela remarked that:

> Before the Vatican II, shall I say, the Church Missions Society and some of these other Protestants were very anti-Catholic, you know? And they didn't like to see you around. But, you see, we always gave them a welcome and in that way, you know, it softened. They changed.

Remarking on other Catholic missionaries, Geraldine remarked that 'anywhere you went, there was a network. More than there was here …we live much more isolated lives here. Sort of, you're on your own'. Barbara talked about the 'camaraderie' and highlighted how much more relaxed relations between missionaries were: 'If one was in the vicinity of other missionaries, one called in on them. There was no standing on ceremony and they were always happy to meet up.' Shades of mission hospitality peppered all the accounts and many of the women drew attention to how well the different nationalities among the missionaries mixed. Indeed, the fact that the women lived abroad with greater numbers of nationalities within their own community and in touch with greater numbers of nationalities through their work was identified by many as one of the most positive aspects of missionary life. It was also one that reflected back on them in 'internationalising' their own outlook.

As was the case elsewhere, missionary religious responded variously to Vatican II. While all the missionary sisters of this study were supportive of those changes which made their daily lives easier, there was discrepancies amongst them concerning how far Vatican II should be taken. Introducing structural changes which aided the day-to-day running of religious life was one thing, redefining religious spirituality was quite another. Of the missionary religious in this study, only Frances talked about Vatican II in terms of the wider project of renewal and reformation. Being on the missions in a small international community headed by an 'enthusiastic and energetic' American constituted, Frances felt, ideal conditions not only to embrace Vatican II but to take it to its natural conclusion: 'We just seemed to be more ready... it was just absolutely right!... So, of course, we took to it... and just went for it!'. She fondly remembered the speed with which missionary sisters were able to adapt to change, admitting that her own group went further than most, encountering opposition along the way: 'We were looked upon as the kind of renegades of the vicariate, you know? "Those people in C____, they've stopped being religious pretty well"' The difference was ever more apparent when she returned to England in 1986: 'I came home and found [the community] stuck in the mud here... They were very slow moving'.

In contrast to Frances' unqualified enthusiasm, a couple of the missionary sisters were ambivalent about the wider implications of Vatican II and the redefinition of religious that appeared to be suggested by it. As was evidenced in Chapter 5, Aisling and Brenda were initially unsure of Vatican II. Each of them felt that being a missionary put them at a *dis*advantage: too remote from the 'core' of the Catholic Church in Rome to be properly instructed. Brenda commented, for example: 'Don't forget, we were very far removed from it all', while Aisling made the following remark:

> [Vatican II] took a long time and we were away out in [Africa] then and, you know what you hear, one person or letter might tell you one thing. There weren't any directors so it was a mixed up kind of time. And you heard what they were doing in Ireland, what they were doing in America or whatever.

Conditions on the missions were sufficiently different from elsewhere for it to have had a significant impact on how Vatican II was experienced. Vatican II occurred during a period of increasing secularisation in the West, particularly Ireland, evidenced in the fall in vocations to and membership of religious congregations. It coincided, therefore, with religious increasingly making a case for their own existence.[25] The position of missionary religious, on the other hand, while often insecure in terms of politics or economics, was more assured in terms of the wider populace relying upon, needing and appreciating them. In addition, the demands of work on the missions mitigated against introspection, especially of a personal nature. As Geraldine put it: 'Work was a big issue. You spent a lot of time working. All your time and energy went into it'. Likewise, Barbara remarked that 'the workload was huge', further distinguishing it from Ireland by adding: 'As against here, there was a sense of urgency about it'. The conditions on the missions were such that Vatican II was less likely to be experienced in terms of individualisation and grand theories of renewal, and more likely to be experienced in terms of practical benefit to daily living and administration of duties.

Missionaries: 'one of us' *vs* white, Western women

The experience of Vatican II for individual congregations as well as for individuals within them depended upon a range of factors, which included the 'corporate' response an institution might have made to Vatican II, the personal views of an individual sister and the social, economic, cultural and geographic location of them both in the world. This was an important element in Vatican II being experienced so differently for the missionary religious than the other sisters in this study. The fact of their being Irish proved a very important theme in the accounts of the women in England. This was less so for the missionaries, which is not to say, however, that ethnicity was not of significance. Far from it, indeed.

Missionaries were distinct from other religious by their 'exile for the sake of the kingdom'.[26] As such, however much missionaries felt 'at one' with the local populace, they were by definition different: from elsewhere. In addition to this, missionaries were set apart by their whiteness, their ethnicity, their religion – often all of these things. Although there were exceptions, it was generally speaking not until Vatican II that mission congregations began to admit indigenous sisters into their ranks. As a result, for most of the women of this study, being a religious on the missions was, until the latter decades of the twentieth century, synonymous with being a white foreigner. Unlike England, where the women's experience of ethnicity was dominated by notions of Irishness and Englishness that were constructed in relation to each other, in the 'third world' a broader frame of reference existed in which the women were positioned as 'white Europeans'. While this did not negate a sense of belonging, it could complicate it: the women were simultaneously both as one with and distinct from the indigenous population.

More than the fact of the women being different was the associations made around the particular attributes that marked them out as different: their whiteness, their Christianity, their Western origins, their consecrated attachment to the Catholic Church. Even Angela, whose narrative so strongly emphasised commonality with the people, recognised not only that colour mattered but that it was weighted. When asked in broad terms what she believed to be the most positive legacy imparted by missionaries, she responded thus:

> I think it was, what shall I call it, a good relationship between cultures. 'Cultural breakdown', if I can call it that... To let them realise that white people are [the same as them]. And that they are just as equal to us as we are to them. We came to them on their level. We accepted them as our own... and treated them as well as ourselves. [On the missions, religious] were just one of the crowd... at everybody else's level... If you weren't, you tried to bring them up to your level... I think that's what we gave back to them.

While Angela did not subscribe to any notion of white superiority (indeed felt the work of missionaries was an attempt to undermine it), her comments at least acknowledged the hierarchical dynamics of race assumed by it. Others felt more keenly the significance of their own whiteness and its effects. Claire, for example, observed that being white was problematic in Africa because 'once there was this colour, there was the association made with money'. Likewise, Geraldine remarked that 'there's something in the mentality that the white is the educated one:... I am white [so] I have access to money'. In addition to being white was the not unrelated and not always distinguishable fact of their being missionaries. Frances felt that as a religious, 'in Africa, you're labelled [as] somebody who's consecrated, somebody special... you're marked out as holy'. Being both white and religious proved to be a double burden for Geraldine:

> You were on a pedestal in Africa in a way that I'm not [in Ireland] or wasn't in England...The people seem to have a more

hierarchical nature [and] seem to hold you in reverence, in awe
...First of all, you're white [so] you stand out...And then, you're a
religious. They call you 'Reverend Sister', so you're up on a
pedestal even by the title... Mostly I was uncomfortable with that.
I preferred to be anonymous [but also] I found the whole thing very
difficult to suss out... I always had that feeling that there's
something I'm missing here...I think there's two sides to the
...way [they] show deference and respect to you. On the outside
[it's] 'you do us a great honour' but underneath there's 'who the
hell do you think you are?'... [I] wonder, you know, really are they
laughing at you? And the two can go together.

The consequence of this for Geraldine was an inability to feel at home
on the missions, although she was in a minority among the
missionary religious of this study in feeling this way. She admitted,
for instance, that she 'never really thoroughly fitted into it...What
I'm really saying is I didn't find it easy to [make] close friends...I was
not known as a person, I was more an image'. Comments such as
these throw the statements by the young boys Brenda taught (see
above) into relief and highlight the innocence of their claim that she
had somehow lost her whiteness. To reiterate, the point is not to
suggest that the women did not feel at home or were falsely alleging
to have fitted in. Rather, these feelings existed *despite* obvious racial,
religious and/or ethnical differences and the associations of wealth,
development and modernisation that were made around them.

The associations around whiteness did not start and end with
money and power. Related to both was the issue of colonialism and
imperialism, as one of the comments from Angela (above) alluded to.
As missionaries, and especially as Irish missionaries, the women
dissociated themselves completely from state or political colonialism,
though they were aware it was a distinction they sometimes had to
impress upon others. For Deirdre, the significant and fundamental
difference between colonialists and missionaries lay in their respective
objectives: missionaries were there to help and serve the people,
colonialists to use and exploit them. Once this distinction was
recognised by locals, missionaries could be accepted:

We'd a very good relationship with [the indigenous population].
Really very good. Now, some of them had some hang-ups with
colonial Europe but [we got past that] because if you're in the
teaching profession or the nursing profession, you're all the time

helping... You're helping them to get well, you're training them to take on work... So, we'd no trouble. And we took to each other and they took to us in a big way. We felt they did.

Some of the women drew connections between themselves and indigenous populations on the basis of a shared history of exploitation. For example, Winnie remarked that the Ugandans were 'like the Irish in a way. Their land is everything to them. And I think the Irish are like that too. Look at the way we fought for it!' A sense of intrinsic Irish anti-colonialism was something questioned only by Pauline and, significantly, only in retrospect:

> The Irish missionaries prided themselves on being one with the people they went to and having no colonial history but in actual fact it's not true. They were far worse with the local people. The colonial authorities had been used to handling local people and putting them in positions and working with them. We were more dismissive of the African [people] really than the colonial person had learned to be.

Nor did the women think of their role as missionaries in terms of religious imperialism. Pre-Vatican II, as sisters, they would not have been directly involved in converting people to Catholicism while, post-Vatican II, the Church's theology placed less emphasis on conversion itself. Instead, its thrust became more to 'bear witness' to Christ's kingdom through the practical delivery of services and, especially, aiding development. As was the case elsewhere, religious missionaries have altered their work practices in the wake of Vatican II. Though many of their institutions remain, religious have moved their work beyond the formality of institutions and structures, into community-based outreach projects which both actually and metaphorically alter the dynamic between religious and the people they serve. The language the women used to discuss the mission project emphasised its emancipatory objective to empower, liberate and help others. As Barbara put it:

> I would say probably from the outset my whole understanding of going out to Africa was to empower people. To enable people in so far as I could and encourage them, I would say more than anything else, to stand on their own two feet. To expose them to the wider world and make them aware of opportunities and then to

encourage them to take up the opportunities. To find ways and means to take up those opportunities.

Lest it be thought this was a one-way relationship, another important theme to emerge from the women's accounts of missionary life was how hugely rewarding mission work was for them personally. For Barbara, the soul that was saved was her own:

> From the missionaries who had come to speak to us... I had this notion that when one went to the mission fields, one would be responsible for the conversion of African people to Christianity. Well, I have to say that my experience was quite other in Africa myself. The reality was very different. The African people in many ways were responsible for my own conversion.[26]

With respect to being Irish, the women experienced their Irishness differently than the religious in England. Many missionaries would have been seen as white Europeans, an identity which served to dilute the specific significance of Irishness, although this obviously depended on their individual situation. Yvonne, for example, found that where she lived, being Irish

> sent your shares up... The[y] loved the Irish. They *loved* them! They were so good to us and so nice to us. They'd had Irish priests. Some of them weren't the best but many of them were very good. I must say... they really love the Irish'.

This would not have been the case for all, however, and in fact, few of the women drew attention to their nationality in recounting their experiences of the missions. This might have suggested it was not important, were it not for the fact that a recurring, albeit submerged, theme in their accounts was the significance of nationality and ethnicity within white European or Western missionary communities and between them. While many of the women noted the internationalism of religious life on the missions and considered it an advantage, there were also several references made to specific and individual nationalities, not always complimentary and, often, stereotypical. Pauline, for instance, remarked that on the missions:

> There was a lot of talk... You'd hear comments saying the Irish got on well with the Africans, the Italians get on well with the Africans.

Like, everyone got on well with everyone except the English couldn't get on with anyone. This was the thing. The English and the Germans were regarded as the races that couldn't get on with anyone!

In addition to the explicit suggestion about 'the' English and 'the' Germans was an implicit message about the greater, natural amiability of other nationalities, including 'the' Irish. Very often, references to non-Irish national stereotypes were recounted in the spirit of good fun but it is impossible to know how non-Irish individuals interpreted these comments themselves. Aisling and Pauline drew attention to the tensions that were the result of a recognised hierarchy within their own congregation which positioned members of the American province below members of the English one, most of whom, ironically, were Irish.

Many of the missionaries stated that their own nationality was not of any significance on the missions. For example, being Irish 'didn't make a difference' to Brenda. More specifically, this meant it was not experienced negatively by them. When Aisling remarked that nationality was 'kind of unimportant really', it was relative to her experience of Irishness in England where, as previously noted, she 'had suffered for it'. Aisling observed, however, that the English accents of St Mildred sisters on the missions could intimidate 'young Irish fathers [and] would put some of the[m] off'. Pauline witnessed Irish priests themselves excluding others during mixed social gatherings of missionaries: 'The [Irish] fathers would start singing all these Irish songs. You know, traditional, Irish songs which are all *full* of hatred for the English…These English sisters, who were working so hard and were such lovely women,… used to slip out and go home'. It was, Pauline declared, 'a side of being Irish that I did not like' but one she distanced herself from both on account of her gender and the fact that she entered a non-Irish congregation: 'We all have a culture [and] are wrapped up in the limits of [it]. Going to England and being trained there helped me to break out of that'.

Reflecting the 'good' history they judged the Irish missionary endeavour to be, many of the women expressed pride in Ireland's heritage as a mission-sending nation, which tended also to inform how, as missionaries, they defined their Irishness. Brenda, for example, commented:

> Maybe I was a dreamer [but] I used to think that the Irish people
> were known as having been the first missionaries. Out away in the
> sixth, seventh, eighth century. Off away in Europe and sharing their
> culture and their gifts of all sorts: art and music. The Book of Kells
> is an example.

Similarly, Joan drew inspiration from the Irish missionaries in her
own congregation who had preceded her, the memories of whom she
found 'so, so powerful. So, so strong'.

The number of Irish and other European missionary sisters has
been in decline since the 1970s while the number of indigenous sisters
in those regions has continued to rise. While this has, and will
continue to have, an impact on the relational and power dynamics
within congregations, it is clear that traditions take time to overturn.
Yvonne, for example, noted that Irish women continued to be over-
represented in positions of authority within the mission community
she was a member of, about which she commented:

> The [indigenous sisters] seemed to love us really... They were very
> kindly disposed to us. I think they were very grateful... They've
> tried appointing a [native] as provincial and it doesn't seem to work
> so well. They seem to have more confidence in somebody who is
> outside their own, you know what I mean?... They seem to prefer
> themselves somebody from outside.

Similarly, the comments Joan made about previous generations of
Irish missionary sisters was thrown into relief by another member of
her congregation who, though not a missionary herself, was, as
provincial, privy to opinions of indigenous sisters in the same
mission community. Lillian recounted a conversation with one of
these sisters which served to illustrate the Asian sisters' desire to
break down what appeared to them to be a hierarchical, if not
domineering, relational dynamic between themselves and Irish
sisters: 'She said, "well, to be quite honest with you, there's a little bit
of feeling amongst some of us that we've had enough now, you
know? We want to be ourselves. Okay, they've contributed and so on
but let's move on."'

Preserving pre-Vatican II naming practices and highlighting the
historical significance of Ireland to the Asian mission, the Irish sisters
were still known within this community as 'Irish Mothers', though
the indigenous religious were known by the less ennobled title 'Sr'.

In this and other cases, however, it is clear that indigenous sisters have begun to make their voices heard, although not without difficulty, as the following example of a St Mildred general chapter illustrates:

> One of the things they did at the chapter was [discuss] the myths that are circulating about each other... The Europeans came across as stingy, very cautious and a few other not so complimentary things [laughter]. And the Africans are people who travel with an awful lot of baggage. But they do! It's partly of course, you know, when they come to this absolute overflowing plenty, whatever, they pick up as much as they can, you know? Just to take it back. [Also] their family ties too are very strong so if they're going anywhere, their family would say bring me back something or other too... What did we think about the Americans? You know, they're the know-alls and running the world and everything else [*laughter*].
>
> And then they had to meet in their own groups to kind of handle this. And the Europeans took it very well and turned it into a kind of joke. *The Africans were terribly hurt*. And that's an interesting kind of human development in us. I mean, the Europeans were all kind of an age anyway and it sort of grows with a secure society, a secure background and everything else. That they were able to make light of it. Whereas the Africans, who have that terrible background... of oppression, dictatorship and a history of being humiliated and so on, it's very hard for them to take. Even though they are highly articulate and sophisticated in themselves. [Frances]

In recounting their experiences of missionary life, the women of this study drew attention to the bonds formed within community, with other missionaries, and with lay peoples. At the same time, however, their narratives revealed the continued significance of race, ethnicity and nationality on the mission fields, where discourses of whiteness, Christianity, the West and Irishness continued to have an impact on their experiences, even if these were not facts about themselves or their experiences the women chose to emphasise.

CONCLUSION

In many respects, Vatican II rewrote the rules of religious life, but how those rules were re-written and their impact on individual religious and communities were influenced as much by external as internal factors. For the women of this study, the fact of their being white, Irish sisters, in communities which were populated by women from similar and different backgrounds, and which existed in societies with histories, cultures and circumstances particular to them, influenced their experience and understanding of Vatican II. Varied as their experience of Vatican II undoubtedly was, the accounts of the women of this study highlighted the continued significance of race, ethnicity, nationality and geography to them all.

NOTES

1 'Decree on the Appropriate Renewal of Religious Life / *Perfectae Caritatis*', reprinted in Abbott, *The Documents of Vatican II*, p. 466.

2 The kind of Irishness being celebrated could be exclusive of Irish women too. Sarah referred to it as 'pseudo-Irish' because it represented to her not the Ireland she had recently left but a nostalgic re-remembering of an Ireland past.

3 On the 30 January 1972, British paratroopers in Derry shot dead thirteen unarmed civilians, an event which became known as 'Bloody Sunday'.

4 Noted also by, for example, Curtis, *Nothing But the Same Old Story*; Hickman and Walter, *Discrimination and the Irish Community*; Hillyard, *Suspect Community*; Walter, *Outsiders Inside*.

5 Hickman and Walter, *Discrimination*, p. 204; Walter, *Outsiders Inside*, p. 169.

6 She did this by highlighting her middle-class background, the fact she had not been educated by religious and by contrasting her own family's subdued practice of Catholicism with the more theatrical devotions of the general Catholic population (whom her father considered 'vulgar').

7 Later on, Vera would cease to privilege ethnicity at all, favouring an identity as a professional woman instead.

8 This is a term Brah uses (*Cartographies of Diaspora*).

9 On December 17th, 1983, an IRA car bomb exploded outside the department store Harrods in London, killing six and injuring ninety others.

10 Hickman and Walter, *Discrimination*, p. 190.

11 Walter, *Outsiders Inside*, pp. 81–105.

12 On 21 November 1974, the IRA detonated bombs in two Birmingham pubs, killing nineteen people and injuring 182.

174 *Made Holy*

13 Walter, *Outsiders Inside*, p. 175.

14 The six men wrongly convicted of the IRA Birmingham bombings who were eventuall released in 1991 having spent sixteeen years in prison.

15 M. Buckley, 'Sitting On Your Politics: The Irish among the British and the Women among the Irish', in J. MacLaughlin (ed.), *Location and Dislocation in Contemporary Irish Society, Emigration and Irish Identities* (Cork: Cork University Press, 1997), pp. 94–132, p. 97.

16 Hickman and Walter, *Discrimination*.

17 K., Miller, *Emigrants and Exiles: Ireland and the Irish Exodus to North America* (Oxford: Oxford University Press, 1985).

18 See, for example, B. Gray, '"The Home of our Mothers and our Birthright for Ages"? Nation, Diaspora and Irish Women', in M. Maynard and J. Purvis (eds), *New Frontiers in Women's Studies: Knowledge, Identity and Nationalism* (London: Taylor & Francis, 1996), pp. 164–88; J. J. Lee, *Ireland, 1912–1985*; and 'Emigration: A Contemporary Perspective', in R. Kearney (ed.), *Migrations, The Irish at Home and Abroad* (Dublin: Wolfhound Press, 1990), pp. 33–44.

19 Only Catherine and Geraldine regarded themselves as part of an Irish community in England. Catherine did so because she worked predominantly with Irish people, although it was only recent to our interviews that she had begun to think of herself in this way. Geraldine qualified her allegiance by noting that contemporary Irish communities tended to revolve around pubs and alcohol, which did not interest her.

20 Annette did not feel she had a choice in undertaking the work she did. Rather, she felt called to it as an 'Irish Christian'. Josephine also felt compelled to work with other Irish people. Although Margaret worked with Irish women, her interest was primarily in working with women. The fact that they were also Irish was incidental.

21 I do not feel comfortable, however, suggesting that they were in some way *not* Irish, as some of their comments might be taken to imply. In their interviews, both Margaret and Vera proposed a more complex relationship with Ireland/Irishness. Simply put, *not* being Irish was not a position they could easily or always inhabit. While they might claim an identity beyond the boundary of their ethnic group or nationality, they often felt positioned by others precisely in these terms.

22 This was mentioned by women in the St Cecile, St Marie, St Louise and St Mildred congregations.

23 Hogan, *The Irish Missionary Movement*, p. 180.

24   The very concept of the mission was expanded such that the work missionaries performed short of conversion (for example, the provision of social, health and educational services) began to be seen as a constitutive element of the drive against 'extreme manifestations of humanity's rejection of God' (Hogan, *The Irish Missionary Movement*, p. 4). Thus, human development was recognised as an end in itself rather than a means to an end, which allowed for indices other than conversions to make it on to the balance sheet and, ultimately, for missionaries to define themselves in less narrow and patrician terms than by the number of souls saved.

25   E. McDevitt, 'Comment', *The Furrow*, 21, 1 (1970), p. 63.

26   Hogan, *The Irish Missionary Movement*, p. 5.

27   Inevitably, the viewpoints expressed here are confined to a select group of women religious, which included neither religious more critical of the mission project nor those seculars who were on the receiving end of it.

Part IV

Return to Ireland

CHAPTER 7

Return and Belonging I: England

'There's something about [being] in your own country and the
sense of belonging'[1]

INTRODUCTION

Return is an important theme in migration literature and diaspora
studies, though often the homeland referred to is imagined, the return
mythic.[2] While the desire to return 'home' is implicit in discourses of
Irish emigration as exile, actual return has not been the majority
experience for Irish emigrants. Reversing a pattern that had been in
place since the Great Famine of the 1840s, it was not until the 1970s
that Ireland recorded net immigration rates, at the time due largely to
returning nationals. The trend 'righted' itself in the recessionary 1980s
although in the last decade of the twentieth century and still today,
Ireland has experienced net immigration, of Irish and non-Irish
nationals, this time on a scale not previously recorded. Between 1991
and 1998 on average 37,000 immigrants arrived in Ireland each year.[3]
It is estimated that between 1991 and 1995, 50,000 Irish people
returned to live in Ireland, more if the children accompanying them
who were born outside Ireland are included. Between 1995 and 2000,
a further 125,000 Irish people immigrated.[4] Though the number of
Irish people returning to live in Ireland is in decline, they still form a
significant proportion of migrants into Ireland.

RETURN MIGRATION AND RETURNING RELIGIOUS: A PRIMER

It is only recently that the stories of return migration have begun to be
excavated.[5] In this small but growing body of literature, religious
have not featured.[6] In much the same way as they are incompatible
with traditional notions of the emigrant, nor do religious fit in to

whatever notion of returning migrant is now emerging. The point of this final section is not to suggest that returning religious are the same as other returning migrants. In many important respects, they are quite distinct from them. Patterns of return migration amongst religious, for example, would not reveal the same information about the Irish economy as reverse migration more generally might. In addition, whatever the circumstances of religious' out-migration, whether they left prior to entering religious life or as professed sisters within Irish or non-Irish congregations, the motives for their return need to be considered within the wider context of their congregation and its requirements also.

Until Vatican II, Irish religious living outside Ireland would have had little power to influence their own return to Ireland, which is not to say this would or did not happen. In its wake, however, individual religious have more freedom, though not carte blanche, over where they live. This is especially the case after retirement. For Irish religious living outside Ireland who are members of Irish congregations or non-Irish congregations with houses in Ireland, movement back to Ireland is aided by the fact that there is already an infrastructure for them to move back into, a practical but important consideration. Returning to Ireland is logistically easier for these women than would be the case if they had no such roots to return to or if they had, as seculars, established roots elsewhere in the form of families. Indeed, this is an important distinguishing feature about religious. Since Vatican II and as they grow older, the opportunities for them to return to Ireland have increased. Irish women emigrants more generally do not tend to return past middle age.[7] This is not to suggest, however, that all religious living outside Ireland wish to return.

The fact that religious often have family members back in Ireland might incline them to return, or it might have the opposite effect. Leaving Ireland to enter congregations elsewhere was shown to be an objective for some of the women in this study and it is likely the case that some religious choose to stay away for the same reason. Familial responsibilities would at one time have been replaced by responsibility to religious life. As some of the testimonies of the women in this study will show, however, this does not occur to the same extent today. In addition, religious may feel the roots they have established elsewhere though not familial, are too strong to be unearthed and remain outside Ireland by choice.

The women upon whose testimonies this book is based lived some, and some all, of their lives as religious outside Ireland. By the time the interviews for this study took place, almost two-thirds of them had returned to live in Ireland. They arrived back over a fifty-year period which ended in 2003, although most had returned in the last decade of the twentieth century or the early years of the twenty-first century. Between them, these returning migrants had spent more than 560 years outside Ireland, individually between twelve and fifty-eight years. Upon their return, they ranged in age from forty-two to seventy-nine but were mostly around sixty. Most had spent more than half their lives as adults, closer to 60 per cent of it as religious, outside Ireland. Of the eighteen who returned, eight had spent most of their time away in England,[8] the rest further afield on the mission fields of Africa and Asia.

This chapter and Chapter 8 will explore the women's experiences of returning to Ireland, focusing on their attitude to and motivation for return, as well as their experience of it. The purpose of this final section is not to 'fit' religious into the wider story of return migration as it is being written. Rather, their experiences of return are considered because they formed a significant theme in the accounts of the women. Nevertheless, the argument will be that the experiences of religious can and do reveal something valuable about Irish society in the late twentieth and early twenty-first century: about Irishness and gendered subjectivity and how the women of this study live their lives in relation to the subjectivities available to them. Writing about return migration, Mary Corcoran[9] was interested in finding out how emigrants made sense of their lives and suggested that return afforded them, depending on their personal circumstances, an opportunity to reflexively re-invent the self. The next two chapters explore the self that is constructed through the women's narratives of return as well as the reference points that are used as navigate this self-actualisation.

Essentially, this chapter and the next explore the themes of belonging and displacement in the women's accounts and the very different tropes and devices individual women used to describe and articulate their own experience of belonging and displacement. This chapter will focus on women returning from England, the next on returned missionaries. While there was no single narrative for either group (in certain incidences, similarities of experiences existed between them), there were sufficient differences to justify examining these groups separately. Both in the context of religious life and beyond it, the missions were conceived of very differently to England. England could not easily be separated from the historical relationship that has existed between it and Ireland or the fact that it was to England that a great number of Irish people both chose and were forced to emigrate.[10] If England in some way represented the failure of the new state, as well as the possible demise of the 'Irish' faith, the missions epitomised its success, the strength of faith amongst Irish people and its potential to influence Catholicism world-wide.

RETURNING FROM ENGLAND

Of the thirty women whose testimonies form the basis of this study, more than two-thirds followed what might be termed one of the more traditional migratory routes out of Ireland: to England. At the time of the interviews, these women lived, or had lived, in England for periods ranging between twelve and fifty-eight years. Eight of them had returned to live in Ireland permanently,[11] while all but two of them made regular trips back to Ireland, many returning more than once a year. In recent years, Irish migration, both in- and out-, has been seized upon in attempts to define and make sense of Ireland and Irishness, though less attention has been given to the experience of returning Irish migrants. The women's experiences are drawn upon to explore how they articulated a sense of self in relation to their experiences of returning to Ireland temporarily and permanently. Themes of belonging, contested belonging and of *not* belonging dominate the accounts, the women's sense of feeling 'at home' in Ireland contingent upon a range of factors both within and outside their control. In particular, the significance is highlighted of gendered and Irish identity to each of these three experiences and the inter-dynamics between the women's sense of self as women and as Irish to enabling, facilitating or impeding 'at homeness' in Ireland.

BELONGING

National identity

Perhaps the strongest theme to emerge from the women's accounts of returning to Ireland, both temporarily and permanently, was an almost immediate sense of belonging. As has been shown earlier, being Irish in England was something that, for most of the women, was tangibly felt – albeit to varying degrees and in different ways. No doubt related to this, the experience of returning to Ireland was articulated as a form of release. Lillian, still living in England, described how she felt returning to Ireland thus:

> When I step off the plane or the boat, I always feel a sense of 'I'm home'... That thing, what it['s] like to be Irish in England, it's just lifted, it's gone. So I must carry that, you know? When I'm in Ireland, I belong... It's something around identity. There's a part of me that I don't have to excuse or feel ashamed of.

Though a sense of being different was not always or necessarily experienced negatively – which is not to say it was not experienced this way at all – it was still a 'burden' from which some felt liberated upon return to Ireland. However Irishness manifested itself in Ireland, be it through accent, physical appearance or cultural values, no longer marked by Irishness, sameness could be assumed. Like Lillian, Geraldine found being in Ireland 'freeing'. Having returned to live in Ireland, it was simply a place she felt 'more comfortable in', adding:

> Coming back to Ireland, the things I enjoy are: the sense of belonging. That I'm 'at home' and I don't have to explain myself. I'm here, I'm me, I'm okay... There's something about [being] in your own country and the sense of belonging. This is where you belong somehow. You're not different... You fit in. You're not 'the Irish one'

Most of the women referred to Ireland as 'home', a 'common parlance', as Josephine put it, for Irish people living in England. Moreover, as illustrated by both Geraldine and Lillian, many of them associated Ireland with a feeling of being 'at home'. 'At home' invokes belonging. It suggests familiarity and feeling at ease, a compatibility with one's surroundings that being foreign can obviate. Being in Ireland facilitated for some a shift from a conscious sense of being other to an unconscious, though appreciated, sense of feeling at one with the people and place that surrounded them. In becoming less conscious of their Irishness, Irishness itself became weightless. Although not, however, meaningless. In fact, it could mean a great deal including community, security, protection and acceptance.

As the quotes above suggest, national identity was key to the women's sense of belonging in Ireland. It was through shared national identity and community with others that the women felt accepted, 'at home'. As has been seen earlier, accent was an important mark by which the women felt recognisable as Irish in England so it was not surprising that it re-surfaced as an important symbol of shared community in Ireland. In Ireland, the women became aware of sounding the same as everyone around them. Whilst national communities are necessarily to some degree imagined, there were material benefits to be had from living among, as Sarah put it, 'your own'. Sarah preferred to be back living in Ireland, having returned there more than ten years before: 'It's less difficult ... [you're] more at ease ... not having to translate some of these phrases and your sayings, and explain them and whatnot'. For Sarah, it was not only accent that separated the Irish from the English, but speech patterns and humour, as well as modes of interpretation, as though a different logic operated in each place.

While one's own people was a crucial element of belonging, national identity often went further and deeper than this. For some, it implied an organic connection with Ireland beyond its people, a relationship with the physical island of Ireland, its geography, past and culture. When talking about Ireland and relating positive experiences of returning to Ireland, the women often talked in abstract terms. For example, May. While she had not requested to return to Ireland – to do so would have conflicted with her sense of obedience – nevertheless, she 'loved' being back. More than this, she felt it 'important' that she had returned:

> Yes, it is [important]. I think now, when you come to my age, it's good ... If there was a need anywhere, I would go ... But I would be happier to stay where I live here now because, you know, it's your own culture in Ireland ... You're back to your roots.

For May, return was important because it allowed for the proper order to be restored – matter back in place, to paraphrase Mary Douglas.[12] Likewise, in Joan's account, return offered the opportunity to right certain anomalies, in particular an unfamiliarity with her capital city:

> Take Dublin as an example. Now, I didn't know Dublin! I didn't know my capital city! ... Then coming back and buying a street map

and getting to know a little, spots of cultural richness. Going up to New Grange and finding little places that, you know, [have] a great tradition. [It] had a great interest for me. I'd be very, very, very much into local history and that kind of thing. So that was great.

For Joan, reacquainting herself with Ireland was part of the joy of return, but implicit in her narrative also was the suggestion that while her connection with Ireland might have lapsed during her time away, it did not and could not expire: the link was unbreakable. Joan was particularly excited by the prospect of voting in Ireland for the first time. By her own admission, she did not hold strong political views but she felt it was important to assert her Irish citizenship at the polling station.

For women who felt a sense of belonging in Ireland, and who used national identity and national community to articulate it, Irishness was an important part of their identity. As previously explored, visits to Ireland could be an important means of expressing that identity. There was no indication that their sense of self as Irish was challenged on their return to Ireland, temporarily or permanently.[13] While this may seem an obvious point to make, in fact, returning migrants often face problems of acceptance if they are seen to have 'changed', especially if they have developed attributes associated with a country not positively conceived of in the home country, as might, in the case of Ireland, be said for England.

In their favour, despite the number of years spent in England, few of the women had lost their Irish accent. Of those whose accents were more neutral, the inflection was definitely upper-class. Of these, Vera actively positioned herself as a foreigner in Ireland so was not seeking to assimilate. Two of the other women whose accents could be interpreted as less definitely Irish (Rebecca and May) had returned to Ireland to live. Neither mentioned their Irishness being questioned in Ireland.[14] While it is impossible to guess if these women spoke as they did before leaving Ireland, the fact that their Irishness appeared not to be challenged on the basis of their accent may be due to class association. In the context of a firmly middle-class congregation in a well-to-do suburb of Dublin, the way Rebecca and May spoke might have been regarded as nothing more than an indication of their elevated class position.

The fact that the women of this study were religious might, in fact, have fortified their Irishness, at least in terms of how they were perceived in Ireland itself. If in Ireland, England on some level continued to be associated with Protestantism or secularism, the women's status as Catholic sisters might be regarded as confirmation of their Irishness, or of an Irishness not yet 'tainted'. Of relevance, too, was the women's situation in England. Their relationship to Ireland and Irishness might be seen to be more concrete than that of other migrants with non-Irish children or partners in England 'challenging' their Irishness. This was a significant factor in the women's experiences of returning to Ireland, where they tended to be re-positioned within their family as daughters, nieces, sisters and aunts, especially so when they reverted to their baptismal name.

Significantly, in the way the women articulated a sense of belonging in Ireland, they alluded heavily to an Ireland that was a place – a sanctuary even – for a particular group of Irish people: those born and bred in Ireland, who looked and sounded Irish and who were white. Though most of the women who returned to Ireland from England drew attention to the increased levels of immigration, a development they saw as hugely positive, and distinguished them-selves from tendencies within Ireland toward racism, their conception of Ireland in terms of their own experiences there seemed not to incorporate the multiple ethnicities they otherwise welcomed.

Irishness as an entry point to belonging was almost universal in the women's accounts, but not total. Rebecca's experience provided a significant exception. Born in Northern Ireland, Rebecca received most of her education in a boarding school in England and remained in England afterwards, initally to attend university and, later, to enter religious life. Growing up, the elevated social standing of Rebecca's family meant they associated and had more in common with the local Protestant elite than northern Catholics. Likewise, Rebecca felt a greater sense of belonging within the well-to-do English Catholic communities she mixed with at boarding school, university and in religious life. She returned to Ireland (to the Republic) in 1954, about which she remarked: 'The thing about me…was I've always felt more different here because I'm from the north than I did in England because I was Irish'. In particular, Rebecca found 'the troubles' a difficult time: 'Since [then]…things are on the television…There was a nun who was rather Republican in the community…For some years I used to listen to the radio [in my room]. Not come down [to join them]'.

This is, of course, the inverse of what some women experienced in the same community in England. Though from Northern Ireland, born one year before the war of independence which would eventually create it, Rebecca had always claimed an identity as Irish and considered her move to Ireland as 'a homecoming'. Her experience of isolation illustrates the complex ways 'insiders' can be positioned as 'outsiders' in their own 'home'. Moreover, it exposes Irishness as a category which cannot be assumed, one with its own internal inconsistencies and contradictions.

Family

In entering religious life when they did and in moving to England, few of the women of this study expected to return to their family again. They knew that most likely, from this point forth, any meetings with family would take place within the convent, either in England where they lived or back in Ireland, where they might one day re-visit. Though most of the women did get the opportunity to visit Ireland prior to Vatican II, it was only in its wake that visits to Ireland could occur with any regularity. At first, visits back occurred perhaps every seven years. In time, every five years. More recently, for most, at least annually. With some notable exceptions, the opportunity to visit family in Ireland was enthusiastically welcomed. It was for many the prime reason for their visits to Ireland and was also one of the significant 'pull' factors for them returning there permanently. Since Vatican II, it has been primarily with family that the religious of this study have stayed when returning to Ireland,[15] representing, as it continues to do, the most cost-efficient holiday available for them. Unsurprisingly then, for many of the women of this study, it was impossible to talk about returning to Ireland without reference to family.

For Frances, Vatican II came along 'just in the nick of time':

> I had a brother married in Dublin and so I said [to him], 'We're going to be coming home now...I'm going to be able to visit you in Dublin'. So, of course, they said 'Come on!'. So, I just had the right opportunity there to get to know them again and to feel part of that family. Whereas, I mean, others must have felt just so completely cut off [by then] that they weren't really interested.

Having lived predominantly outside Ireland since the age of ten, establishing a foothold with her family in Ireland was the prime reason Frances gave for considering Ireland home, for visiting Ireland and for keeping open the possibility of returning to live there permanently. For those that had moved back, already, family was integral to that experience. For Norah, being near family was the most positive aspect of return while Teresa, who had also returned to live in Ireland, 'loved coming home and...getting involved with [my nieces and nephews] and, I suppose, just re-entering into their lives again, you know?...There's a huge intimacy around that'. Eileen was 'of course, delighted to come home' to live in the 1960s, more so because of the greater opportunities afforded by Vatican II to re-establish relations with her family, reunion with whom proved emotional:

> I always remember coming in on the boat. I'd been green [with illness] as I came across on the boat. I'm not a good sailor. But the sight of my family...was a great joy. And I was very happy to be in close contact with my family and to meet brothers-in-law and sisters-in-law. It was something.

Sarah, who prized her Irish identity above all others,[16] was, like Eileen, 'delighted' to be back. She was especially pleased to be in close contact with her family again, though they lived in an entirely different part of the country to her. When Sarah talked about being closer to her family, she meant sharing the same national space – and media. The fact that certain 'big' events in Ireland might be ignored or interpreted differently in England had reinforced her feeling of being away from home. Although still geographically separated from her family, she felt psychologically closer to them in Ireland.

As nation did, family invoked roots, belonging and at homeness. For those living in England, family copper-fastened the relationship they had with Ireland, making real and more material their connection with it. The women's relationship with family transcended their being away from Ireland as much as it facilitated their return to it. For many, Ireland was home because that was where family was. Referring once more to the good timing of Vatican II, Frances remarked that her 'home was still there', meaning Ireland and the fact that her family lived there. For Lillian, Ireland was 'definitely' home because 'it's where my family are, it's where my roots are'. When she visited Ireland, which she 'loved' to do, Lillian returned to the family home, the house she grew up in: 'When I go to

Ireland, I go "home". I'm not, like, going to a brother or sister, like some people do. I have my own room at home, some of my stuff is there. So, it's very much going "home"'.

Spending time with family, immediate and extended, was elemental to Lillian's experience of Ireland as home: 'because that's all 'home', isn't it?...When I say I'm going home, home is all that'. There was both corporeal and material aspects to her belonging: she had a place in the family and a room in the family home. Likewise, Catherine made reference to her roots, both familial and ethnic, when discussing her conception of home:

> Home [is] Ireland. Isn't that strange? Yeah. After all those years...I *love* going home. And I love, I love just being at home. And I love the fields and I love the, just the feel [of home]...Home is Ireland. And home is my own home where I was born...I'm part of my family. We're a very close family, you know? I would ring them every week or they would ring me. And I can talk like this to them about *anything*...[So] I would consider them home...I think there's this natural bond as well, that people are bonded with flesh and blood. Not with rules and regulations. And no matter what society you join...I don't think you can get away from that earthy, fleshy thing, you know?...I'm very, very proud of my Irishness. My roots. My heritage. Because I think I bring a lot of richness, I bring that culture with me. I bring that sort of warmth, sort of hospitality...I [get] my nature [from my Irishness and] from my family as well.

For those women who had returned permanently, as well as those still living in England, Ireland and family in Ireland might be particularly associated with a sense of belonging and homeness considering the ambulant lifestyle many religious lead. With the exception of Elaine, who worked in the same hospital ward for forty years before reluctantly taking retirement, the women of this study moved between five and fifteen times, across counties, countries and continents. The women's living arrangements also changed in each new location, living with smaller or larger communities of different women. When they were not moving, those around them often were. In a material sense, there was no permanence to the homes they established. As members of community, they owned things in common, including, very often, the houses they lived in and its furnishings. When they moved, they tended to take only their personal possessions with them.[17] The point has already been made that religious do not have families of their own. Though many regarded the religious community as a family, not all did. Even when they did, however, qualifications had to be made about the extent to which the community might be said to replace the family. Conceptually, while similarities could be drawn, the family and religious life were not synonymous.

Family did not automatically equate to belonging, even for those who felt a sense of belonging in Ireland. For some, in fact, family complicated their experience of return. With family came responsibility, something religious life, at least pre-Vatican II and at least when lived outside Ireland, tended to minimise. Returning home, the demands of family could be re-imposed. While Joan enjoyed a good relationship with her family, she found the lack of independence with regard to them difficult to get used to upon her return: 'With relation to my family...now I'm here in [Ireland], you're expected to [*clicks fingers*], you know, [be] at the beck and call and give a reaction and I suppose it's something that needs a lot more reflection on my part, you know?' The significance of family in the women's narratives of returning to Ireland and to their concomitant sense of belonging in Ireland are not presented here as a case to argue the inseparability of Ireland and family. Rather, it is to highlight that while a sense of belonging in Ireland was not dependent upon close relations with family, it was, at least for the women of this study, often strengthened by it.

CONTESTED BELONGING

Though, as Irish, many of the women felt an immediate rapport in Ireland, ethnicity had no monopoly on acceptance. Many of the women felt that a true sense of belonging in Ireland was attenuated by other factors. This sense of contested belonging was a complex theme in their accounts, one that needed to be unpacked on several levels. For many, belonging was complicated by the fact of their being religious – significantly, in different ways. Some of the women felt they could not be accepted in Ireland because religious themselves were no longer accepted; others, that their notion of religious life was incompatible with current discourses of religious life, positive and negative, in Ireland. For women of either persuasion, whether they tended towards the traditional or modern in their views of religious life, there was a sense in their accounts that they were being denied a space in Ireland to claim the subjectivity they wanted, either as religious or as women. In order to feel a sense of belonging, one needs to feel a sense of acceptance. Belonging needs reciprocity in the form of acceptance, is a two-way relationship. It is not enough to *think* you might belong, you must *receive* belonging in return. While not necessarily with respect to a shared sense of Irishness, in relation to other subjectivities, the women felt their sense of belonging inhibited in Ireland.

Of significance, there was a contextual specificity to the women's accounts with respect to both England and Ireland. One of the recurrent themes in the women's accounts of life in England was the very different attitude toward and position of religious in England compared to Ireland. This was especially noticeable in transit. Travelling from one place to the other, it was possible to identify where one was by the treatment one received from the wider populace. Initially, for example, in Ireland, payment for public transport would not have been accepted. In England, this rarely occurred, though derogatory comments about religious were commonplace on public transport. Catherine compared the different reactions she received collecting money for her congregation in each place. In England, the public were reticent and Catherine had to explain the objectives of her collection in great detail before money was proffered, if at all. By contrast, 'before you came to the door in Ireland, they'd be coming out with the money to you'.

This was, however, 'back then'. The situation had since changed, suspicion and negativity towards religious in England becoming less palpable. Never having carried the significance it did in Ireland, being a religious in England had become less relevant. In addition, the position of religious 'other' had been taken over by non-Christian religions. As Lillian put it, 'I don't think people give a damn [that you're a religious]'. The consensus was also that attitudes towards religious in Ireland had changed. Reflecting its secularism, religious were not held in such high esteem, except perhaps by 'traditional' Catholics, many of whom were reluctant to accept the modernisation that had occurred in religious life since Vatican II. For certain other sections of the population, religious had come to represent a history of Catholic dominance and oppression, nuns a form of passive womanhood considered outdated and archaic. Most serious, of course, were the allegations of abuse by religious, both sexual and physical. In Ireland, according to Irene, 'things are totally different [for religious] now'. As Josephine put it, the 'pendulum has swung completely the other way'. Though few of the women lamented the powerful position once enjoyed by the Church (May, for instance, felt the Church had been forced to change 'but maybe for the better and it's been purified and I think that's no harm'), attitudes towards religious in Ireland had a definite impact on their experiences there.

Of those women who themselves might be described as more traditional in their outlook, many felt Ireland had become, as Kate and Hannah described it 'anti-religious', Kate suggesting further that religious there were 'under siege'. Though the women talked about this in general terms, they also gave specific examples of the personal experience of antipathy towards religious. More significant than the events themselves were the women's interpretation of them as being directly related to the fact of their being sisters:

> I noticed [the attitude towards religious] very much, just the last time I was home. I was trying to cross the road, I'd come out of the church from mass, this was Sunday mass, and the cars were all just coming round [the corner]. There's no crossing, nowhere you can cross. You just have to wait for a car to let you go. And there must have been thirty cars passed before I got across. That wouldn't have happened three or four years ago. And I was wearing my habit and all, so I mean, not that I would be looking for any special privilege because of that but again, it was raining as well. But I just thought, you know, people just wouldn't speak, don't speak to you in Ireland like the way they would long ago.

In the same vein, Hannah felt overlooked and excluded: '[In Ireland] they'd ignore you. You might as well...be invisible...Whereas here [in England] somebody will speak to you. They might be a Shi'ite or something but if you say good morning, they'll answer you. In Ireland they just went by as if [you] were dead...I think there's a very definite swing against religious'.

In addition, some of the women felt religious were not appreciated for the work they did in Ireland. Catherine had returned there to work for a period in the late 1970s and found it harder to work there than in England: 'They wanted the pound of flesh more'. She had heard similar sentiments, and worse, from co-religious who had returned more recently. Traditionally, religious in Ireland were considered to be different to other members of society and super-human expectations were placed on them as a result, both by themselves and others.[18] Equally, they were accorded a status above others. Given the allegations of abuse, however, religious were now seen to have reneged on their side of the arrangement and consequently to 'owe' Irish society a great debt.

On the other hand, the religious of this study who who were less traditional in either their work, dress or outlook felt under pressure in Ireland to conform to particular notions of religious life that they themselves did not hold. Although, generally speaking, younger generations tended not to be so concerned, particular elements of what might be termed Catholic Ireland continued to hold on to a fixed view of 'proper' religious which was challenged by the ways the women chose to live their lives. For example, several of the women[19] gave specific examples of being admonished for choosing not to wear a habit. The problem was, as Josephine identified, that in Ireland 'you're a nun first... Then you're a woman – if you graduate to that level, of which you're not at all certain!'. This was in contrast to the situation she described for herself in England:

> Like, we live in a street here. Now, they all know we're religious. They know damn all about us so they don't make any presumptions. Or expectations. You can come and go and do what you like, and all the rest. And they're all very friendly and we all chat over the fence and have a laugh and all the rest of it but that's it... Here they meet you, you're a woman, they deal with you. [Josephine]

Having returned to live in Ireland, Sarah 'struggled' with the pressure to conform: 'They might want you to be "the sister" and to be acting "the sister" and what-not. To be looking like "the sister" and all this'. She found herself being more careful in the language she used and in the views she expressed around others who knew she was a religious for fear of giving offence. Though pleased to be back in Ireland, Sarah identified a fundamental difference in the set up of religious life in both places. She was of the opinion that because religious had been so powerful in Ireland, especially in the areas of health and education, it was more difficult for them to change on an organisational if not individual basis. Due to the external pressure to conform, as well as internal power dynamics, she felt that religious institutions in Ireland were more resistant to modernisation:

I suppose it was harder for religious women here to move into the changes and move into not being institutionalised and to move away from institutions [and an] institutional outlook. Far more difficult [in Ireland] because the populous [*sic*] kind of expected you to be wearing a habit and there'd be comments about that kind of thing that you wouldn't get in England, because people wouldn't have been as familiar with religion.

Expectations placed upon them as religious in Ireland prevented some of the women of this study from being themselves which is at heart what a sense of belonging is all about. Though this feeling might be the result of any one of several factors, it was significant that the women of this study identified the fact of their being religious as the prime reason for it. Of all the women, it was Teresa who felt it most acutely. Having been 'very settled' in England, where she moved to enter religious life in the early 1960s (aged 17), she found returning to live in Ireland almost twenty-five years later 'absolutely dreadful...I missed my work, I missed my social [life], my friends, my whole life'. During her first year back, she bought two one-way tickets back to England but relented each time: 'It felt like being on alien ground...I just can't sufficiently express the struggle that it was. It was huge'.

Her skills not easily convertible to the Irish social welfare system, Teresa faced re-entering the job market at entry level. Principally, however, was the fact of her being a religious in a hostile environment:

I think there's huge rejection...of religious. A lot of religious would still be seen to be doing a lot of damage, you know?...I find that a lot of people have been so hurt by religious in the past, so damaged at school or whatever [that] when you say you're a religious, that's what they dump on you straight away. You're immediately associated with this Church which is totally out of touch, or which has all the control...People's notion of religious is that they're out of touch and...outdated [and] old-fashioned...It really is very negative...Even here now, I find it terribly, *incredibly* hard here to be a religious.

Critical of both the Catholic Church and its religious, Teresa did not feel the opinions she held were accepted by non-religious. Instead, she felt dismissed by non-religious as 'part of it' or 'one of them'.

In particular, a number of the women felt prevented from claiming a subjectivity as women not dominated by their status as religious, a concern expressed in several of the interviews. Josephine's comment about graduating to womanhood (above) is illustrative of this. As explored in Chapter 5, being regarded primarily or exclusively as religious limited the women's freedom to claim a gendered subjectivity of their own: as feminists, sexual beings or 'ordinary women'. Such limitations tended, in fact, to be experienced more acutely in Ireland due to the continued significance of religious life there and the varied, often conflicting, meanings attached to it. 'We just can't win in Ireland...if I'm in Ireland and I go around just as myself and I sit around in jeans or I express opinions about women and women's rights and what I feel about patriarchy [I am not accepted]' (Lillian). If marked by their Irishness in Britain, the women were equally though differently marked by their status as religious in Ireland. Interestingly, the women used similar language to describe their feelings of being other as Irish in England as they did their experiences of being other as religious in Ireland: Lillian 'carried' her Irishness with her in England, while Josephine felt a 'weight' on top of her as a religious in Ireland.

Many of the women described their experience of being a religious in Ireland in terms of proprietorship. Although Vatican II changed the organisation of religious life within the congregation, in Ireland, authority continued to be levied to some degree from outside. The relationship between religious and Irish society was in reality quite complex: even the elevated position religious once held needed to be legitimated by the society they served and could be challenged or revoked by it. Although not equal, a reciprocal relationship existed between the two: 'They *owned* you. Okay, you ran the schools and hospitals and everything else but you were *owned*...and you had to meet people's expectations [and] fulfil [their ideals]' (Josephine).

The result was that some of the women felt, as Geraldine did, 'public property...I suppose they have a sense of ownership of you in a way that they wouldn't otherwise'. By not fulfilling the expectations of others, the women's authenticity as religious was challenged and they felt made feel inauthentic: not *proper* religious. This is also, indeed, how some more traditional religious tended to regard modern nuns, even in jest. Of course, individuals and groups often feel sidelined in society. In addition, migration can serve to heighten an awareness of exclusion. Of significance, however, is the way these women interpreted their own experiences of exclusion as specifically related to the fact of their being religious and the distinction they made between Ireland and England.

For those women still living in England, experiences of returning to Ireland temporarily affected their desire to return there permanently. Indeed, when the interviews took place, only one of the women living in England – Annette – was sure she wanted to return to Ireland to live. Although few of the other women had or could have ruled this out, it was not an ambition for any of them. Annette's experiences as an Irish woman living in England were particularly trying and she tended to position Ireland and the Irish in opposition to England and the English: the Irish were 'warm', the English 'cold'; Ireland was 'religious', England 'pagan'. For Annette, Ireland was home so it followed that England could not be.

The rest of the women tended to have a more complex and less fixed notion of where home was and, by extension, where they felt they belonged. For the most part, this related to the changed and changing meanings attached to religious life in Ireland, and in England, over the course of their lives as religious. Speaking of the possibility of return, Josephine remarked 'I'm actually not so sure I could take the intrusion, you know? I really couldn't stand it'. Likewise, Lillian thought it would be 'too difficult to be a religious in Ireland now', while Hannah was not the only one to state simply that it was 'easier' to be a religious in England. In contrast to her experiences as a religious in Ireland, Lillian felt she could 'be myself a lot more [in England]'. A very different binary was being set up between Ireland and England than was suggested earlier, in which England now became the more accepting nation. Hannah described England as a friendlier and more accepting place than Ireland. For Lillian, London was a place where no one belonged, but equally, no one felt excluded:

> I love just being lost in London. I love to be able to go out the door and meet no one and just get lost. Whereas if I'm [at home], my mother will say 'Oh, you might meet so and so in the town or you might meet..'. *I hate that!* I mean, I'm just a very introvert person anyway and I just love to be free to just not think that I'm going to be bumping into people and all that kind of stuff. Or if I do meet them, kind of, 'this is so and so's daughter and she's the nun'. *I hate all that!* Now, what's that all about I don't know, but I [hate it]. Maybe I just hate having to live up to anybody's expectations.

Several of the women talked about their community in particular as the place they could really 'be myself' (Geraldine) and 'feel at home' (Catherine). Indeed, with the exception of Annette, for all of the women living in England, where they lived was the place they referred to as home and was also, significantly, a place they felt *at* home. As Kate put it: 'Ireland is home but I'm "at home" in England'.

For those women who lived in England but continued to visit Ireland, continued to see themselves as Irish and continued to consider Ireland home, belonging there was made difficult by their experiences as religious women. By contrast, in this respect, where they lived in England represented home, belonging and acceptance. Brah[20] recognises the importance of multiple homes in the migrant identity but the women of this study rarely identified more than one home at once. Ireland as home was arrived at through a very different route than was England as home. Initially, home was assumed to refer to ethnicity; only later was this unpacked in terms of religious or gendered identity. Certainly, Ireland was where most of them felt at home in terms of ethnicity, but this was not the only medium through which they experienced feeling at home. Regarding the freedoms to live their life as religious and, significantly, as women, where they lived in England was also home. Indeed, for some, the significance of their home in England took precedence over home in Ireland.

One further complexity could be identified. When describing where they lived as home, the women rarely mentioned England. Instead, they talked about 'here' or 'this house'. Perhaps in an abstract way, England remained Ireland's opposite and was more difficult to identify as home than the actual surroundings of everyday life in which the women felt at home. As mentioned in Chapter 6, a traditional incompatibility, linguistically and psychologically, has existed between Irish and British/English identities. Indeed, recognising England as the primary home was not a position easily arrived at by the women. Few of the women seemed comfortable admitting to me, another Irish woman at that time living in England and whose plans to stay or return they could not know, that they had no ambitions to return. It seemed the wrong answer. Kate, for example, initially went very quiet and would speak only very hesitantly about not wanting to return until she was assured it was 'okay' to hold that opinion.

Breda Gray has identified the various and limiting acceptable discourses surrounding emigration in Ireland. She found, for example, that, because Ireland was assumed to be 'the best place on earth', leaving had to be legitimated by economic necessity or to pursue economic success.[21] Moreover, she found that emigration for women was deemed especially 'unnatural' given the role women play in reproducing children and, therefore, the nation.[22] Though celibate, the narratives of the women of this study revealed a similar discomfort, if not reluctance, surrounding their desire to remain migrants. This reinforces Gray's point about the limitations of emigration discourses which continue to construct Irish women in terms of their reproductive capacities and duty to the nation, leaving little alternative space to claim a woman-centred Irish subjectivity. For the women of this study, identifying England as home was complicated by remembered processes of othering on the basis of being Irish experienced elsewhere. Directly after remarking that as a woman, she felt accepted in England, Josephine added the caveat: 'you might be an *Irish* woman'. Similarly Lillian, after describing Ireland as a place she felt she belonged, added 'whether it rejects me as being religious...I mean, there's all that'.

For those that had returned to Ireland to live, the response was often to conceal a religious identity. Both Teresa and Sarah began to do this when they returned to live in Ireland: Sarah, because she felt she could not be accepted as a 'normal' woman, Teresa, because religious were considered 'out of touch' and for fear of being associated with abuse. Moreover, Teresa also believed that her status as a religious was having a direct and negative effect on her ability to secure employment in Ireland:

> I don't admit to a lot of people that I'm a religious. First of all, I kind of want to be accepted as a woman, as a person, [as an] equal...I think it is really to do with the baggage nuns are carrying nowadays, you know? Every group you join you're wondering, God, when will they find out?...Even job-wise, I feel religious don't get jobs because they're religious, you know? I was interviewed for a job here last week and I was scared stiff in case they found out I was a religious. I certainly wouldn't put it on my CV.

Since the 1970s, the women's movement in Ireland has significantly altered the position of women,[23] often by confronting and challenging 'traditional' and/or Catholic notions of woman-hood.[24] However, the movement itself, its aims and achievements, have not always been seen as relevant to women religious (which is not to say women religious have shared this opinion themselves or were not part of that movement also).[25] Exploring concepts of womanhood in Ireland in the late twentieth century, Pat O'Connor suggested that dominant constructions of Irish womanhood tended to fix women in functionalist relationships with society as wives, mothers and daughters but that, reflecting achievements made by the women's movement, a newer discourse has begun to emerge, one of personhood.[26] This emerging discourse recognises women's subjectivity as workers, feminists and so on, while taking into account also the importance of family and other relationships through which the self is defined in Irish society. Religious life is not a subjectivity that O'Connor explores but it would seem that for the women of this study, personhood was not a subjectivity they felt was available to them.

NOT BELONGING

Three women, in recounting their stories of returning to Ireland, spoke not of belonging but of *not* belonging. There were various reasons for this, most of which have already been touched upon. What differentiated these women's experiences, however, was that their sense of dislocation was not balanced out by acceptance in other respects. Nora, for example, had returned to Ireland only a few months before our interview. By her own admission, she had been 'very much settled in England', where she had lived for over sixty years since leaving to enter religious life as a teenager in the early 1940s. On temporary visits back to Ireland she admitted to feeling like a 'fish out of water'. Returning in her late seventies, slightly under duress,[27] there were many adjustments to make. Studies of return migration show that the first year of return is generally the hardest and certainly it was proving so for Norah. Her problems, however, were not to do with the pace of life in Ireland or the fact that attitudes to religious had changed, as other returning migrants have found,[28] but more specifically, the organisation of religious life in Ireland, which she considered to be 'absolutely' pre-Vatican II:

> I think sisters [here] continued to stay in the old set-up much longer than we did in England. I think in England we were always much more open…[Here,] they are very much at the stage where the superior is very important. Now, I've been in shared leadership

set-ups all my life now…where everybody would take responsibility for what was going on…But I find [it] very difficult now.
That [people] make a fuss of [the superior]…I [have] found that
very difficult. I really do. Because we've moved away from it so
much.[29]

While Norah's situation might ease over time, it had been many years
since either Margaret or Vera felt any sense of belonging in Ireland.
Vera admitted she 'wouldn't go back to Ireland. I would find life too
restricting. The fact that everybody knows everybody else…Here [in
England], you can be anonymous…you can mind your own business
and people don't interfere with you. There is still that mentality [in
Ireland], there is'.

Significantly, Vera was not close to her family, remarking 'when I
left Ireland, I left it for good and when I left my family, I left them for
good'. Likewise, Margaret did not feel close to her family, though she
thought this 'an awful' thing to admit to. While she still visited
Ireland, this was more out of obligation than desire and she admitted
to being 'bored stiff' when there. In particular, Margaret felt
pressurised by others' notion of religious life:

> It was very uncomfortable going to weddings or anything because
> you were just sat there in a corner on your own. Everybody was
> dancing and, you know, you couldn't do anything. If you got up and
> danced, you'd scandalise everybody. If you had a drink, you'd
> scandalise everybody. So, they wanted you there but doing what
> they wanted you to do and looking the way they wanted you to look.

Margaret drew a distinction between her own spirituality and
Catholicism as she saw it being practised in rural Ireland, where she
came from: 'I think religiously and spiritually they're infants. They
have no sophistication when it comes to their faith, you know?…
They're living…like children…There's a lack of sophistication about
their faith, there's a lack of taking responsibility for the way they live
their lives'. As others had, she described her experiences in terms of
ownership: 'It was like they owned us…and they could dictate what
we would wear, what time we went to bed, what time we got up,
what we should do with our lives [and] were quite miffed that we
decided to do things differently'. In the accounts of the women who
felt they no longer belonged in Ireland, as was the case for all the
women who recounted their experiences of return, there was an

inherent suggestion of a mono-ethnic Ireland. While younger generations might not adhere to the teachings of the Catholic Church to the same extent, there was little sense of a country actually or significantly changed by increased levels of immigration of non-Irish nationals or a growing number of Irish nationals with differing ethnic background to the majority.

CONCLUSION

With notable exceptions, the women of this study who returned to Ireland from England, temporarily or permanently, associated Ireland with a sense of belonging. It was their Irishness too that prevented them from feeling at home in England. However, their sense of belonging in Ireland was complicated by their status as religious, which directly affected their freedom to claim the gendered subjectivity they wanted to, whether that be the more 'traditional' form of religious life which had at one time been esteemed in Irish society, or a more personal and individual notion of womanhood not prescribed by membership of a religious congregation. In each place, albeit in different ways, the women's sense of self was refracted through their positioning as women, religious and Irish. This positioning could be experienced unconsciously or consciously, depending on the situation.

In relating their stories of returning to Ireland from England, the major theme to emerge from the women's accounts was belonging: belonging, contested belonging and not belonging. Integral to their experiences of one and all of these positions was a sense of self as Irish, especially in relation to nation and family, and as religious and/or women. This is not to suggest that being Irish or female or religious was the only means of experiencing belonging but to draw attention to the fact that it was principally in relation to these subjectivities that the women articulated their experience of these emotions. That these women talked about returning to Ireland in terms of belonging (or not belonging or contested belonging) and that they chose to do so through particular subjectivities as Irish and women/religious might seem an obvious point to make. In fact, however, as the following chapter will illustrate, there were alternative ways of presenting a narrative of return.

NOTES

1 Geraldine.
2 See, for example, M. Anwar, *The Myth of Return* (London: Heinnemann, 1979); Brah, *Cartographies of Diaspora;* G. Buijs (ed.), *Migrant Women, Crossing Boundaries and Changing Identities* (Rhode Island, NJ: Berg Press, 1993); and J. Clifford, 'Diasporas' *Cultural Anthropology,* 9, 3 (1994), pp. 302–38.
3 M. P. Corcoran, 'The Process of Migration and the Reinvention of Self: The Experiences of Returning Irish Emigrants', *Eire/Ireland,* Spring/Summer (2002), pp. 175–91.
4 Walter, B. 'Irish Emigrants and Irish Communities Abroad: A Study of the Existing Sources of Information and Analysis', research undertaken for the *Task Force on Policy Regarding Emigration* (Dublin: Department of Foreign Affairs, 2002). See also *Annual Population and Migration Estimates, 1991–1998* (Dublin: Central Statistics Office, 1999).
5 F. McGrath, 'The Economic, Social and Cultural Impacts of Return Migration to Achill Island', in R. King (ed.), *Contemporary Irish Migration* (Dublin: Trinity College Dublin, Geographical Society of Ireland Special Publications No. 6, 1991), pp. 55–69, p. 55.
6 See, for example, McGrath, 'The Economic, Social and Cultural Impacts'; G. Gmelch, 'The Readjustment of Return Migrants in Western Ireland', in R. King (ed.), *Return Migration and Regional Economic Problems* (London: Croom Helm, 1986), pp. 152–69; and Corcoran, 'The Process of Migration'.
7 See Walter, 'Irish Emigrants and Irish Communities Abroad'.
8 May had spent an equal amount of time (twenty-three years) in France as she had in England.
9 Corcoran, 'The Process of Migration', p. 177.
10 As noted in Chapter six, the women living in England rarely considered themselves part of an Irish migrant or ethnic community.
11 In so far as it is possible to use the term permanently given the tendency of religious to move location frequently, even after they have officially retired.
12 M. Douglas, *Purity and Danger, An Analysis of the Concepts of Pollution and Taboo* (London: Routledge, 1991) (first published 1966), p. 35.
13 Only one of the women mentioned any difficulty being accepted as Irish upon her return to Ireland. Teresa had adopted an English accent to 'fit in' in England but this was not found to be acceptable when she moved back to Ireland where she was 'insulted' by colleagues at work for being 'a snob'. On the basis of her changed

accent, Teresa's authenticity as Irish was being questioned. The insults suggested that Teresa's attempts at 'ethnic fade' were a strategy of upward social mobility, which implied also her complicity in positioning Irish and Irishness as inferior in relation to English and Englishness. Shortly after her return, Teresa regained her Irish accent and, since then, had found no difficulty being accepted as Irish.

14 As will be seen, Rebecca felt on occasion that her 'brand' of Irishness was different from that of other women in the congregation.

15 There were some exceptions to this, most often if immediate family had moved outside Ireland or had died. Annette used her holidays in Ireland to visit the families of prisoners whom she worked with in England.

16 The only woman in this study to do so.

17 Before Vatican II, the women would not even have had personal possessions.

18 Indeed, the position religious held in Ireland was bestowed upon them at least partly because of the work they did. Equally, that work was fundamental to their being accepted by society in the nineteenth century.

19 Among them Josephine, Lillian, Norah, Geraldine, Margaret, Sarah, Teresa and Frances.

20 Brah, *Cartographies of Diaspora.*

21 B. Gray, 'Locations of Irishness: Irish Women's Accounts of National Identity', p. 167; and 'Unmasking Irishness: Irish Women, the Irish Nation and the Irish diaspora', in J. MacLaughlin (ed.), *Location and Dislocation in Contemporary Irish Society, Emigration and Irish Identities* (Cork: Cork University Press, 1997), pp. 209–35, pp. 213–16.

22 B. Gray, '"The Home of our Mothers"', p. 172; and 'Unmasking Irishness', pp. 210–11.

23 L. Connolly, 'The Women's Movement in Ireland, 1970–1995: A Social Movements Analysis', *Irish Journal of Feminist Studies,* 1, 1 (1996), pp. 43–77 and *The Irish Women's Movement.*

24 See, for example, U. Berry 'Women in Ireland', *Women's Studies International Forum,* 11, 4 (1988), pp. 317–22; and E. Mahon, 'The Impasse of Irish Feminism: Women's Rights and Catholicism in Ireland', *New Left Review,* 166 (1987), pp. 53–77.

25 M. MacCurtain, 'Women – Irish style', *Doctrine and Life,* 24, 4 (1974), pp. 182–97.

26 O'Connor, P., *Emerging Voices.*

27 Norah's family were concerned by her failing physical health and wished for her to return.

28   See, for example, Corcoran, 'The Process of Migration'.
29   It is important to remember that this study is based only on religious who have lived outside Ireland. It is not my intention to make any claims about the responses religious who remained in Ireland made to Vatican II, whose opinions may differ considerably from the accounts of the women represented here. Rather, the point is to highlight the experiences of the women of this study alone and to draw attention to how they interpreted and made sense of those experiences.

CHAPTER 8

Return and Belonging II: The Missions

'It's a different world to come back to'[1]

INTRODUCTION

One of the arguments advanced in this book is that the experiences of religious abroad are part of the history and reality of Irish migration, though they have, for the most part, been overlooked. This is not to suggest, however, that there are not significant or important factors which distinguish religious from other Irish migrants or, indeed, from each other. In the last chapter, the experiences of returning to Ireland from England for women religious, both temporarily and permanently, were considered. In this chapter, attention will be turned to missionary sisters, in particular the ten missionary sisters who had, at the time of the interviews, returned to live permanently in Ireland.[2] The accounts of missionary sisters provide another perspective from which to explore the experience of return migration and, through them, to offer up different themes which have implications for our understanding of how Irishness and belonging are constructed, conceived and experienced.[3]

There were obvious differences between missionary religious and those who stayed closer to home: not only the distance they had travelled but the organisation of religious life they lived and worked within. Within the context of this study, there were certain other aspects specific to returned missionaries which set them apart from the women who had returned from England, differences not always reducible to the fact of their being missionaries. First, the missionaries tended to have been more recent returnees to Ireland. Though the group of women who had returned from England had spent roughly the same length of time outside Ireland (thirty one as against thirty-two years) less time had lapsed between missionaries' return to Ireland and the interviews taking place than was the case with the sisters who had returned from England. Returnees from England had returned on average sixteen years prior to the interview taking place, half of them within the previous ten years. The missionary sisters, by contrast, had returned on average ten years before they were interviewed, more than 70 per cent of them having returned in less than that time. Second, the missionary sisters were, generally speaking, older than the women from England, both when they returned to Ireland and at the time of the interviews: the women from England were most likely to have been in their forties when they returned, the missionaries in their fifties, sixties or seventies. At the time the interviews took place, most of the women who had returned from England were in their fifties, whereas the missionaries were mostly in their eighties. In addition, the missionary sisters were more sure their return to Ireland was permanent than those from England were or could be. The extent to which these differences had an impact on the women's narratives is a question worth bearing in mind, though in themselves, the differences did not, it will be argued, determine the discrepancies in those accounts

MAKING A BREAK FOR IT

One striking difference between the returned missionaries' accounts and those given by women who had returned from England was that the returned missionaries placed far greater emphasis on leaving the missions and returning to Ireland than the women from England had. In fact, return was a major theme in their accounts and much space was given to describing, in detail, the circumstances prompting their return, the preparation involved in organising it and their experiences following it. It was, as one woman put it, 'a very big deal'. Missionaries had, of course, travelled further afield, not just geographically, but socially and culturally also. For this reason alone, return was rarely straightforward, either for them or their communities. The situation in each place was rarely commensurate to the extent that movement from one to the other could be seamless. Both institutionally and socially, there were differences in the type of work communities were involved in, as well as in the ways they carried out that work.

The fact that, logistically speaking, movement from the missions back home involved a greater degree of planning and forethought than was the case for religious moving back from England might perhaps have granted returning missionaries a recognition not extended to those who returned from England. Though neither were regarded as traditional migrants, nor tended to regard themselves as such, the acknowledgement of the missionaries' homecoming as 'a big deal' gave them a validation as returnees – albeit as returned *missionaries* rather than returned *migrants* – the women who returned from England did not receive.

Returned missionaries were able to draw upon a range of discourses when talking about their experiences of return. Policies adopted by their own congregation in relation to return provided one such discourse: 'Well, [there] was a policy in Africa [for the missionary sisters to return, because the congregation] did not want [us]... to be getting older and older there and [then] not be able to do the work. Then come home and [find that we] didn't fit into anything, [or] weren't able to do anything [here either]. There were all those practical things' (Aisling).

These policies were adopted not only for the benefit of individual missionaries but to secure the survival of the mission project through indigenous peoples. They reflected also, however, changes in the interpretation and objective of the mission project itself, which became, especially in the wake of Vatican II, both less imperialistic and less paternal in its approach. As others did, Deirdre talked about the importance of western missionaries retreating from the areas they missioned to: 'It's important that we don't stay on...We have to [move out]. We knew that it was the right thing to do. That we should be letting the local people take responsibility for things'

Discourses such as these were repeated, referred to and relied upon by the women when describing their own experience of return, many of whom claimed the decision to leave as their own. Winnie, Angela and Rosemary emphasised their own agency in their accounts of departure. For each, their decision was prompted by a desire to withdraw while still in full possession of their faculties. As Winnie put it: 'I could have stayed on but in a way I thought it was better [to leave]...I said, well, really, if I am going to come back [to Ireland], I'll have to come when I still have something, that I can give'. Likewise, Angela felt she would rather not 'come home in a wheelchair, not knowing who's pushing me around'. Her advice to others would be 'to get home a year or two before they go senile!'. Rosemary made a promise to herself not to remain on the missions after she turned 70:

'I don't know, I felt just I was old at that stage'. True to her promise, she left Africa on her seventieth birthday, having lived there for almost forty years.

These women had in mind a very specific notion of the person they did not want to be: the returned, retired, redundant missionary, too incapacitated to find a niche for themselves in Ireland. It was a theme that pervaded Yvonne's account also, though she felt she had already left it too late. The twentieth century had not yet reached its midpoint when Yvonne first left Ireland in 1949. By the time she returned, urged on by family due to her own ill-health, more than half a century had passed. It was, she felt in retrospect, 'too long':

> Because you're too old really to take up a different career in Ireland and you really would need that. I think, anyway...The wiser decision would be to come earlier when you were more able to play a kind of an active role. Nobody prevents me from playing an active role but... my faculties are not as alive and as awake as they used to be. So I don't sort of trust myself...You really *don't* know what's going on.

Barbara also claimed the decision to return as her own. An illness in the family had brought her back to Ireland on a temporary basis which she decided to make permanent, despite 'lots of opportunities and requests to return'. For her, it was 'important that the expatriates kind of back away and allow [the native population] to forge their own destiny and find their own identity'. A relatively youthful fifty-eight when she left, Barbara exemplified the new thinking towards the mission project, putting the theory of retreating Westerners into practice herself.

A number of the returned missionaries could not claim the decision to return as their own, nor would they have wanted to. Obedience, or loyalty to a sense of obedience, prevented some from doing so while for others circumstances neither of their making nor their choosing forced departure upon them, often reluctantly. Aisling had returned to England for a vacation in 1975 but ran into difficulty renewing her visa. She took up a temporary position hoping the matter would be resolved but it was not and she was soon recalled to Ireland. The situation 'upset me a lot because I never thought of staying at home'. Though she dearly wanted to return to Africa, Aisling did not request that more be done on her behalf, nor enquire about the possibility of being sent elsewhere in Africa, though she was aware that 'other people I know now would have pushed and maybe found another opening'. She rationalised her situation in terms of a sense of duty to obedience:

> I was brought up in my own home [to believe] that whatever happens is the will of God. Whatever will be, will be, kind of thing. And I suppose [in religious life too] we were brought up to do what we were told, kind of thing. Whatever your superior decides'.

Although Vatican II had occurred more than a decade previously, Aisling's thinking was still very much pre-Vatican II. Then in her - mid-fifties, she further consoled herself that 'at that age', she would soon be leaving the missions regardless. Neither Deirdre nor Claire were quite so philosophical about their respective departures, Deirdre to take up a position within the community in Ireland, Claire to be closer to her unmarried sister whose health was failing. It was firmly in the context of external factors that Claire positioned her own return, remarking on several occasions that she would otherwise 'still be there... *No way* would I be home yet!'. Deirdre's response to the news that she was being called back to Ireland was utter disappointment, indeed she took exception to the very idea that she would have chosen to return herself:

> I didn't [ask to] come back! I would *never*, I wouldn't [ever] have thought of coming back!... I was called home to work and I did that ...I cried my eyes out! I didn't like it at all! I didn't want to go back to Ireland. I wanted to stay in Africa and, if I had been assigned to another African country...I wouldn't have minded. But I minded coming back to Ireland. I really didn't want to come back... Going out, I felt, was for life, you know? I really did think I'd be there till I wasn't able to work anymore.

Only one woman, Brenda, talked about return in terms of positive pull factors to Ireland: 'the call to be, to come home'. She drew on romantic representations of Ireland to elaborate: '"The Hills of Donegal", and "The Nights of the Kerry Dancing", and all the songs that were Irish, "When Irish Eyes are Smiling", 'twas that sense of "this is home"'.

With two exceptions (Brenda and Rosemary), the dominant theme pervading the women's accounts of leaving the missions was the pain involved. This was in contrast to the women from England who rarely described their departure in such terms, though many of them experienced difficulties settling back in Ireland. Being back in Ireland was for Winnie 'a struggle. More than I expected!'. Similarly, Aisling 'found it *very* difficult'. Unsurprisingly, those who had returned not by their own volition were upset about the circumstances of their departure, but they were not the only ones who expressed regret. 'There are times', Barbara admitted, 'when I say to myself, "what am I doing here?"'. Winnie also found herself 'for a long time afterwards [asking] myself "what have I done?"'. It took Claire 'about two years to get over the fact that I was home', during which time she could not 'see a Kenyan stamp, but I would cry'. Such was the enormity of the act of leaving and the strength required to do it that many of the women talked about having to 'make a break for it' (Angela) or, finally having left, needing to 'put it at arm's length' (Claire) by not returning to the missions, even for a visit. The very detailed, personal and emotive accounts the women gave, only a taste of which can be offered here, were testimony to the seismic event leaving the missions was in their lives. As Deirdre remarked simply but poignantly: 'They were the happiest years of my life.'

CULTURE SHOCK IN REVERSE: EXPERIENCES OF RETURN

Three of the returned missionary sisters had come back to Ireland in the late 1970s, one in the early 1990s, the rest between 1997 and 2003. They had spent between fifteen and fifty years on the missions. If there was a dominant theme concerning their experiences of return, it was the difficulty they encountered readjusting to life in a country they neither recognised nor identified with. Though the women from England had felt a degree of displacement back in Ireland, this was complicated by, because it was coupled with, a sense of belonging – often, as has been seen, on the basis of a shared sense of national community and identity. For the women returning from the missions, the feeling of displacement was presented as more totalising. As Yvonne put it, 'You're out of it [here], that's for sure'. More than displacement, the women spoke of culture shock. For most, going on the missions represented their first trip outside Ireland and was presented, as seen in Chapter 4, as a very different life but one they quickly adjusted to. Though it might have been expected that the outbound trip would be the one they associated with culture shock, this was not the case. Asked about her first impressions of Africa, Barbara had responded thus: 'I didn't find that the dislocation was as big an experience as maybe the return to Ireland and feeling out of it [in Ireland]...Coming back to Ireland, it's a very different ballgame'.

A further irony was that during the women's time on the missions, the world had, supposedly, become smaller. Before they went, their knowledge of the missions was received second hand, through magazines and the stories of returned missionaries. While living away, they returned to Ireland with increasingly regularity and were, as a result of developments in communication and travel, increasingly less remote from it and the rest of the world. And yet, Barbara was not the only woman to have experienced a greater sense of culture shock on her return to Ireland. For Aisling, moving back was such a 'huge change' that she found she 'just couldn't settle down'. Deirdre found it, in a word, 'overwhelming'.

The women explained their sense of culture shock on the basis that Ireland had changed, as had they themselves. Without doubt, Ireland *had* changed: not only economically, but culturally and demographically. It had modernised and secularised. Things that mattered previously, mattered less now. Concerns not given an airing before, now dominated.[4] Perhaps the most noticeable difference the women were cognisant of was the decline in religious observance in Ireland, a fact noted by them all. Aisling, for example, contrasted the 'age of great faith' she had grown up in with an Ireland where 'the faith is really at the bottom'. Many were particularly aware of a growing anti-clericalism in Ireland, especially within the media. Yvonne found the media's attitude to the Church 'really very painful', as well as 'exaggerated. They never miss a chance...[for] Church-bashing'. Which is not to say either that the women were unquestioning supporters of the Church or that they lamented the position of authority it once had. Used to a less formal Church structure on the missions, many felt the Church had abused its position in Ireland and was receiving its rightful comeuppance. Though she professed to having a high regard for individual clergy, Rosemary, for instance, described the Church as 'pathetic'. Angela thought 'the hammering' the Church was getting might be 'a good thing'.

As was the case with the accounts from women who had returned from England, the accounts from returned missionaries were framed very much in the context of the mission fields where they had lived. More often than not, implicitly if not explicitly, comparisons were drawn between 'here' and 'there'. Religion was a case in point: though the missions had been considered 'godless', they were presented in the women's accounts as more spiritual places than the new Ireland. While many of the women had lived and worked almost entirely with non-Christian populations, they were not *anti*-Christian, as some felt Ireland had become. Aisling, for example, drew a distinction between the school children she taught upon her return and those she had previously taught in Africa:

> They didn't have the same religious sense [as they did in Africa]...I remember one child, I was doing the gospel of Saint Luke and she threw the gospel like this across the room, [saying] 'what's that?' It came as such a shock...There was that sense of irreverence, I suppose, and rebellion probably.

As with declining religious observance, Ireland's greater wealth was something all the women commented on, some making a causal link between the two. The women remarked not just upon the fact of Irish people having more money, but the effect it was having on values and attitudes. Most of them described Ireland, as Barbara did, as 'a more materialistic country', Brenda opining that materialism had 'taken dominance [and] has to a large extent overcome our spiritual thrust'. Certainly, describing Ireland in such terms was not intended as a compliment.

Ireland's wealth provided another point of contrast with the missions, as well as between Irish society and the women themselves. Stories exemplifying Ireland's affluence were usually set against stories of life on the missions, which further served to highlight the women's own sense of displacement in Ireland. Barbara, for example, talked about the cavalier attitude she witnessed in Ireland towards material objects, a folly only the prosperous could afford. This had made her 'very aware of the waste... *incredible* waste [in Ireland]. Waste of time, waste of energy, waste of materials'. Not only did she differentiate between Ireland and the missions in this respect ('it certainly would *not* have been the case in Africa!'), she described herself in opposition to it also: 'You'll find that I tend to recycle everything'. Likewise, Deirdre found the variety of consumer goods in Ireland particularly difficult to fathom, describing visits to the supermarket as 'just *awful*'. Variety reflected Ireland's wealth, but pointed to a more demanding society also. Once again, the distinction was with the missions, where, as Deidre put it, 'you wouldn't have choices', adding:

> If you were told to go out and buy cheese, there was one thing there and you bought it. If you were buying toothpaste or a bar of soap, it would be the same. There wouldn't be ten different varieties or something like that. I found that very [difficult, when I came back]. I found we had too much...I didn't even want to see town or go near the shops or anything like that because it was too much.

Nor was there any desire to adapt to Irish society and the new values and priorities it seemed to now hold. Rather, apparent in the women's accounts was a tendency to present themselves as *not* of this society at all.

Another consequence of Ireland's increased wealth and materialism identified by the returned missionaries was the greater level of individualism in Irish society. At the expense of community, people in Ireland had become more concerned with themselves and with protecting and advancing their own position, materially and socially. Deirdre talked of a 'selfishness' within society while its more individualistic nature Barbara had found 'difficult to take, when I returned'. Neither woman could be sure the extent to which Irish society had actually changed or if they were simply more aware of it given their experiences on the missions. One point identified by the returned missionaries also, though it was also noted by those from England, was the increased number of immigrants in Ireland. Many of the returned missionaries regarded this positively, especially when they met migrants from countries in which they had lived. They regretted, however, the less than positive reception extended to these immigrants in Ireland generally.

One particularly negative impact of the changing nature of Irish society was the effect it was having on children. Nearly all the returned missionaries voiced fears about the manners, materialistic attitude and lack of respect exhibited by children. Angela for example, when asked how she felt Ireland had changed remarked simply 'I think children have too much', adding 'the result is... they're always wanting more and more and more. I think that's the hard, sad thing'. It was an opinion shared by most of the women, the behaviour of children seeming to represent the natural outcome of a society whose values revolved around materialism. Once again, the contrast was with the missions, where children 'have *nothing*' (Deirdre). Again, Deirdre wondered if her opinion on children in Ireland were formed by changes in Ireland itself or her own exposure to non-Irish children's lives elsewhere.

In addition to 'new' Ireland, there was a recognition of past truths about Ireland which had previously been hidden. Though many of the returned missionaries mentioned the cases and allegations of abuse levied against the Church and religious orders, they did so at one step removed from them. Few, of course, had been in Ireland during the period the abuse cases were, or were alleged, to have been perpetrated, or when they came to light, so it was not surprising that they distanced themselves from them. In addition, however, it became another distinguishing feature of the women's lives as missionaries. Remarking on the abuse cases, for example, Rosemary said 'It's a desperate situation, this abuse. [It] has really shocked me. It has sickened me...Because that's unheard of outside [i.e. on the missions], you know?'

The point in their life cycle when the returned missionaries went back to Ireland was significant in their experience of it, especially in terms of dislocation and displacement. For most, returning to Ireland represented a stage in their retirement, whether or not they had wanted or known this would be the case. If going on the missions represented a step forward in their career, often a giant leap, return tended to imply the opposite. For many people, not least religious, sense of self is entwined with work. This is arguably more so the case for missionary religious whose identity is so intrinsically bound to providing services for the needy. For returning missionaries, work was an important theme in their accounts because it had been so fundamental to their sense of personal worth on the missions. A point identified by many, it was perhaps felt most acutely by Yvonne whose difficult experience of return she associated principally with not finding a comparable role for herself back in Ireland: 'You have to get used to [the fact that] you're on the shelf, you know?...I found it *very* painful'.

Redundancy, especially involuntary redundancy, can make a person feel surplus to the requirements of society. This was certainly how Claire felt. Despite the experience she gained working for refugees in Africa, she found her skills not easily transferable to the Irish situation, which required formal qualifications she did not have: 'You see, you have to be trained and you have to be a social worker and you have to be all sorts'. Likewise, Barbara, who had returned from the missions before retirement age, 'encountered...huge difficulty' entering the job market which she felt had a direct and negative impact on her sense of self: 'I became a non-person. What I had to offer was not of significance'.[5]

Once more, the contrast was with the missions where, as Yvonne noted, 'there was always work for everybody'. In addition to need, there was a great appreciation of the work missionaries did. Rosemary was of the opinion that the job she returned to in Ireland had eased her own settlement back, identifying, at the same time, that lack of employment was '...what upset a lot of the sisters. Like, [on the missions] they're doing a great job and there's a lot of people depending on them and they're really needed. And [then] they come home and they've no work'. Pauline made a connection between this and the poor mental health some missionary religious experienced upon return:

> I've been told there are an awful lot of sisters in Ireland at the moment, returned missionaries, with terrible depression and getting treatment...Because they're not needed. Like there is that. When you're out on the missions, there's no doubt about it...if you weren't there, nobody else was going to do the work you were doing. And the kids wouldn't have got their exams or they wouldn't have been able to get on. There was nobody else to do it. And you were [used to] being needed. Talk about being needed!

Barbara not only found it difficult to find work upon return from the missions, but considered the work that she was experiencing difficulty in securing less valuable than that she had undertaken on the missions. Prior to her return, she regarded herself as 'someone [who was] making a difference to people's lives...In the African context, one was responding to a need that was expressed: we need a school here, we need a workshop here. Can you help us? Can you help us to set up a library? And so on and so forth'. By contrast, back in Ireland, Barbara found herself trying to resist 'do[ing] something for the sake of doing something [or] that was coming out of my own needs'. The discourses of selflessness and motivation that Barbara drew on highlighted once more the differences, as she saw them, between Ireland and the missions.

Although these quotes might suggest otherwise, the returned missionaries were not unhappy in Ireland. In fact, despite their comments, they remained mostly positive in their outlook. Though Brenda lamented the fact that Ireland, her 'land of saints', had become, instead, 'a country to be redeemed', or that Yvonne regarded the decline in religious observance to be her 'biggest sadness', neither they nor any of the returned missionaries allowed themselves to be pessimistic about Ireland in general nor Irish people in particular. Not only were the women positive about Ireland's future, they identified many positive aspects of Irish society and its people. Aisling, for example, remarked that the situation in Ireland, 'though it could' did *not* depress her, adding that she 'really believe[d] everything is going to work out'. Likewise, Angela felt that 'it will come out right in the end'. Several of the women commented on people in Ireland being, at heart, 'good', 'moral' or, indeed, ultimately 'faithful', to a sense of right and wrong, if not an organised Church. In addition, many of them commented on the benefits of being in close contact with family. For Deirdre, this was 'the most positive aspect of being back'. Similarly, Angela thought it 'marvellous' to be back in the family fold, remarking that she was 'spending [her] time reconnecting with nieces and grandnieces and great-grandnieces... No matter what cockfight is on, I have to be there. It's great really. It's lovely'.

DISPLACEMENT AND HOME: HERE VERSUS ELSEWHERE

The missionaries' narratives of return were neither a negative assessment of Irish society or a judgement of its decline. Rather, they served a different purpose, which was to make explicit the difference between Ireland and the missions and where it was that the women positioned themselves in relation to that binary. The contrast the women made between here and there highlighted their own sense of displacement in Ireland at the same time as suggesting an elsewhere where this was not the case. Their accounts of life on the missions were replete with references to acceptance and belonging. By contrast, their accounts of return emphasised dislocation. Dislocation was not, or was not in the case of these women, necessarily the same as not belonging: the missions occupied a place in their accounts as the absent present (sometimes the *present* present) where they belonged. Nor was it necessarily problematic or entirely negative. In fact, dislocation in Ireland was a subject position many of the women clung to because it allowed them to hold on to their identity as missionaries and gave them an actual, material connection to a particular and named elsewhere.

The importance of an identity as a missionary was much in evidence in the returned missionaries' discussion of where they considered home to be. Though living in Ireland, return to the missions at best improbable, if not impossible, the women's accounts pointed to an ambiguity concerning its location.[6] Winnie, for example, seemed reluctant to claim Ireland as home, though, by the time of her interview, she had been living in Ireland for over ten years: 'I suppose my home is here now. But my home was in [Africa] and I've such a longing for my home [there], you know? There's no doubt about it, I have a special love for [it]'.

Winnie had spent thirty years, almost half her life as a religious, in Africa. Though she had not wanted to go on the missions and was shocked to find herself being sent there sixteen years into her life as a religious, the extent to which she embraced the mission life was clear. Claire described Africa, where she had lived for thirty years, 'very much' as home. Though she had returned six years prior to being interviewed, her 'heart [was] there really'. Nor was it the case, however, that time spent on the missions determined where home was. Although Deirdre entered a missionary congregation with the hopes of living always on the missions, in fact, she spent only fifteen of her forty-four years as a religious outside Ireland and had returned to Ireland permanently two years before we met.[7] For her, Africa was still home: 'Now? At this stage? [Home] would be Africa. And I wouldn't mind where it was. But I would *love* to live in Africa, I really would. I *loved* the simplicity of the life there'.

For some of the returned missionaries, home was more than one place. Though Ireland was home for Yvonne, the places she had lived on the missions were equally: 'Yes, they would be home certainly'. Barbara, on the other hand, was reluctant to fix home geographically:

> I don't see home as restricted to one specific place. I went back to Africa now this year...and it was like a homecoming. But then again, when I am with family and friends, I feel at home. For me, home is more being at ease in relationships than something that's well defined. 'At home' doesn't mean for me four walls or curtains and chairs. It's more a sense of well-being with people...in a way, I think we carry home with us.

Only two of the returning missionaries were unequivocal about home being Ireland and Ireland alone. Brenda always referred to Ireland as home, her desire to return, as has been seen, a 'call to...come home'. Though she had spent forty years of her life, over 90 per cent of her life as a religious, in Africa, Rosemary 'did not' consider Africa home. Instead, though she had not until recently lived there, the congregation's motherhouse in Ireland was where she 'always thought of...as home...Let me put it this way. This'll answer your question...If I was asked, which I was, where would I like to be buried, I'd say *definitely* I'd like to be buried at home [in Ireland]...I wouldn't have liked to be buried in [Africa]'

Along with Brenda, Rosemary's narrative contradicted the discourse of pain so prevalent in other accounts. Though her attraction to religious life had been specifically to the missions, and while she was appreciative of the opportunity she had to go on the missions, Rosemary nevertheless described missionary life as 'awfully hard. *Awfully* hard'. She was perhaps the only woman who seemed able to put a distance between the missions and home when she returned for temporary visits, and found this to be the case also when she left for good:

> I had always the capacity, when I came home, to forget about it all. I was not in the airport [to leave for good] when I had forgotten all about it. You know, a lot of our sisters here would be bringing it up and bringing it up and bringing it up, you know? I wouldn't. No. Even though I was very happy, I liked the people and I got a good response from them, I was able to help them. But I'm happy to be back. I've no regrets. I have absolutely no regrets. But I wouldn't want to go back. Now, even, I've saw [sic] sisters coming back for golden jubilees and certain things, you know? Openings of church and that. And coming back, very enthusiastic. I wouldn't be interested in going back...In my head, [I'm] certainly not there.

ROOTS AND ROUTES

Perhaps significantly, Brenda and Rosemary were the only two returned missionaries who claimed a strong and exclusively Irish national identity. Brenda remarked that she 'couldn't be anything else *but* Irish' while Rosemary said she 'would want to be identified as Irish – *very* much'. By contrast, Barbara described herself as not 'specifically Irish' but 'international', the fact of her Irishness dismissed as 'an accident of history'. For Aisling, Irishness was 'not that important' on the missions, even less so now she had returned to Ireland. Although being Irish was not something Yvonne would 'shy away from', neither was it something she felt was important to her sense of self. While Deirdre was 'proud' of being both Irish and a Dubliner, and Angela 'liked' being Irish, both these women also identified strongly with the missions. Neither Winnie nor Claire claimed Irishness as an important part of their identity.

For the returned missionaries, the fact of their Irishness and the shared sense of community associated with it was far less important a theme in their accounts, both of migration and return, than was the case for those women returning from England. Unlike the women returned from England, for whom belonging was a major theme in their narratives of return, the returned missionaries spoke of displacement. It was a displacement, however, that hinted of belonging elsewhere. Hence, there was no great search for belonging in Ireland. For the missionaries, the frame of reference was more global than local. A common theme in their accounts was a tendency to distinguish between 'the West' and 'the rest' and to locate themselves as belonging more on the missions within a non-Western sensibility than 'at home' in Ireland.

Also in contrast to the women who returned from England, and though they were certainly aware of the declining status of religious in Ireland, the returned missionaries did not refer to the position of religious as relevant to their experience of return. Few mentioned negative attitudes towards religious generally, none personally. Though Aisling confessed to being 'delighted not to be recognised as a nun' on public transport, this had more to do with the snobbish associations made around her congregation than her fear of adverse comment against religious generally (she confessed also, despite the socio-economic roots of her congregation, that she preferred to work with and for 'the lower classes, working class...why should we be putting our energy into the people who have all the money anyway?').

None of the returning missionaries concealed their religious identity, in the way that those from England did.[8] As Deirdre, put it: 'I wouldn't be trying to hide [the fact that I'm a religious] anywhere. No matter where I am'. Generally speaking, in fact, the women took pride in their identity as a religious and, with the exception of Barbara, mentioned it specifically when describing themselves. This is not to suggest that the returned missionaries were necessarily traditional: few wore a habit and many, in fact, saw themselves as slightly *extraordinary*, the fact of their being missionaries and their experiences on the missions presented as proof of this. The women's adventurous nature was also highlighted in the way they talked about needing to be a 'certain kind of person' (Barbara) to survive the missions. Their experience of modernisation, however, was influenced by its context, that is, the mission societies and communities themselves.

Nor did the returned missionaries, in contrast to many of the non-missionary women, state, suggest or even imply that access to gendered subjectivity was compromised by their status as religious. In fact, the returned missionaries were far less likely to claim womanhood as a possible identity at all. Pauline was the only returned missionary to describe herself as a feminist, though this was an identity she had embraced only after returning to Ireland in the late 1970s. Winnie, Angela, Brenda and Claire ignored 'woman' as a option of self identity when it was proffered while Rosemary stated it simply as a fact without expanding on what it meant to her to be a gendered subject. As pointed out in Chapter 5, Deirdre was 'proud' of being a woman but did not seem to take the option of 'woman' as an identity seriously.

On balance, the returned missionaries seemed more accepting of their less than central position in Irish society than those women who had returned from England. In part, this may have related to their age and the fact that they were retired, but it could not be entirely attributed to it: some of those who had or still lived in England were also retired. Alternatively, their sidelined position – still 'matter out of place'[9] to some extent – could serve to augment their displaced identity, keeping safe their subjectivity as missionary sister which was so important to them. Women returning from England were very conscious of the way they felt Irish society responded to them, the levels – or not – of acceptance. For returned missionaries, their issues with Irish society were less specific to them as individual women religious, perceived more as a fundamental schism between themselves as missionaries and the kind of society Ireland had become.

CONCLUSION

As this chapter has shown, the experience of leaving the missions, returning to and living in Ireland for the missionary sisters was intrinsically bound to their identity as missionaries. In recounting their stories of life back in Ireland, the missions were ever present. As with those women who had returned or continued to return to Ireland from England, suggesting that returned missionaries' experience of return was deeply informed by their experiences on the missions might seem to be stating the obvious. Well worth highlighting, however, is how very differently the women from the missions narrated their story of return compared to the women from England.

Oral history is necessarily about memory. It asks a person to give an account of themselves by drawing on their memory. As this and the previous chapter have illustrated, memory is as much a creative process as a recollective one. The very different narrative accounts offered in these two chapters point to some, though certainly not all, of the devices or tropes individual Irish women religious draw on to make sense of their experience of returning to Ireland and in so doing, point to the significance of context to the construction of self identity and how we as individuals inhabit, experience and express a sense of self.

NOTES

1   Winnie.
2   Though Frances, Margaret, Geraldine and Joan had each spent time on the missions, this was short compared to the time they had each spent in England. Their stories of return to Ireland were told in the context of life in England more than elsewhere and, therefore, appear in Chapter 7.
3   It is worth pointing out once more that no accounts of temporary return from the missions are included in this study.
4   While the women would have been aware of changes in Ireland on visits home, those visits were often very busy and spent immersed in the fold of family and friends. They tended to be recounted as almost unreal episodes such that the full changes of Irish society, the machinations that underscored them and the impact of them personally were rarely fully appreciated until the women came home to live.
5   Unlike Teresa (Chapter 7), Barbara made no connection between this and the fact of her being a religious.

6   While some of the women *in* England tended to be ambiguous about
     home, those who had returned from there were not.
7   In two separate terms of duty (one of seven, the other of eight years)
     spent in two different African countries.
8   Though, as noted in Chapter 5, Barbara tended not to identify
     herself as a religious and considered herself 'unchurched'.
9   Douglas, *Purity And Danger*.

CONCLUSION

'As ubiquitous as the pint of Guinness'

When making contact with individual religious for the purposes of this research, the most common response I received was incredulity: *Why* did I want to know about the lives of religious and how, 'in God's name', had someone of my age ever become interested in such a topic? Missionary religious were slightly less surprised, but only until they learned I was more interested in their personal experiences than in the impact of their congregation abroad. It was a reaction that seemed to affirm the near acceptance, even by religious themselves, that they occupy a space outside what is deemed vital, relevant or even worthy of study. And yet, the figure of the nun continued to loom large in the popular image of Ireland and Irish womanhood, both in Ireland and its diaspora.

Not long ago, England-born writer Pete McCarthy went in search of his Irish roots by way of every pub he came to in Ireland owned or run by a McCarthy, collecting his experiences in the best-selling book *McCarthy's Bar*. On the book's front and back cover, as well as on its inside front cover, there is a picture of a pint of Guinness. There is also a picture of a nun. The Irish nun, it seems, is as ubiquitous as a pint of the black stuff, and no more transparent. The curious status of religious as icon more than person was invoked in the introduction to this book and it seems appropriate to return to it now to ask, in conclusion, what is revealed when the focus shifts not just to include but to centre on the experiences of Irish women religious

Growing up, the women of this study formed their sense of self as women in response to several factors. These included dominant though fluctuating notions of Irish womanhood and femininity, a process of negotiation that occurred not in one moment but was on-going throughout their lives. Their experiences of girlhood and early adulthood developed in them an awareness of the gendered structures that existed in the Irish society in which they were born and grew up. They recognised the limitations placed upon them as girls and women and were able to identify the particular roles they were expected to assume in response. Significantly, for them, nuns embodied a lifestyle that represented an attractive alternative to marriage and motherhood. The meanings the women of this study attached to religious life illustrated they had strong ideas about what it would offer them, which extended far beyond warding off spinsterhood, one of the common assumptions made about Irish women's entry to religious life.[1] The way they differentiated between congregations and individual religious further revealed them to be discriminating in their decision-making processes and conscious of the possibilities religious life offered them personally, professionally and spiritually.

The women of this study had negotiated and reconfigured their religious identity throughout their lives. Although, as girls, the women experienced their Catholicism as natural and innate, in reality it was both constructed and learned. Catholicism was also, for most of them, intrinsically linked to nationhood, Irishness and their family. Their accounts indicated that mothers and fathers took on distinct but important roles in passing religion on to their children, challenging the assumption that mothers were more 'religious' figures than fathers. Fathers were presented as being imbued with an ethereal spirituality superior to the mere attending to tasks, producing a dichotomy between the roles assumed by parents. The 'other-worldliness' of the women's vocation for religious life, moreover, tended to be situated closer to the spirituality of their fathers, while the obligations of motherhood were presented as onerous and less attractive by comparison.

Few of the women in this study distinguished between Catholic and Irish as they were growing up, although some refused to be labelled as 'traditional Irish Catholics'. This mixing of ethnic and religious identities suggested the women were influenced by the post-colonial Irish identity that was promoted in the newly independent state or by their parents' rejection of it. Most of them had a very strong sense of the alien other (especially non-Catholics in Ireland and elsewhere) while some occupied this position themselves as Catholics in Northern Ireland. The association between Catholicism and Ireland or Irishness did not prevent, and indeed sometimes provoked, the women to enter religious congregations that took them outside Ireland. Traditional constructions of Irish national identity have idealised women's 'natural' place in the home and 'at home' in Ireland. For the women of this study, however, loyalty to vocation and personal choices for particular congregations overrode that to family and nation.

Though some of the women drew upon discourses of self-sacrifice in describing their vocation, they each presented their entry into religious life as an act of personal agency. In so doing, they laid claim to an individuality and freedom from family obligation which challenges previous representations of religious as mere cultural dupes, responding passively to the needs of a patriarchal Church. Their agency also raises questions about the migration of women who left Ireland to enter congregations in England or entered congregations in Ireland knowing they would be required at some point to live outside it. Sharon Lambert[2] has argued that the Irish women migrants she interviewed in Lancaster, who left Ireland at approximately the same time as the women of this study, did so not to pursue individual aspirations but because their movement benefited the family unit. For the women of this study, by contrast, religious life and its concomitant migration was more of an individual act, a communication between themselves and the divine, one that family might benefit from but rarely felt able to stand in the way of. By choosing to enter congregations which required them to spend time outside Ireland, the women were able to articulate a positive desire for travel which traditional discourses of emigration have tended to exclude. For missionary religious, moreover, emigration was a symbol of their commitment to Irish Catholicism and the international project it had set itself. Nor was the women's movement out of Ireland regarded as a threat to their Irishness or their Irish womanhood. This makes nuns who lived outside Ireland a very specific group of emigrants whose experiences might also be said to contradict the conventional narrative of Irish women's emigration during this period as selfish opportunism, cultural abandonment or the road to ruin.

The process by which women became nuns within religious life was entirely gendered. Entrants were expected to embrace and inhabit a particular form of womanhood rooted in notions of woman's inferior mental capacity and dangerous physical capabilities. Although religious life has often been associated with the forsaking of womanhood, an examination of the pre-Vatican II regime revealed that religious life continually marked its members out precisely as women. The key distinction, however, was that it did so while at the same time denying them any investment in femininity. Religious life was never about shedding gender or becoming 'half-women'.[3] In fact, it served to reinforce gender, albeit in very particular ways. Although some of the women of this study retrospectively identified the pre-Vatican II regime as restrictive with respect to the gendered identity it imposed upon them, at the time, they had accepted it. Their acceptance reflected a commitment to obedience and, for many, an investment in the way religious life defined womanhood.

While also gendered, religious life defined religious identity. Entry into it required that the women reconfigure their religious identity, concepts of family and nation as a means of defining their Catholicism being replaced by religious life itself. More so than was the case regarding the forms of womanhood available in the pre-Vatican II period, the women recognised the religious regime as restrictive in retrospect, both physically and psychologically demanding, though it was one they chose to remain within. They were also able to identify, however, the rewards of religious life, not only the opportunity to pursue educational or employment ambitions, but the spiritual rewards of a life lived within community and devoted to prayer. Although obedience was intrinsic to the regime, accounts of resistance, however small, revealed an attempted renegotiation of the prescribed religious identity.

The strictures of pre-Vatican II life and the rule books that defined that life in such intricate detail would suggest that religious life, while 'in' the natural world, was not really 'of' that world. The significance of place to the women's experience of religious life, however, high-lighted the extent to which congregations were also human institutions, influenced by the socio-historical and socio-political conditions in which they existed, as were the individuals who populated them. Contrary to the stated aims of the pre-Vatican II regime, ethnicity was shown to be of great significance within religious life, the experiences of the women in this study affected by their choice of congregation, In particular, whether that congregation was a minority- or majority-Irish congregation in England, or one that took them out of that archipelago, altogether, to the mission fields of Africa and Asia. Processes of othering and being othered were central to the experiences of Irish women in England, while for those on the missions, hospitality and community served to temporarily, if somewhat superficially, gloss over cultural, language, religious and racial differences.

The subjective understandings and expressions of religious identity by and among women religious is an under-explored area of research, especially so with respect to Vatican II. For the women of this study, Vatican II was shown to have had a major impact on their lives and prompted them to reconfigure their identity as religious in its wake, sometimes reluctantly. For many, Vatican II enabled a more positive re-evaluation of what it meant to be a nun, one that was defined as much by the self as the institution of religious life.

Post-conciliar changes introduced into religious life gave women who chose to profit from them an opportunity to claim forms of womanhood not previously available to them. The women of this study expressed this in various ways: by reverting to their secular name, in the clothes they wore, in the titles they preferred (or not) to use, and through forming group identities with other non-religious women. A significant feature for some was their re-investment in femininity and physical appearance. Others also adopted feminist and sexual identities which would have been refused them prior to Vatican II. The freedom to assert such identities was not, however, absolute. A number of the women felt their right to be the kind of woman they wanted was contested, sometimes denied, by others. Although not fixed in any sense beforehand, Vatican II has provided the space for contestation and negotiation around gender and what it means to be a female religious.

For those women who have clung to the rules and regulations of religious life as an elemental part of it, Vatican II represents a challenge to the essence of religious life which is neither easy to accept nor understand. The women's accounts also pointed to tensions that continue to surround Vatican II and its consequences within religious life. It has demanded an on-going and as yet unresolved re-think about what it means to be a religious and how that identity should be inhabited and displayed. In the course of this redefinition, religious identity has become less easy to locate than was the case either under the pre-Vatican II regime, or in the mis-remembered intrinsic and organic Catholicism of the women's youth. That religious life has been in such flux since Vatican II challenges the notion of it, and religious themselves, as stagnant or fixed.

Vatican II enabled and in some cases encouraged congregations to confront internal practices of exclusion. Initially, however, greater freedoms within religious life served to enforce divisions or to make individuals aware of them in the first place. As was the case prior to

Vatican II, the experience of it and of religious life since, has been affected by *where* it has been experienced. For women in England, Vatican II coincided with increased levels of hostility directed against Irish people living there. While the Northern Irish peace process and Ireland's economic success has much improved the position of Irish people in England, the women of this study living in England continue to feel conscious of their Irishness. Their awareness of being other to the majority suggested a specifically 'Irish-in-England' identity and illustrated once more the importance of emigration to their construction of self, even though they tended not to define themselves as Irish emigrants. For the missionaries, Vatican II was both conceived of and understood differently, the women's interpretation of it shaped by the demands and needs of where they lived locally, as well as their geopolitical location within the 'third world'.

One experience shared by all the women who took part in this study was that they each experienced religious life outside Ireland. Close to two-thirds of them had returned to Ireland to live while, with two exceptions, the rest continued to visit Ireland, many regularly. Home and belonging were the reference points the women used to describe return to Ireland temporarily and permanently, though they used them in significantly different ways. The women who had or continued to return from England articulated differing notions of belonging along different axes. On the basis of ethnicity, most felt at home in Ireland, where their ethnicity ceased to be consciously felt. However, this was not the only mode by which they experienced belonging and many of the women felt more at home, as well as greater freedoms to be themselves as religious and as women, in England than in Ireland. Although their narratives suggested a multi-located sense of belonging, this did not amount to an unlimited or open-ended sense of belonging everywhere but pointed, instead, to contestation around where and in what circumstances they could feel at home. For the missionary sisters, belonging was almost uncontested, wherever they had been on mission representing for most its locus.

The purpose of synopsising in this conclusion the salient points made in previous chapters enables a brief suggestion of some of the wider themes that have emerged from focusing on Irish women religious. As was pointed out in the beginning, while the oral histories upon which this book is based were in effect created jointly by myself and the women who took part in this study, in the process of their being written into book form, decisions had to be made about what parts of the women's lives to focus on, what parts to exclude. If any of the women who were involved in this research, or, indeed, anybody else had written a book based on the same interviews, no doubt the result would have been very different, not only in content but also in emphasis. This is not a book that charts the complete lives of the women of this study, nor is it its intention to provide a biography of them. Instead, it uses their stories, partial as they necessarily are, to discuss issues beyond them. Drawing on individual and unique experiences, it speaks more generally about the 'macro' experience of being Irish, woman and religious.

Less concerned with facts and figures, this book is best described as an exploration of identity and subjectivity, about the complex and interdependent ways they are formed and expressed. More specifically, this is a book about gendered subjectivities and one of its guiding aims has been to contribute to our knowledge of gendered Irish subjectivities. Via the women's subjectivities as Irish women religious this is a book about class and domesticity, about the private and the public, about femininity and respectability, about work and the identities that are formed around them, about nationality and ethnicity, about religion and spirituality, about conformity and non-conformity.

Oral histories collect the daily lives of ordinary people. The testimonies of ordinary people are located within the wider historical context that shape them and reveal much to us about their context, as well as the responses individuals make to them. The oral histories that this book draws from disclose much about the women themselves, but also about the society they were born and grew up in, the ones they moved to and the Ireland many returned to, societies that shaped them, as they shaped those societies in return.

Since the 1960s, the number of Irish women entering religious life has declined, as has the status and authority of the Catholic Church in Ireland. Simultaneously, the position of women in Ireland has altered. While its duration cannot be predicted, the economic success that Ireland has recently enjoyed has had an impact upon Irish migration, shifting the balance from out- to in-migration. Issues of Irishness are now being debated within Ireland, while reports of discrimination and racism against new immigrant groups illustrate the difficult transition the country is undergoing.

The women of this study represent the end of an era, the end of the near phenomenon that was Irish women's entry into religious life in the first six decades of the twentieth century, and the departure of many of them out of Ireland. This puts greater stress on the importance of documenting their experiences now. As professed sisters of the Catholic Church, these women represent a distinct group of Irish emigrant women, not only for who they are, but also for what they are not: not wives or mothers or economically vulnerable.

To return to a point made several times in this book, the women of this study were not born nuns, but became them. Their accounts of growing up and making decisions about their future, which encompassed both entry into religious life and leaving Ireland, of temporary and permanent return, are stories about Irish society, Irish womanhood and Irish migration. Not only in the pre-Vatican II period, and especially not since then, were these women ever exclusively nuns. Though some of their experiences were specific to religious life, many of them involved a confrontation with issues of ethnicity and gender that have relevance beyond it. The women's accounts are unique, giving an insight into a group of women previously disregarded. They also serve to highlight the inextricable, interdependent and conditional nature of identity formation.

One of the stated aims of this research, and the principal reason oral history was chosen as its method, was to let the voices of Irish women religious be heard, voices generally silent in accounts of Irish women at home or abroad. In light of this, I had thought that the most appropriate way of drawing this book to a final conclusion would be to use a quote from one of the respondents, one that epitomised what this research has been about. Poring over the many pages of interviews, I realised that this would prove an impossible task. The reality is that from the lives of thirty women, there could be no such final encapsulation. Perhaps this, however, is the point to end on, to reiterate once more the complexity and range of experiences among a group of women thus far disregarded, of which this book represents not the final word but a first step in exploring.

NOTES

1   MacCurtain, 'Late in the Field', p. 58.
2   Lambert, *Irish Women in Lancashire*, p. 24.
3   C. Clear, *Nuns in Nineteenth Century Ireland* (Dublin: Gill & Macmillan, 1987), p. xviii.

Brief Biographies of Respondents

In order to preserve confidentiality, respondents are identified by first and congregational name only, both of which are pseudonyms. Where precise details were unclear, the lowest estimated figure has been given, beside which appears an asterisk in brackets. Places of birth are given at county level only. Where the women's background was middle-class or above, it is so noted. Otherwise, assume a lower middle-class/working-class background.

Annette b. 1919, Galway. One older brother. Rural, middle-class background. Entered with the St Louise (Fr.) congregation in Ireland in 1939 (aged 19) and trained to be a teacher. Left Ireland for England in 1957 and lived there until her death in 2002.

Bernadette b. 1911, Offaly. Seven siblings, two of whom did not survive childhood. Eldest of four brothers and one sister. Rural background. Father died when Bernadette was in her early teens, her youngest sister still an infant. Entered with the St Nadine (Fr.) congregation in Ireland in 1931 (aged 19), qualifying as a nurse a number of years later. Left Ireland for England in 1943. d. England, 2003.

Catherine b. 1941, Longford. Second eldest of four children: two boys, two girls. Rural background. Left Ireland in 1959 (aged 18) to enter with the St Cecile (Fr/Eng.) congregation, undertaking nursing training twelve years later. At the time of the interviews, was living in England.

Vera b. 1931, Leitrim. Second youngest of nine children, of whom two were boys, seven were girls. Rural, middle-class background. Having worked for some years in Ireland, Vera left in 1955 (aged 24) to enter with the St Mildred (Eng.) congregation, where she re-trained as a teacher. At the time of the interviews, was living in England.

Elaine b. 1922, Cork. Eldest of six children: one boy and five girls. Rural background. Qualified as a nurse before leaving Ireland to work in England in 1941. Elaine entered with the St Mildred (Eng.) congregation four years later, aged 23. At the time of the interviews, was living in England.

Frances b. 1930, Waterford. Tenth of eleven children: five girls, six boys. Mother widowed at a young age. Rural background. Left Ireland aged 10, for boarding school in England run by the St Mildred (Eng.) congregation. Entered with the same congregation in 1948 (aged 18) where she trained as a teacher. At the time of the interviews, was living in England.

Geraldine b. 1945, Monaghan. Middle of six children, one older sister a nun also. Rural background. Having worked in Ireland for a few years, Geraldine left Ireland for England in 1964 (aged 19) to enter with the St Mildred (Eng.) congregation. Re-trained as a teacher within the congregation. Spent eight years back in Ireland, and five years on the missions, before leaving England to return to live in Ireland in 2000.

Hannah b. 1933, Westmeath. Eldest of two girls. Comfortable, rural background. Left Ireland in 1951 (aged 18) to enter with the St Mildred (Eng.) congregation in England. Trained as a teacher. Worked predominantly in England, where she was still living at the time of the interviews.

Irene b. 1939, Donegal. One, older (invalid) brother. Rural background. Left Ireland in 1956 (aged 17) to enter with the St Cecile (Fr./Eng.) congregation in England. Received domestic training. At the time of the interviews, was living in England.

Josephine b. 1950, Kilkenny. Eldest girl of five boys and two girls. Rural background. Entered with the St Marie (Fr.) congregation in 1970 (aged 20) and left Ireland for England two years later. Trained as a social worker. At the time of the interviews, was living in England.

Kate b. 1936, Roscommon. Middle of three children: one older sister, one younger brother. Rural background. Left Ireland for England in

1955 seeking employment and teacher training. Having qualified as a teacher a couple of years previously, Kate entered with the St Louise (Fr.) congregation in England in 1963, aged 27.

Lillian b. 1947, Limerick. Eldest of six children: four brothers and one sister. Rural background. Entered with the St Marie (Fr.) congregation in Ireland in 1965 (aged 18), leaving for England two years later. Trained as a teacher.

Margaret b. 1942, Derry. Second eldest, and eldest girl, of seven children. Rural background. Educated by the St Marie congregation, Margaret entered the same congregation in Ireland in 1962 (aged 18) and left Ireland for England two years later. She spent seven years as a missionary sister in Latin America in two separate terms of duty. She returned to England in 1982 and was still living there at the time of the interviews.

Norah b. 1922, Kerry. One older brother and six younger siblings. Rural background. Left Ireland for England in 1941 (aged 19) to enter with the St Marie (Fr.) congregation. Trained as a teacher. Returned to live in Ireland in 1999.

Eileen b. 1932, Dublin. Five (*) siblings. Mother widowed at a young age. Left Ireland in 1952 (aged 20) to enter with the St Mildred (Eng.) congregation in England. Trained as a teacher. Returned to Ireland to live in 1976.

Pauline b. 1930, Dublin. One older brother. Left Ireland in 1948 (aged 17) to enter with the St Mildred (Eng.) congregation in England, where she trained as a teacher. Spent twenty years in Africa before returning to England, in 1976, and to Ireland one year later. Pauline was still living in Ireland at the time of the interviews.

May b. 1920, Dublin. Two (*) siblings. Comfortable background. Left Ireland in 1938 (aged 18) to enter with the St Mildred (Eng.) congregation in England, where she received teacher training. May spent an equal number of years (twenty-three) in France as in England, as well as some years in Ireland, before finally returning to Ireland to live in 1993.

Rebecca b. 1918, Tyrone. One older sister. Very comfortable background. Left Ireland for boarding school in England run by the St Mildred (Eng.) congregation in 1931 (aged 13). Attended university in England before joining the St Mildred congregation in 1938 where she completed teacher training. Returned to live in Ireland in 1953.

Sarah b. 1944, Galway. Four (*) siblings: three sisters and one brother. Rural background. Educated by the St Louise (Fr.) congregation in Ireland, leaving to enter with the same congregation in England in 1961/62 (aged 17). Trained as a teacher. Sarah returned to Ireland to study between 1965 and 1969 and to study 1971 and 1978. She returned to live in Ireland permanently in 1987.

Teresa b. 1944, 'rural Ireland'. Two (*) sisters, at least one of whom was older than Teresa. She left Ireland in 1961/62 (aged 17) to enter with the St Marie (Fr.) congregation in England, where she trained as a social worker. Teresa returned to live in Ireland in 1986.

Joan b. 1930 (*), Dublin. Two (*) sisters, one of whom was older than Joan. Joan left Ireland in 1949 aged 18, following her sister into the St Marie (Fr.) congregation in England where she trained as a teacher. Spent two years in Asia between 1993 and 1995 before returning to live in Ireland in 1995.

Barbara b. 1945, 'rural Ireland'. Two (*) siblings. Entered with the St Gemma (Ir.) congregation in Ireland in 1963 (aged 18), the same congregation she had been educated by. Barbara trained as a teacher and spent between 1976 and 1998 in Africa, with the exception of a year's sabbatical in the United States. She returned to live in Ireland in 1998.

Winnie b. 1929, Louth. Four siblings: three sisters and one brother. Rural background. Attended boarding school run by the St Gemma (Ir.) congregation and entered with them, in Ireland, in 1946 (aged 17). Trained as a teacher. Winnie spent thirty-four years as a missionary sister in Africa before returning to live in Ireland in 1992.

Aisling b. 1923, Mayo. At least two siblings, one of whom was a priest and one a religious sister. Aisling entered with the St Mildred (Eng.) congregation in Ireland in 1941 (aged 18), moving to England six months later. She trained as a teacher and spent between 1954 and

1976 as a missionary sister in Africa. She returned to England in 1978 and moved back to Ireland the same year.

Yvonne b. 1921, Wicklow. Three brothers, all older than herself. Comfortable background. Educated by the St Helen congregation (Ir.), entering with them in Ireland in 1943 (aged 22). Trained as a teacher in Ireland. Yvonne left for the missions in 1949 and returned to live in Ireland in 2000.

Rosemary b. 1933, Antrim. Three brothers and one sister, also a nun. Rosemary trained as a nurse before entering with the St Brigid (Ir.) congregation in Ireland in 1961 (aged 28). She spent between 1964 and 2003 as a missionary sister in Africa before returning to live in Ireland (the Republic).

Angela b. 1923, Roscommon. Seven siblings, of whom her twin brother became a priest. Rural background. Entered with St Brigid (Ir.) congregation in Ireland in 1941 (aged 18), where she trained as a nurse. Leaving for Africa first in 1944, Angela spent a total of fifty-three years there before returning to Ireland for good in 2000.

Brenda b. 1919, Dublin. Eldest of three children: one brother, one sister. Very comfortable background. Entered with the St Gemma (Fr.) congregation in 1937 (aged 18), having spent the final years of her education in one of their boarding schools in Ireland. Brenda trained as a teacher and spent nine years as a missionary sister in Africa, as well a smaller number of years in North America, before returning to live in Ireland in 1989.

Claire b. 1933, Kildare. Second eldest and eldest girl of four children – two girls, two boys – one of whom became a priest. Having spent four years living and working in England, Claire returned to Ireland to enter with the St Anne (Ir.) congregation in 1956 (aged 22). Trained as a nurse. In 1967, Claire went to Africa where she spent thirty years as a missionary religious before returning to Ireland to live in 1997.

Deirdre b. 1936, Dublin. Eldest of seven children. Urban, working-class background. Having worked in an office for five years, Deirdre entered with the St Brigid (Ir.) congregation in 1959 (aged 23) undertaking mostly administrative work within the congregation. She spent fifteen years between 1976 and 2001 as a missionary in Africa.

BIBLIOGRAPHY

Abbott, W. M. *The Documents of Vatican II* (London: Geoffrey Chapman, 1965).

Akenson, D. H. *The Irish Diaspora, A Primer* (Belfast: Institute of Irish Studies, 1993).

Alcott, L. and Potter, E. *Feminist Epistemologies* (New York: Routledge, 1993).

Anderson, B., *Imagined Communities, Reflections on the Origin and Spread of Nationalism* (London: Verso, rev. edn, 1991).

Anderson, K. and Jack, D. C. 'Learning to Listen: Interviewing Techniques and Analyses', in S. Berger Gluck and D. Patai (eds), *Women's Words: The Feminist Practice of Oral History* (London: Routledge, 1991), pp. 11–26.

Annual Population and Migration Estimates, 1991–1998 (Dublin: Central Statistics Office, 1999).

Anson, P. F. *The Religious Orders and Congregations of Great Britain and Ireland* (Worcester: Stanbrook Abbey, 1949).

Anthias, F. and Yuval-Davis, N. *Racialized Boundaries: Race, Nation, Gender, Colour and Class and the Anti-Racist Struggle* (London: Routledge, 1992).

Anwar, M. *The Myth of Return* (London: Heinemann, 1979).

Anzaldúa, G. *Borderlands/La Frontera* (San Francisco, CA: Aunt Lude Book Company, 1987).

Arensberg, C. M. and Kimball, S. T. *Family and Community in Ireland* (Cambridge, MA: Harvard University Press, 1968) (first published 1940).

Armstrong, K. *Through the Narrow Gate, A Nun's Story* (London: Flamingo, 1979).

Austin, W. G. and Worchel, S. *The Social Psychology of Intergroup Relations* (Belmont, CA: Wadsworth Publishing Company, 1979).

Badham, P. (ed.) *Religion, State and Society in Modern Britain* (New York: Edwin Mellen Press, 1989).

Bagley, C. and Binitie, S. 'Alcoholism and Schizophrenia in Irishmen in Britain', *British Journal of Addiction*, 65 (1970), pp. 3–5.

Baldwin, M. *I Leap Over the Wall* (London: Hamish Hamilton, 1949).

Barrington, C. *Irish Women in England: An Annotated Bibliography* (Dublin: Women's Education Research and Resource Centre, UCD, 1997).

Barth, F. *Ethnic Groups and Boundaries: The Social Organisation of Cultural Difference* (London: George Allen & Unwin, 1969).

Battersby, W. J. 'Educational Work of the Religious Orders of Women, 1850–1950', in G. A. Beck (ed.), *The English Catholics, 1850–1950* (London: Burns & Oates, 1950), pp. 337–64.

Baum, W. K. and Dunaway, D. K. (eds) *Oral History: An Interdisciplinary Anthology* (Nashville, TN: Altamira Press, 1996).

Bauman, Z. *Thinking Sociologically* (Oxford: Blackwell, 1990).

Beale, J. *Women in Ireland, Voices of Change* (Bloomington and Indianapolis, IN: Indiana University Press, 1987).

Beattie, M. *St Augustine* (Dublin: Authanian Press, 1945).

Beaumont, C. 'Women and the Politics of Equality: the Irish Women's Movement, 1930–1943', in M. G. Valiulis and M. O'Dowd (eds), *Women and Irish History* (Dublin: Wolfhound, 1997), pp. 173–88.

Beaumont, C. 'Gender, Citizenship and the State in Ireland, 1922–1990', in S. Brewster, V. Crossman, F. Becket, and D. Alderson (eds), *Ireland in Proximity: History, Gender, Space* (London: Routledge, 1999), pp. 94–108.

Beck, G. A. (ed.), *The English Catholics, 1850–1950* (London: Burns Oates, 1950).

Beck, U. and E. Beck-Gernsheim, E. *Individualization* (London: Sage, 2002).

Bell, C. and Roberts, H. (eds) *Social Researching: Politics, Problems, Practice* (London: Routledge and Kegan Paul, 1984).

Bennett, C. *The Housing of the Irish in London* (London: Polytechnic of North London Press, 1988).

Berger Gluck, S. and Patai, D. (eds), *Women's Words: The Feminist Practice of Oral History* (London: Routledge, 1991).

Bernstein, M. *Nuns* (London: Fount Publishers, 1978).

Berry, U. 'Women in Ireland', Women's Studies International Forum, 11, 4 (1988), pp. 317–22.

Bielenberg, A. (ed.) *The Irish Diaspora* (Essex: Longman, 2000).

Bishop, P. *The Irish Empire* (London: Boxtree/Macmillan, 1988).

Bourdieu, P. *Outline of a Theory of Practice* (trans. R. Nice) (Cambridge: Cambridge University Press, 1977).

Bourdieu, P. 'The Forms of Capital', in J. G. Richardson (ed.), *Handbook of Theory and Research for the Sociology of Education* (New York: Greenwood Press, 1983), pp. 241–58.

Bourdieu, P. *Distinction: A Social Critique of the Judgement of Taste* (London: Routledge, 1984).

Bourdieu, P. 'The Genesis and Concepts of Habitus and Field' (trans. C. Newman), *Sociocriticisms*, Vol 2 (1985), pp. 11–24.

Bourdieu, P. 'What Makes a Good Social Class? On the Theoretical and

Practical Existence of Groups', *Berkeley Journal of Sociology*, 32 (1987), pp. 1–18.

Bourdieu, P. 'Genesis and Structure of the Religious Field', *Comparative Social Research*, 13, 3 (1991), pp. 1–44.

Bourdieu, P. and Wacquart, L. J. D. *An Invitation to Reflexive Sociology* (Cambridge: Polity Press, 1992).

Boyle, P. and Halfacree, K. (eds) *Migration and Gender in the Developed World* (London: Routledge, 1999).

Bradley, A. and Valiulis, M. G. (eds) *Gender and Sexuality in Modern Ireland* (Amherst, Massachusetts: University of Massachusetts, 1997).

Brah, A. *Cartographies of Diaspora: Contesting Identities* (London: Routledge, 1996).

Brewster, S., Crossman, V., Becket, F., and Alderson, D. (eds) *Ireland in Proximity: History, Gender, Space* (London: Routledge, 1999).

Brown, S. J. *Emigration from Ireland* (Dublin: The Standard, 1953).

Brown, S. J. and Miller, D. W. (eds) *Piety and Power in Ireland, 1760–1960* (Notre Dame, IN: University of Notre Dame Press, 2000).

Brown, T. *Ireland: A Social and Cultural History 1922–2002* (London: Harper Perennial, 2004) (first published in 1981).

Buchanan, T. and Conway, M. *Political Catholicism in Europe, 1918–1965* (Oxford: Clarendon Press, 1996).

Buckley, M. 'Sitting on Your Politics: the Irish among the British and the Women among the Irish', in J. MacLaughlin (ed.), *Location and Dislocation in Contemporary Irish Society, Emigration and Irish Identities* (Cork: Cork University Press, 1997), pp. 94–132.

Buijs, G. (ed.) *Migrant Women, Crossing Boundaries and Changing Identities* (Rhode Island, NJ: Berg Press, 1993).

Bull, G. *Vatican Politics at the Second Vatican Council, 1962–5* (Oxford: Oxford University Press, 1966).

Burke, A. W. (1976), 'Attempted Suicide among the Irish-Born Population in Birmingham', *British Journal of Psychology* 128 (1976), pp. 534–7.

Byrne, A. 'Single Women in Ireland: A Re-Examination of the Sociological Evidence', in A. Byrne and M. Leonard (eds), *Women and Irish Society: A Sociological Reader* (Belfast: Beyond the Pale, 1997), pp. 415–30.

Byrne, A. and Leonard, M. (eds), *Women and Irish Society, A Sociological Reader* (Belfast: Beyond the Pale, 1997).

Byrne, A. and Lentin, R. (eds), *(Re)Searching Women, Feminist Research Methodologies in the Social Sciences in Ireland* (Dublin: Institute of Public Administration, 2000)

Campbell-Jones, S. *In Habit, An Anthropological Study of Working Nuns* (London: Faber & Faber, 1979).

Carr, M. *From Here to Maternity: A Study of Irish Women's Experiences of Maternity Services in Brent* (London: Brent Equal Access, 1996).

Chamberlain, M. 'Gender and Memory: Oral History and Women's History', in V. Shepherd, B. Brereton and B. Bailey (eds), *Engendering History: Caribbean Women in Historical Perspective* (Kingston: Ian Randle Publishers, 1995), pp. 94–110.

Chambers, I. *Migrancy, Culture, Identity* (London: Routledge, 1994).

Chance, J. 'The Irish in London: An Exploration of Ethnic Boundary Maintenance', in P. Jackson (ed.), *Race and Racism: Essays in Social Geography* (London: Allen & Unwin, 1987), pp. 124–60.

Clancy, M., Clear, C. and NicGiolla Choille, T. (eds) *Women's Studies Review, 7, Oral History and Biography* (Galway: Women's Studies Centre, 2000).

Clarke, C., Ley, D., and Peach, C. (eds), *Geography and Ethnic Pluralism* (London: Allen & Unwin, 1984).

Clarke, S. *No Faith in the System* (Cork: Mercier Press, 1995).

Clear, C. *Nuns in Nineteenth Century Ireland* (Dublin: Gill & Macmillan, 1987).

Clear, C. 'Walls Within Walls – Nuns in Nineteenth Century Ireland', in C. Curtin, P. Jackson, and B. O'Connor (eds) *Gender in Irish Society* (Galway: Galway University Press, 1987), pp. 134–51.

Clear, C. 'The Limits of Female Autonomy: Nuns in Nineteenth-Century Ireland', in M. Luddy and C. Murphy (eds), *Women Surviving: Studies in Irish Women's History in the Nineteenth and Twentieth Century* (Dublin: Poolbeg Press, 1989), pp. 15–50.

Clear, C. *Women of the House: Women's Household Work in Ireland, 1922–1961 Discourses, Experiences, Memories* (Dublin: Irish Academic Press, 2000).

Clifford, J. 'Diasporas', *Cultural Anthropology*, 9, 3 (1994), pp. 302–38.

Clear, C. *Routes, Travel and Translations in the Late Twentieth Century* (Cambridge, MA: Harvard University Press, 1997).

Cohen, R. *Frontiers of Identity, The British and the Others* (Essex: Longman, 1994).

Cohen, R. *Global Diasporas: An Introduction* (London: University College, London Press, 1997).

Collinge, W. J. *Historical Dictionary of Catholicism* (Maryland: Scarecrow Press, 1997).

Coman, P. *Catholics and the Welfare State* (London: Longman, 1977).

Connolly, L. 'The Women's Movement in Ireland, 1970–1995: A Social Movements Analysis', *Irish Journal of Feminist Studies*, 1, 1 (1996), pp. 43–77.

Connolly, L. *The Irish Women's Movement from Revolution to Devolution* (Hampshire and New York: Palgrave, 2002).

Connor, T. *The London Irish* (London: London Strategic Policy Unit, 1987).

Conway, S. *The Faraway Hills are Green: Voices of Irish Women in Canada*

(Ontario: Women's Press, 1992).

Coogan, T. P. *The I.R.A.* (London: Harper Collins, 1987).

Corcoran, M. 'Of Emigrants, 'Eirepreneurs' and Opportunists', *The Irish Reporter*, 13, 1 (1994), pp. 5–8.

Corcoran, M. 'Heroes of the Diaspora', in M. Peillon and E. Slater (eds), *Encounters with Modern Ireland, A Sociological Chronicle, 1995–6* (Dublin: Institute of Public Administration, 1998), pp. 135–43.

Corcoran, M. 'The Process of Migration and the Reinvention of Self: The Experiences of Returning Irish Emigrants', *Eire/Ireland*, Spring/Summer (2002), pp. 175–91.

Cotel, P. *A Catechism of the Vows for the Use of Religious* (London: Burns, Oates and Washbourne, 1926).

Cotterill, P. 'Interviewing Women: Issues of Friendship, Vulnerability and Power', *Women's Studies International Forum*, 15, 5/6 (1992), pp. 593–606.

Cruise, D. E. 'The Development of the Religious Orders' in G. A. Beck (ed.) *The English Catholics, 1850–1950* (London: Burns Oates, 1950), pp. 442–74.

Cullen, M. (ed.) *Girls Don't Do Honours: Irish Women in Education in the 19th and 20th Centuries* (Dublin: WEB, 1987).

Cullen, M. and Luddy, M. (eds), *Women, Power and Consciousness in 19th Century Ireland* (Dublin: Attic Press, 1995).

Cullen, M. and Luddy, M. (eds), *Female Activists, Irish Women and Change 1900–1960* (Wicklow: The Woodfield Press, 2001).

Curran, M. J. *'Across the Water'*, *A Guide for Young Irish People Going to Britain* (London: Irish Chaplaincy in Britain, 1995).

Curtin, C., Jackson, P., and O'Connor, B. (eds), *Gender in Irish Society* (Galway: Galway University Press, 1987).

Curtis, L. *Nothing But the Same Old Story* (Dublin: Information on Ireland, 1984).

Curtis, L., O'Brien, J., O'Keefe, J. and Keeting, C. *Hearts and Minds / Anam agus Intinn: the Cultural Life of London's Irish Community* (London: London Strategic Policy Unit, 1987).

Daly, M. E. 'Women in the Irish Workforce from Pre-Industrial to Modern Times', *Saothar*, 7 (1981), pp. 74–82.

Daly, M. E. '"Turn on the Tap": the State, Irish Women and Running Water', in M. G. Valiulis and M. O'Dowd (eds), *Women and Irish History* (Dublin: Wolfhound, 1997), pp. 206–19.

Daly, M. E. '"Oh, Kathleen Ni Houlihan, Your Way's a Thorny Way!" The Condition of Women in Twentieth-Century Ireland', in A. Bradley and M. G. Valiulis (eds), *Gender and Sexuality in Modern Ireland* (Massachusetts: University of Massachusetts, 1997), pp. 102–25.

Daniels, M. 'Exile or Opportunity? Irish Nurses and Wirral Midwives',

Irish Studies Review, 5, 4 (1993), pp. 4–8.

Danylewycz, M. *Taking the Veil: An Alternative to Marriage, Motherhood and Spinsterhood in Quebec, 1840–1920* (Ontario: McClelland & Stewart, 1987).

Darr, D. 'Change and Irish Identity', *Doctrine and Life*, 24, 1 (1974), pp. 3–16.

Davis, G. *The Irish in Britain, 1915–1914* (Dublin: Gill & Macmillan, 1991).

Delaney, E. *Demography, State and Society, Irish Migration to Britain, 1921–71* (Liverpool: Liverpool University Press, 2000).

De Rosa, P. *Vicars of Christ* (London: Bantam Press, 1988).

Desmond, H. *Religious Life in England and Wales, an Historical Background* (Herts: Signum Publications, 1982).

Diner, H. R. *Erin's Daughters in America, Irish Immigrant Women in the Nineteenth Century* (Baltimore, MA: John Hopkins University Press, 1983).

Donnelly Jnr, J. S. 'The Peak of Marianism in Ireland, 1930–60', in S. J. Brown and D. W. Miller (eds), *Piety and Power in Ireland, 1760–1960* (Notre Dame, IN: University of Notre Dame Press, 2000), pp. 252–83.

Douglas, M. *Purity And Danger, An Analysis of the Concepts of Pollution and Taboo* (London: Routledge 1991) (first published 1966).

Douglas, R., Harte, L. and O'Hara, J. *Drawing Conclusions, A Cartoon History of Anglo-Irish Relations, 1798–1998* (Belfast: Blackstaff Press, 1998).

duGay, P., Evans, J. and Redman, P. (eds) *Identity: A Reader* (London: Sage, 2000).

Dunaway, D. K. 'Method and Theory in the Oral Biography', *Oral History*, 20, 2 (1992), pp. 40–4.

Egan, K. and Tilki, M. *Limited Opportunities: Economic Disadvantage and Access to Housing for Single Irish Women* (London: Cara Irish Housing Agency, 1995).

Enloe, C. 'Religion and Ethnicity', in P. Sugar (ed.), *Ethnic Diversity and Conflict in Eastern Europe* (Santa Barbara, CA: ABC-Clio Press, 1980), pp. 347–71.

Fahey, T. 'Nuns in the Catholic Church in Ireland in the Nineteenth Century', in M. Cullen (ed.), *Girls Don't Do Honours: Irish Women in Education in the 19th and 20th Centuries* (Dublin: WEB, 1987), pp. 7–30.

Fanning, C. (ed.) *New Perspectives on the Irish Diaspora* (Carbondale, Southern Illinois: Southern Illinois University Press, 2000).

Farmer, D. H. *Oxford Dictionary of Saints* (Oxford: Oxford University Press, 4th edn, 1997).

Faubion, J. D. *Michel Foucault: Power, The Essential Works* (London: Penguin, 1994).

Fennell, D. *The Changing Face of Catholic Ireland* (London: Geoffrey

Chapman, 1968).

Ferriter, D. *The Transformation of Ireland, 1900–2000* (London: Profile Books, 2004).

Fielding, S. *Class and Ethnicity, Irish Catholics in England, 1880–1939* (Buckingham: Open University Press, 1993).

Finch, J. '"It's Great to Have Someone to Talk to": The Ethics and Politics of Interviewing Women', in C. Bell and H. Roberts (eds), *Social Researching: Politics, Problems, Practice* (London: Routledge and Kegan Paul, 1984), pp. 70–87.

Fitzpatrick, D. *Irish Emigration, 1801–1921* (Dublin: The Economic and Social History Society of Ireland, 1984).

Fitzpatrick, D. *Oceans of Consolation, Personal Accounts of Irish Migration to Australia* (Cork: Cork University Press, 1994).

Foucault, M. *Discipline and Punish. The Birth of the Prison* (Harmondsworth: Penguin, 1975).

Foucault, M. *The History of Sexuality, Volume I* (London: Penguin, 1976).

Fuller, L. *Irish Catholicism Since 1950: The Undoing of a Culture* (Dublin: Gill & Macmillan, 2002).

Gaffney, G. *Emigration to England, What You Should Know About It, Advice to Irish Girls* (Dublin: Irish Independent Newspapers, 1937).

Gelsthorpe, L. 'Responses to Martyn Hammersky's Paper on "Feminist Methodology"', *Sociology*, 26, 2 (1992), pp. 213–18.

Gilley, S. and Sheils, W. T. *A History of Religion in Britain: Practice and Belief from Pre-Roman Times to the Present* (Oxford: Blackwell, 1994).

Gilroy, P. *The Black Atlantic, Modernity and Double Consciousness* (London: Verso. 1993).

Gilroy, P. 'Diaspora and the Detours of Identity', in K. Woodward (ed.), *Identity and Difference* (London/Milton Keynes: Sage/Open University Press, 1997), pp. 299–346.

Gittens, A. *Modernity and Self-Identity, Self and Society in the Late Modern Age* (Cambridge: Polity, 1991)

Gmelch, G. 'The Readjustment of Return Migrants in Western Ireland', in R. King (ed.), *Return Migration and Regional Economic Problems* (London: Croom Helm, 1986), pp. 152–69.

Goffman, E. *The Presentation of Self in Everyday Life* (New York: Doubleday, 1959).

Goffman, E. *Asylums* (New York: Doubleday, 1961).

Good, A. 'Listening to my Grandmother: (Re)Connecting Nationalism and Feminism through Intellectual Biography', *Auto/Biography*, 4, 1/2 (1998), pp. 39–44.

Graham. C. and Kirkland, R. (eds) *Ireland and Cultural Theory, The Mechanics of Authenticity* (London: Macmillan, 1999).

Grant, J. (ed.) *Women, Migration and Empire* (Stoke-on-Trent: Trentham

Books, 1996).

Gray, B. '"The Home of our Mothers and our Birthright for Ages"? Nation, Diaspora and Irish Women', in M. Maynard and J. Purvis (eds), *New Frontiers in Women's Studies: Knowledge, Identity and Nationalism* (London: Taylor and Francis, 1996), pp. 164–88.

Gray, B. 'Accounts of Displacement – Irish Migrant Women in London', *Youth and Policy: The Journal of Critical Analysis*, 52, 2 (1996), pp. 22–9.

Gray, B. 'Irishness, A Global and Gendered Identity', *Irish Studies Review*, 16, 3 (1996), pp. 24–8.

Gray, B. 'Irish Women in London: National or Hybrid Diasporic Identities?', *National Women's Studies Association Journal*, 8, 1 (Spring, 1996), pp. 85–109.

Gray, B. 'Locations of Irishness: Irish Women's Accounts of National Identity' (Lancaster University: unpublished PhD thesis, 1997).

Gray, B. 'Unmasking Irishness: Irish Women, the Irish Nation and the Irish Diaspora', in J. MacLaughlin (ed.), *Location and Dislocation in Contemporary Irish Society, Emigration and Irish Identities* (Cork: Cork University Press, 1997), pp. 209–35.

Gray, B. 'Modes of National Belonging: Emigration and Irish National Identity', *Auto/Biography*, 4, 1/2 (1998), pp. 145–55.

Gray, B. 'Longings and Belongings – Gendered Spatialities of Irishness', *Irish Studies Review*, 7, 2 (1999), pp. 193–210.

Gray, B. 'From "Ethnicity" to "Diaspora": 1980s Emigration and "Multicultural" London', in A. Bielenberg (ed.), *The Irish Diaspora* (Essex: Longman, 2000), pp. 65–88.

Gray, B. 'Gendering the Irish Diaspora: Questions of Enrichment, Hybridization and Return', *Women's Studies International Forum*, 23, 2 (2000), pp. 167–85.

Gray, B. *Women and the Irish Diaspora* (London: Routledge, 2004).

Grele, R. J. 'Movement Without Aim: Methodological and Theoretical Problems in Oral History', in R. Perks and A. Thomson (eds), *The Oral History Reader* (London: Routledge, 1998), pp. 38–52.

Guinnaine, T. W. *The Vanishing Irish, Households, Migration and the Rural Economy in Ireland 1880–1914* (Princeton, NJ: Princeton University Press, 1997).

Gwynn, D. 'The Irish Immigration', in G. A. Beck (ed.), *The English Catholics 1850–1950* (London: Burns Oates, 1950), pp. 265–90.

Hall, S. 'Cultural Identity and Diaspora', in J. Rutherford (ed.), *Identity: Community, Culture, Difference* (London: Lawrence and Wishart, 1990), pp. 222–37.

Hall, S. 'Introduction: Who Needs Identity?', in S. Hall and P. duGay (eds), *Questions of Cultural Identity* (London: Sage, 1996), pp. 1–17.

Hall, S. and duGay, P. (eds) *Questions of Cultural Identity* (London: Sage,

1996).

Handley, J. E. *The Irish in Scotland, 1798–1845* (Cork: Cork University Press, 1943).

Handley, J. E. *The Irish in Modern Scotland* (Cork: Cork University Press, 1947).

Hannan, D. *Rural Exodus, A Study of the Forces Influencing the Large-Scale Migration of Irish Rural Youth* (London: Geoffrey Chapman, 1970).

Harding, S. (ed.) *Feminism and Methodology* (Milton Keynes: Open University Press, 1987).

Harrison, L. and Carr Hill, R. *Alcohol and Disadvantage Amongst the Irish in England* (London: FIS, 1992).

Hastings, A. H. *Modern Catholicism, Vatican II and After* (London: SPCK, 1991).

Hazelkorn, E. *Irish Immigrants Today* (London: Polytechnic of North London Press, 1990).

Henagan, J. *Father Damien, Exemplar of Noble Deeds* (Dublin: Clonmore & Reynolds, 1954).

Hesse-Biber, S., Gilmartin, C. and Lydenberg, R. (eds), *Feminist Approaches to Theory and Methodology: An Interdisciplinary Reader* (New York: Oxford University Press, 1999).

Hickman, M. J. *Religion, Class and Identity: The State, the Catholic Church and the Education of the Irish in Britain* (Hampshire: Avebury Press, 1995).

Hickman, M. J. and Smyth, A. *Feminist Review Special Edition, The Irish Issue: The British Question*, 50, 2 (1995).

Hickman, M. J. and Walter, B. 'Deconstructing Whiteness: Irish Women in Britain', *Feminist Review*, 50, 2 (1995), pp. 5–19.

Hickman, M. J. *The Irish Community in Britain: Myth or Reality?* (London: University of North London Press, 1996).

Hickman, M. J. and Walter, B. *Discrimination and the Irish Community in Britain: A Report of Research Undertaken for the Commission for Racial Equality* (London: Commission for Racial Equality, 1997).

Hill, M. *A Sociological Yearbook of Religion in Britain*, 5 (London: SCM Press, 1972).

Hillyard, P. *Suspect Community: People's Experience of the Prevention of Terrorism Act in Britain* (London: Pluto, 1993).

Hoff, J. and Coulter, M. (eds), *Irish Women's Voices Past and Present* (Bloomington and Indianapolis, IN: Indiana University Press, 1995).

Hogan, E. M. *The Irish Missionary Movement: A Historical Survey, 1830–1980* (Dublin: Gill & Macmillan, 1990).

Holland, J. and Blair, M. (eds) *Debates and Issues in Feminist Research and Pedagogy* (Milton Keynes: Open University Press, 1995).

Holm, J. *Women in Religion* (London: Pinter, 1994).

Holmes, C. (ed.), *Immigrants and Minorities in British Society* (London: George Allen & Unwin, 1978).

Holmes, C. *John Bull's Island: Immigration and British Society, 1871–1971* (Hampshire: Macmillan, 1988).

Holmes, C. *A Tolerant Country? Immigrants, Refugees and Minorities in Britain* (London: Faber & Faber, 1991).

Holohan, A. *Working Lives, The Irish in Britain* (Middlesex: The Irish Post, 1995).

Hornsby-Smith, M. P. *Roman Catholics in England, Studies in Social Structure Since the Second World War* (Cambridge: Cambridge University Press, 1987).

Hoy, S. and MacCurtain, M. *From Dublin to New Orleans: The Journey of Nora and Alice* (Dublin: Attic Press, 1994).

Hoy, S. 'The Journey Out: the Recruitment and Emigration of Irish Religious Women to the United States, 1812–1914', *Journal of Women's History*, 6, 4 (1995), pp. 64–98.

Hug, C. *The Politics of Sexual Morality in Ireland* (Hampshire: Macmillan Press, 1999).

Hulme, K. *The Nun's Story* (London: Muller, 1977) (first published 1956).

Ignatiev, N. *How the Irish Became White* (New York: Routledge, 1995).

Inglis, T. 'Decline in Numbers of Priests and Religious in Ireland: Report on Recent Surveys', *Doctrine and Life*, 30, 2 (1979), pp. 79–98.

Inglis, T. *Moral Monopoly, The Rise and Fall of the Catholic Church in Modern Ireland* (Dublin: University College Dublin Press, 1998) (first published 1987).

Inglis, T. *Truth, Power and Lies, Irish Society and the Case of the Kerry Babies* (Dublin: University College Dublin Press, 2003)

Jackson, J. A. *The Irish in Britain* (London: Routledge & Kegan Paul, 1963).

Jackson, P. (eds), *Race and Racism: Essays in Social Geography* (London: Allen & Unwin, 1987).

Kaiser, R. B. *Inside the Council, The Story of Vatican II* (London: Burns & Oates, 1963).

Kanya-Forstner, M. 'Defining Womanhood: Irish Women and the Catholic Church in Victorian Liverpool', in D. MacRaild (ed.), *The Great Famine and Beyond, Irish Migrants in Britain in the Nineteenth and Twentieth Centuries* (Dublin: Irish Academic Press, 2000), pp. 168–88.

Keaney, M. *They Brought the Good News, Modern Irish Missionaries* (Dublin: Veritas, 1980).

Kearney, R. (ed.), *Migrations, The Irish at Home and Abroad* (Dublin: Wolfhound Press, 1990).

Kells, M. *Ethnic Identity Amongst Young Irish Middle Class Migrants in London* (London: University of North London Press, 1995).

Kells, M. 'Ethnicity in the 1990s: Irish Immigration in London', in

U. Kockel (ed.), *Landscape, Heritage and Identity, Case Studies in Irish Ethnography* (Liverpool: Liverpool University Press, 1995), pp. 223–35.

Kells, M. '"I'm Myself and Nobody Else": Gender and Ethnicity among Young Middle-Class Irish Women in London', in P. O'Sullivan (ed.), *Irish Women and Irish Migration* (London: Leicester University Press, 1995), pp. 201–34.

Kells, M. 'Ethnicity and Individuality, Irish Migrants in London, 1980s–1990s' (LSE, University of London: unpublished PhD thesis, 2000).

Kelly, K. and NicGiolla Choille, T. *Emigration Matters for Women* (Dublin: Attic Press, 1990).

Kelly, K. and NicGiolla Choille, T. 'Listening and Learning: Experiences in an Emigrant Advice Agency', in P. O'Sullivan (ed.), *Irish Women and Irish Migration* (London: Leicester University Press, 1995), pp. 168–91.

Kennedy, R. E. *The Irish: Emigration, Marriage and Fertility* (Berkeley California: University of California Press, 1973).

Kenny, K. *The American Irish, A History* (Harlow: Pearson Education, 2000).

Keogh, D. *Twentieth-Century Ireland: Nation and State* (Dublin: Gill & Macmillan, 1994).

Kestelman, E. *The Irish Women's Project* (Islington: Islington Women's Counselling Centre, 1995).

King, R., Shuttleworth, I. and Strachan, A. 'The Irish in Coventry: the Social Geography of a Relict Community', *Irish Geography*, 22, 2 (1989), pp. 64–78.

King, R. (ed.), *Contemporary Irish Migration* (Dublin: Geographical Society of Ireland, Special Publication, 6, 1991).

King, R. and O'Connor, H. 'Migration and Gender, Irish Women in Leicester', *Geography*, 81, 4 (1996), pp. 311–25.

King, U. *Religion and Gender* (Oxford: Blackwell, 1995).

Kirby, P. *Is Irish Catholicism Dying?* (Cork: Mercier Press, 1984).

Kockel, U. (ed.), *Landscape, Heritage and Identity, Case Studies in Irish Ethnography* (Liverpool: Liverpool University Press, 1995).

Kofman, E., Phizacklea, A., Raghuram, P. and Sales, R. *Gender and International Migration in Europe, Employment, Welfare and Politics* (London: Routledge, 2000).

Kondo, D. K. *Crafting Selves: Power, Gender, and Discourses of Identity in a Japanese Workplace* (Chicago, IL: Chicago University Press, 1990).

Kowarzik, U. *Developing a Community Response: The Service Needs of the Irish Community in Britain* (London: AGIY and FIS, 1994).

Kowarzik, U. *Standardised Information Systems for Irish Service Providers, Annual Report* (London: AGIY and FIS, 1996).

Lambert, S. 'Female Emigration from Post-Independent Ireland: An Oral

History of Irish Women in Lancaster, 1922–60' (University of Lancaster: unpublished PhD thesis, 1997).

Lambert, S. *Irish Women in Lancashire 1922–1960: Their Story* (Lancashire: Centre for North-West Regional Studies, University of Lancaster, 2001).

Larkin, E. 'The Devotional Revolution in Ireland, 1850–75', *American Historical Review*, 77, 3 (1972), pp. 625–52.

Lawless, G. *Augustine of Hippo and his Monastic Rule* (Oxford: Clarendon Press, 1987).

Lee, J. J. 'Women and the Church since the Famine', in M. MacCurtain and D. O'Corrain (eds), *Women in Irish Society, The Historical Dimension* (Dublin: Arlen House, 1978), pp. 37–57.

Lee, J. J. (ed.), *Ireland 1945–70* (Dublin: Gill and Macmillan, 1979).

Lee, J. J. *Ireland, 1912–1985* (Cambridge: Cambridge University Press, 1989).

Lee, J. J. 'Emigration: A Contemporary Perspective', in R. Kearney (ed.), *Migrations, The Irish at Home and Abroad* (Dublin: Wolfhound Press, 1990), pp. 33–44.

Lees, L. H. *Exiles of Erin, Irish Migrants in Victorian London* (Manchester: Manchester University Press, 1979).

Lennon, J., Ryan, L., MacGreil, M., Drake, N. and Perera, C. (1972) 'Survey of Catholic Clergy and Religious Personnel', *Irish Journal of Sociology*, 1, 1 (1972), pp. 137–234.

Lennon, M. 'Off the Boat', *Spare Rib*, 94 (1980), pp. 52–5.

Lennon, M. 'A Haemorrhage from the Land: a History of Irish Women's Emigration to Britain', *Spare Rib*, 118 (1982), pp. 38–9.

Lennon, M., McAdam, M. and O'Brien, J. *Across the Water: Irish Women's Lives in Britain* (London: Virago, 1988).

Lentin, R. 'Feminist Research Methodologies – A Separate Paradigm? Notes for a Debate', *Irish Journal of Sociology*, 3 (1993), pp. 119–38.

Letford, L. and Pooley, C. 'Geographies of Migration and Religion: Irish Women in Mid-Nineteenth Century Liverpool', in P. O'Sullivan (ed.), *Irish Women and Irish Migration* (London: Leicester University Press, 1995), pp. 89–112.

Lloyd, C. *The Irish Community in Britain: Discrimination, Disadvantage and Racism, an Annotated Bibliography* (London: University of North London Press, 1995).

Lloyd, D. 'Making Sense of the Dispersal', *Irish Reporter*, 13, 1 (1994), pp. 3–4.

Loudon, M. *Unveiled, Nuns Talking* (London: Vintage, 1992).

Lovell, T. 'Thinking Feminism With and Against Bourdieu', *Feminist Theory*, 1, 1 (2000), pp. 11–32.

Lowe, W. J. *The Irish in Mid-Victorian Lancashire: The Shaping of a Working-*

Class Community (New York: Peter Lang, 1989).

Luddy, M. and Murphy, C. (eds) *Women Surviving: Studies in Irish Women's History in the Nineteenth and Twentieth Centuries* (Dublin: Poolbeg Press, 1989).

Lynch, A. *The Irish in Exile: Stories of Emigration* (London: Ethnic Communities Oral History Project, 1988).

McAdam, G. 'Willing Women and the Rise of Convents in Nineteenth-Century England', *Women's History Review*, 8, 3 (1999), pp. 411–41.

McAdam, M. 'Hidden from History', *The Irish Reporter*, 13, 1 (1994), pp. 12–13.

McBrien, R. P. *Harper Collins Encyclopedia of Catholicism* (San Francisco, CA: Harper Collins, 1995).

McCall, L. 'Does Gender Fit? Bourdieu, Feminism and Conceptions of Social Order', *Theory and Society*, 21, 6 (1992), pp. 837–67.

McCarthy, P. *McCarthy's Bar* (London: Hodder & Stoughton, 2000).

MacCurtain, M. 'Women – Irish Style', *Doctrine and Life*, 24, 4 (1974), pp. 182–97.

MacCurtain, M. 'Towards an Appraisal of the Religious Image of Women', *The Crane Bag: Images of the Irish Woman*, 4, 1 (1980), pp. 26–30.

MacCurtain, M. 'Late in the Field: Catholic Sisters in Twentieth-Century Ireland and the New Religious History', in M. O'Dowd and S. Wichert (eds), *Chattel, Servant or Citizen, Women's Status in Church, State and Society* (Belfast: Institute of Irish Studies, Queen's University Press, 1995), pp. 34–44.

MacCurtain, M. 'Godly Burden, Catholic Sisterhoods in Twentieth Century Ireland', in A. Bradley and M. G. Valiulis (eds), *Gender and Sexuality in Modern Ireland* (Amherst, Massachusetts: University of Massachusetts, 1997), pp. 245–56.

McDevitt, E. Comment, *The Furrow*, 21, 1 (1970), p. 63.

McGrath, F. 'The Economic, Social and Cultural Impacts of Return Migration to Achill Island', in R. King (ed.), *Contemporary Irish Migration* (Dublin: Trinity College Dublin, Geographical Society of Ireland Special Publications, 6, 1991), pp. 55–69.

McGrath, M. S. *These Women? Women Religious in the History of Australia, The Sisters of Mercy, Parramatta, 1888–1988* (New South Wales: New South Wales University Press, 1990).

McHale, J. *On the Wing: The Story of the Pittsburgh Sisters of Mercy, 1843–1968* (New York: Seabury Press, 1980).

McKenna, Y. 'Entering Religious Life, Claiming Subjectivity: Irish Nuns, 1930s–1960s', *Women's History Review*, Vol 15, No. 2, April 2006, pp. 189–211.

McKenna, Y. 'A Gendered Revolution: Vatican II and Irish Women Religious', *Irish Feminist Review*, 1, 1 (2006), pp. 75–93.

McKenna, Y. 'Forgotten Migrants: Irish Women Religious in England, 1930s–1960s', *International Journal of Population Geography*, 9 (2003), pp. 295–308.

McKenna, Y. '"Sisterhood"? Exploring Power Relations in the Collection of Oral Histories', *Oral History*, 31, 1 (2003), pp. 65–72.

MacLaughlin, J. 'Social Characteristics and Destinations of Recent Emigrants from Selected Regions in the West of Ireland', *Geoforum*, 22, 3 (1991), pp. 319–31.

MacLaughlin, J. *Ireland: The Emigrant Nursery and the World Economy* (Cork: Cork University Press, 1994).

MacLaughlin, J. *Historical and Recent Irish Emigration* (London: University of North London Press, 1994).

MacLaughlin, J. 'Outwardly Mobile: the Sanitisation of Emigration', *Irish Reporter*, 13, 1 (1994), pp. 9–11.

MacLaughlin, J. (ed.) *Location and Dislocation in Contemporary Irish Society, Emigration and Irish Identities* (Cork: Cork University Press, 1997).

MacLaughlin, J. '"Pestilence on their Backs, Famine in their Stomachs": The Racial Construction of Irishness and the Irish in Victorian Britain', in C. Graham and R. Kirkland (eds), *Ireland and Cultural Theory, The Mechanics of Authenticity* (London: Macmillan, 1999), pp. 50–76.

McNamara, J. A. K. *Sisters in Arms: Catholic Nuns through Two Millennia* (Cambridge, MA: Harvard University Press, 1996).

MacRaild, D. *Culture, Conflict and Migration: The Irish in Victorian Cumbria* (Liverpool: Liverpool University Press, 1998).

MacRaild, D. *Irish Migrants in Modern Britain, 1750–1922* (Hampshire: Macmillan, 1999).

MacRaild, D. (ed.) *The Great Famine and Beyond, Irish Migrants in Britain in the Nineteenth and Twentieth Centuries* (Dublin: Irish Academic Press, 2000).

Magray, M. P. *The Transforming Power of the Nuns: Women, Religion and Cultural Change in Ireland, 1750–1900* (New York: Oxford University Press, 1998).

Mahon, E. 'The Impasse of Irish Feminism: Women's Rights and Catholicism in Ireland', *New Left Review*, 166, 6 (1987), pp. 53–77.

Maguire, M. *The Irish in Ealing: an Invisible Community* (Brent: Brent Irish Advisory Service, 1989).

Marks, L. *Working Wives and Working Mothers, A Comparative Study of Irish and East European Jewish Married Women's Work and Motherhood in East London, 1870–1914* (London: Polytechnic of North London Press, 1990).

Marks, L. '"The Luckless Waifs and Strays of Humanity": Irish and Jewish Immigrant Unwed Mothers in London, 1870–1939', *Twentieth Century British History*, 3, 2 (1992), pp. 113–37.

Martin, A. K. 'The Practice of Identity and an Irish Sense of Place',

Gender, Place and Culture, A Journal of Feminist Geography, 4, 1 (1997), pp. 89–113.

Mathew, D. *Catholicism in England, 1535–1935: Portrait of a Minority, its Cultures and Tradition* (London: Catholic Book Club, 1938).

Maynard, M. and Purvis, J. (eds) *Researching Women's Lives from a Feminist Perspective* (London: Taylor & Francis, 1994).

Maynard, M. and Purvis, J. (eds), *New Frontiers in Women's Studies: Knowledge, Identity and Nationalism* (London: Taylor & Francis, 1996).

Maynes, P. 'Counselling Irish Women in Britain', *Women's Health Newsletter*, February (1995), pp. 4–6.

Maynes, P. 'Irish Women in Britain', in R. Perkins, Z. Nadirshaw, J. Copperman and C. Andrews (eds), *Women in Context, Good Practice in Mental Health Services for Women* (London: Good Practices in Mental Health, 1996), pp. 43–6.

Meaney, G. 'Sex and Nation: Women in Irish Culture and Politics', in A. Smyth (ed.), *Irish Women's Studies Reader* (Dublin: Attic Press, 1993), pp. 230–44.

Midgley, C. (ed.), *Gender and Imperialism* (Manchester: Manchester University Press, 1998).

Miller, K. *Emigrants and Exiles: Ireland and the Irish Exodus to North America* (Oxford: Oxford University Press, 1985).

Minister, K. (1991) 'A Feminist Frame for the Oral History Interview', in S. Berger Gluck and D. Patai (eds) *Women's Words: The Feminist Practice of Oral History* (London: Routledge, 1991), pp. 27–41.

Moi, T. 'Appropriating Bourdieu: Feminist Theory and Pierre Bourdieu's Sociology of Culture', *New Literary History*, 22, 4 (1991), pp. 1017–49.

Moorhouse, G. *Against All Reason* (Kent: Sceptre, 1986) (first published 1969).

Murphy, C. C. *An Introduction to Christian Feminism* (Dublin: Dominican Publications, 1994).

Murphy, J. N. *Terra Incognita, or the Convents of the United Kingdom* (London: Burns & Oates, 1876) (first published 1873).

Murphy, M. 'The Fionnuala Factor: Irish Sibling Emigration at the Turn of the Century', in A. Bradley and M. G. Valiulis (eds), *Gender and Sexuality in Modern Ireland* (Amherst, Massachusetts: University of Massachusetts, 1997), pp. 85–101.

National Enconomic and Social Council, *The Economic and Social Implications of Emigration* (Dublin, NESC, 1991).

NiLaoire, C. 'Gender Issues in Irish Rural Out-Migration', in P. Boyle and K. Halfacree (eds), *Migration and Gender in the Developed World* (London: Routledge, 1999), pp. 223–37.

Nolan, J. A. *Ourselves Alone, Women's Emigration from Ireland, 1885–1920* (Lexington, Kentucky: University Press of Kentucky, 1989).

Oakley, A. 'Interviewing Women: a Contradiction in Terms?', in H. Roberts (ed.), *Doing Feminist Research* (London: Routledge & Kegan Paul, 1981), pp. 30–61.

Oakley, A. *Experiments in Knowing, Gender and Method in the Social Sciences* (Cambridge: Polity Press, 2000).

O'Brien, J. and Travers, P. (eds), *The Irish Emigrant Experience in Australia* (Dublin: Poolbeg Press, 1991).

O'Brien, J. A. *The Vanishing Irish, The Enigma of the Modern World* (London: W. H. Allen, 1954).

O'Brien, O. *Assessing the Impact of HIV on the Irish Community in Britain: An Examination of Current Issues and Service Provision* (London: Positively Irish Action on Aids, 1993).

O'Brien, S. 'Terra Incognita: the Nun in Nineteenth Century England', *Past and Present*, 121 (1988), pp. 123–8.

O'Brien, S. 'Lay-Sisters and Good Mothers: Working-Class Women in English Convents, 1840–1910', in W. J. Sheils and D. Woods (eds), *Women in the Church, Studies in Church History* (Oxford: Basil Blackwell, 1990), pp. 453–65.

O'Carroll, I. *Models for Movers: Irish Women's Emigration to America* (Dublin: Attic Press, 1990).

O'Connor, P. *Emerging Voices, Women in Contemporary Irish Society* (Dublin: Institute of Public Administration, 1998).

O'Donoghue, H. 'Women's Congregations 25 Years after Vatican II', *Religious Life Review*, 30, 3 (1991), pp. 115–23.

O'Dowd, L. 'Church, State and Women: the Aftermath of Partition', in C. Curtin, P. Jackson, and B. O'Connor (eds), *Gender in Irish Society* (Galway: Galway University Press, 1987), pp. 3–36.

O'Dowd, M. and Wichert, S. (eds), *Chattel, Servant or Citizen, Women's Status in Church, State and Society* (Belfast: Institute of Irish Studies, 1995).

Offen, K., Pierson, R. and Rendall, J. (eds), *Writing Women's History, International Perspectives* (London: Macmillan, 1991).

O'Flynn, E. *Under Piccadilly's Neon: Irish and Homeless in London* (London: Piccadilly Advice Centre, 1991).

O'Flynn, J. *Identity Crisis: Access to Social Security and ID Checks* (London: AGIY, 1993).

O'Flynn, J. *Racial Attacks and Harassment of Irish People* (London: AGIY, n.d.)

Ó Gráda, C. *On Two Aspects of Post-War Irish Emigration* (London: Centre for Economic Policy Research, 1985).

Gráda, C. *Ireland Before and After the Famine: An Exploration in Economic History, 1800–1925* (Manchester: Manchester University Press, 1993).

O'Grady, A. *Irish Migration to London in the 1940s and 1950s* (London:

Polytechnic of North London Press, 1988).

Olson, K. and Shopes, L. 'Crossing Boundaries, Building Bridges: Doing Oral History among Working-Class Women and Men', in S. Berger Gluck and D. Patai (eds), *Women's Words: The Feminist Practice of Oral History* (London: Routledge, 1991), pp. 189–204.

Örsy, L. M. *Open to the Spirit: Religious Life after Vatican II* (London: Geoffrey Chapman, 1968).

O'Sullivan, P. *Terrain and Tactics* (London: Greenwood Press, 1991).

O'Sullivan, P. (ed.), *Patterns of Migration, Volume 1, The Irish World Wide Series* (Leicester: Leicester University Press, 1992).

O'Sullivan, P. (ed.), *The Irish in the New Communities, Volume 2, The Irish World Wide Series* (Leicester: Leicester University Press, 1992).

O'Sullivan, P. (ed.), *The Creative Migrant, Volume 3, The Irish World Wide Series* (Leicester: Leicester University Press, 1994).

O'Sullivan, P. 'Picturing Ireland', *Irish Studies Review*, 12, 3 (1995), pp. 42–4.

O'Sullivan, P. (ed.), *Irish Women and Irish Migration, Volume 4, The Irish World Wide Series* (Leicester: Leicester University Press, 1995).

O'Sullivan, P. (ed.), *Religion and Identity, Volume 5, The Irish World Wide Series* (Leicester: Leicester University Press, 1996).

O'Sullivan, P. (ed.), *The Meaning of the Famine, Volume 6, The Irish World Wide Series* (Leicester: Leicester University Press, 1997).

O'Sullivan, P. Review article of R. H. Bayor and T. J. Meagher (eds), *The New York Irish, Irish Studies Review*, 6, 1 (1998), pp. 82–4.

Passerini, L. 'Work Ideology and Consensus under Italian Fascism', *History Workshop Journal*, 8 (1979), pp. 84–92.

Patai, D. 'U.S. Academics and Third World Women: Is Ethical Research Possible?', in S. Berger Gluck and D. Patai (eds), *Women's Words: The Feminist Practice of Oral History* (London: Routledge, 1991), pp. 137–53.

Paul, K. *Whitewashing Britain: Race and Citizenship in the Post-War Era* (New York: Cornell University Press, 1997).

Pearson, M., Madden, M. and Greenslade, L. *Generations of an Invisible Minority, Occasional Papers in Irish Studies No. 2* (Liverpool: The Institute of Irish Studies, University of Liverpool, 1991).

Peillon, M. and Slater, E. (eds), *Encounters with Modern Ireland, A Sociological Chronicle, 1995–6* (Dublin: Institute of Public Administration, 1998).

Perkins, R., Nadirshaw, Z., Copperman, J. and Andrews, C. (eds), *Women in Context: Good Practice in Mental Health Services for Women* (London: Good Practices in Mental Health, 1996).

Perks, R. and Thomson, A. (eds), *The Oral History Reader* (London: Routledge, 1998).

Plummer, K. *Documents of Life: An Introduction to the Problems and*

Literature of the Humanistic Method (London: George Allen & Unwin, 1983).

Pooley, C. G. 'From Londonderry to London: Identity and Sense of Place for a Protestant Northern Irish Woman in the 1930s', in D. MacRaild (ed.), *The Great Famine and Beyond, Irish Migrants in Britain in the Nineteenth and Twentieth Centuries* (Dublin: Irish Academic Press, 2000), pp. 189–213.

Poovey, M. *Making a Social Body, British Cultural Formation, 1830–1864* (Chicago, IL: University of Chicago Press, 1995).

Portelli, A. 'The Peculiarities of Oral History', *History Workshop*, 12 (1981), pp. 96–107.

Portelli, A. *The Death of Luigi Tragtulli and Other Stories, Form and Meaning of Oral History* (New York: State University of New York Press, 1991).

Portelli, A. *The Battle of Valle Giulia, Oral History and the Art of Dialogue* (Wisconsin: University of Wisconsin Press, 1997).

Probyn, E. *Outside Belongings* (New York: Routledge, 1996).

Reinharz, S. *Feminist Methods in Social Research* (Oxford: Oxford University Press, 1992).

Richardson, J. G. (ed.) *Handbook of Theory and Research for the Sociology of Education* (New York: Greenwood Press, 1983).

Robbins, D. *Bourdieu and Culture* (London: Sage, 2000).

Roberts, E. *A Woman's Place, An Oral History of Working-Class Women 1890–1940* (Oxford: Basil Blackwell, 1984).

Roberts, E. *Women and Families, An Oral History 1940–1970* (Oxford: Blackwell, 1995).

Roberts, H. (ed.), *Doing Feminist Research* (London: Routledge & Kegan Paul, 1981).

Rossiter, A. 'Bringing the Margins into the Centre: A Review of Aspects of Irish Women's Emigration', in A. Smyth (ed.), *Irish Women's Studies Reader* (Dublin: Attic Press, 1993), pp. 177–202.

Rossiter, A. 'In Search of Mary's Past: Placing Nineteenth-Century Irish Immigrant Women in British Feminist History', in J. Grant (ed.), *Women, Migration and Empire* (Stoke-on-Trent: Trentham Books, 1996), pp. 1–29.

Ruether, R. R. (ed.) *Religion and Sexism: Images of Women in the Jewish and Christian Traditions* (New York: Simon & Schuster, 1974).

Rutherford, J. (ed.), *Identity: Community, Culture, Difference* (London: Lawrence & Wishart, 1990).

Ryan, L. 'Irish Emigration to Britain since World War II', in R. Kearney (ed.), *Migrations, The Irish at Home and Abroad* (Dublin: Wolfhound Press, 1990), pp. 45–68.

Ryan, L. 'Irish Female Emigration in the 1930s: Transgressing Space and Culture', *Gender, Place and Culture*, 8, 3 (2001), pp. 271–82.

Safran, W. 'Diasporas in Modern Societies', *Diaspora*, 1, 1 (1991), pp. 83–99.

Said, E. W. *Orientalism, Western Conceptions of the Orient* (London: Penguin, 1978).

Sangster, J. 'Telling our Stories: Feminist Debates and the Use of Oral History', *Women's History Review*, 3, 1 (1994), pp. 5–28.

Scott, G. *The R.C.'s: A Report on Roman Catholics in Britain Today* (London: Hutchinson, 1967).

Scott, J. W. 'The Evidence of Experience', *Critical Inquiry*, 178, 3 (1991), pp. 773–97.

Sheils, W. J. and Woods, D. (eds), *Women in the Church, Studies in Church History* (Oxford: Basil Blackwell, 1990).

Shepherd, V., Brereton, B. and Bailey, B. (eds), *Engendering History: Caribbean Women in Historical Perspective* (Kingston: Ian Randle, 1995).

Skeggs, B. (ed.), *Feminist Cultural Theory: Process and Production* (Manchester: Manchester University Press, 1995).

Skeggs, B. *Formations of Class and Gender, Becoming Respectable* (London: Sage, 1997).

Smith, A. D. *The Ethnic Origins of Nations* (Oxford: Blackwell, 1986).

Smith, D. *The Everyday World as Problematic, A Feminist Sociology* (Milton Keynes: Open University Press, 1987).

Smyth. A. (ed.), *Irish Women's Studies Reader* (Dublin: Attic Press, 1993).

Smyth, E. 'Labour Market Structures and Women's Employment in the Republic of Ireland', in A. Byrne and M. Leonard (eds), *Women and Irish Society, A Sociological Reader* (Belfast: Beyond the Pale, 1997), pp. 63–80.

Stacey, J. 'Can There Be a Feminist Ethnography?', in S. Berger Gluck and D. Patai (eds), *Women's Words: The Feminist Practice of Oral History* (London: Routledge, 1991), pp. 111–19.

Stacpoole, A. *Vatican II By Those Who Were There* (London: Geoffrey Chapman, 1986).

Stanley, L. *Feminist Praxis: Research, Theory and Epistemology in Feminist Sociology* (London: Routledge 1990).

Stanley, L. and Wise, S. *Breaking Out: Feminist Consciousness and Feminist Research* (London: Routledge & Kegan Paul, 1983).

Stanley, L. and Wise, S. *Breaking Out Again: Feminist Ontology and Epistemology* (London: Routledge, 1993).

Steele, F. M. *The Convents of Great Britain and Ireland* (London: Sands & Co, 1901).

Sugar, P. (ed.) *Ethnic Diversity and Conflict in Eastern Europe* (Santa Barbara, CA: ABC-Clio Press, 1980).

Summerfield, P. *Reconstructing Women's Wartime Lives, Discourse and Subjectivity in Oral Histories of the Second World War* (Manchester: Manchester University Press, 1998).

Swift, R. and Gilley, S. (eds), *The Irish in the Victorian City* (London: Croom Helm, 1985).

Swift, R. and Gilley, S. (eds), *The Irish in Britain, 1815–1939* (London: Pinter, 1989).

Swift, R. and Gilley, S. (eds), *The Irish in Victorian Britain, The Local Dimension* (Dublin: Four Courts Press, 1999).

Tajfel, H. and Turner, J. 'An Integrative Theory of Inter-Group Conflict', in W. G. Austin and S. Worchel (eds), *The Social Psychology of Intergroup Relations* (Belmont: Wadsworth, 1979), pp. 33–47.

Taylor, S. *Smalltown Boys and Girls: Emigrant Irish Youth in London* (London: Polytechnic of North London Press, 1988).

Thompson, P. *The Voice of the Past, Oral History* (Oxford: Oxford University Press, 1988) (first published 1978).

Tranter, J. 'The Irish Dimension of an Australian Religious Sisterhood: the Sisters of Saint Joseph', in P. O'Sullivan (ed.), *Religion and Identity* (Leicester: Leicester University Press, 2000), pp. 234–55.

Travers, P. '"There Was Nothing for Me There": Irish Female Emigration, 1922–71', in P. O'Sullivan (ed.), *Irish Women and Irish Migration* (Leicester: Leicester University Press, 1995), pp. 146–67.

Turnbull, A. 'Collaboration and Censorship in the Oral History Interview', *International Journal of Social Research Methodology*, 3, 1 (2000), pp. 15–34.

Valiulis, M. G. 'Power, Gender, and Identity in the Irish Free State', in J. Hoff and M. Coulter (eds), *Irish Women's Voices Past and Present* (Bloomington and Indianapolis, IN: Indiana University Press, 1995), pp. 117–36.

Valiulis, M. G. 'Neither Feminist nor Flapper: The Ecclesiastical Construction of the Ideal Irish Woman', in M. O'Dowd and S. Wichert (eds), *Chattel, Servant or Citizen, Women's Status in Church, State and Society* (Belfast: Institute of Irish Studies, Queen's University Belfast 1995), pp. 168–78.

Valiulis, M. G. 'Engendering Citizenship: Women's Relationship to the State in Ireland and the United States in the Post-Suffrage Period', in M. G. Valiulis and M. O'Dowd (eds), *Women and Irish History* (Dublin: Wolfhound, 1997), pp. 159–72.

Valiulis, M. G. and O'Dowd, M. (eds), *Women and Irish History* (Dublin: Wolfhound. 1997).

Walby, S. 'Is Citizenship Gendered?', *Sociology*, 28, 2 (1990), pp. 379–95.

Wall, R. *Leading Lives, Irish Women in Britain* (Dublin: Attic Press, 1991).

Wallace, R. A. 'New Roles for Women in the Catholic Church', in H. R. Ebaugh (ed.), *Religion and the Social Order, New Developments in Theory and Practice*, Volume II (Greenwich, Connecticut: JAI Press, 1991) pp. 123–36.

Walls, P. *Researching Irish Mental Health: Issues and Evidence; A Study of the Mental Health of the Irish Community in Haringey* (London: Muintearas, Irish Mental Health Group 1996).

Walsh, B. *Roman Catholic Nuns in England and Wales, 1800–1937 A Social History* (Dublind: Irish Academic Press, 2002).

Walsh, J. A. *To Go or Not to Go: The Migration Intentions of Leaving Certificate Students* (Dublin: Carysfort College, Department of Geography, 1984).

Walter, B. 'Time Space Patterns of Second-Wave Irish Migration into Two British Towns', *Transactions of the Institute of British Geographers*, 5, 3 (1980), pp. 297–317.

Walter, B. 'Tradition and Ethnic Interaction: Second-Wave Irish Settlement in Luton and Bolton', in C. Clarke, D. Ley and C. Peach (eds), *Geography and Ethnic Pluralism* (London: Allen & Unwin, 1984), pp. 258–83.

Walter, B. *Irish Women in London* (London: London Strategic Policy Unit, 1988).

Walter, B. *Irish Women in London, The Ealing Dimension* (London: London Borough of Ealing Women's Unit, 1989).

Walter, B. *Gender and Irish Migration to Britain* (Cambridge: Anglia Working Paper 4, 1989).

Walter, B. 'Gender and Recent Migration to Britain', in R. King (ed.), *Contemporary Irish Migration* (Dublin: Geographical Society of Ireland, Special Publication no. 6, 1991), pp. 11–20.

Walter, B. 'Irishness, Gender and Place', *Environment and Planning, D: Society and Space*, 13 (1995), pp. 35–50.

Walter, B. 'Contemporary Irish Settlement in London: Women's Worlds, Men's Worlds', in J. MacLaughlin (ed.), *Location and Dislocation in Contemporary Irish Society, Emigration and Irish Identities* (Cork: Cork University Press, 1997), pp. 61–93.

Walter, B. 'Gendered Irishness in Britain: Changing Constructions', in C. Graham and R. Kirkland (eds), *Ireland and Cultural Theory, The Mechanics of Authenticity* (London: Macmillan, 1999), pp. 77–98.

Walter, B. 'Inside and Outside the Pale: Diaspora Experiences of Irish Women', in P. Boyle and K. Halfacree (eds), *Migration and Gender in the Developed World* (London: Routledge, 1999), pp. 310–24.

Walter, B. *Outsiders Inside, Whiteness, Place and Irish Women* (London: Routledge, 2001).

Walter, B. 'Irish Immigrants and Irish Communities Abroad: A Study of Existing Sources of Information and Analysis', research undertaken for the Task Force on Policy Regarding Emigration (Dublin: Department of Foreign Affairs, 2002).

Ward, M. *Unmanageable Revolutionaries* (London: Pluto Press, 1989).

Ward, M. 'National Liberation Movements and the Question of Women's Liberation: The Irish Experience', in C. Midgley (ed.), *Gender and Imperialism* (Manchester: Manchester University Press, 1998), pp. 104–22.

Ward, M. 'Irish Immigrants and Irish Communities Abroad: A Study of Existing Sources of Information and Analysis', research undertaken for the *Task Force on Policy Regarding Emigration* (Dublin: Department of Foreign Affairs, 2002).

Webster, W. *Imagining Home, Gender, 'Race' and National Identity, 1945–64* (London: University College London Press, 1998).

Whyte, J. H. Church, State and Society, 1950–70, in J. J. Lee (ed.), *Ireland 1945–70* (Dublin: Gill & Macmillan, 1979), pp. 73–82.

Whyte, J. H. *Church and State in Modern Ireland, 1923–1979* (Dublin: Gill & Macmillan, 1980).

Wiesner, M. E. *Women and Gender in Early Modern Europe* (Cambridge: Cambridge University Press, 1993).

Wilkinson, S. and Kitzinger, C. (eds) *Feminism and Discourse: Psychological Perspectives* (London: Sage, 1995).

Wilkinson, S. and Kitzinger, C. (eds) *Representing the Other: A Feminism and Psychology Reader* (London: Sage, 1996).

Wittberg, P. *The Rise and Decline of Catholic Religious Orders: A Social Movement Perspective* (New York: State University of New York, 1994).

Woodward, K. (ed.) *Identity and Difference* (London/Milton Keynes: Sage/Open University Press, 1997)

Woolf, V. *Three Guineas* (London: The Hogarth Press, 1938).

Wright, C. 'Representing the "Other": Some Thoughts', *Indian Journal of Gender Studies*, 4, 1 (1997), pp. 83–9.

Reports:

Action Group for Irish Youth (AGIY) (1988) *Young and Irish: Meeting the Need*, London: AGIY.

(1989) *A Programme for Action*, London: AGIY/TIDE.

(1994) *Developing a Community Response: The Service Needs of the Irish Community in Camden*, Conference Report, London: AGIY.

(1997) *The Irish Community: Discrimination and the Criminal Justice System*, London: AGIY.

Brent Irish Advisory Service (BIAS) (1988) *Irish Homeless Families in London, A Report*, London: BIAS.

Brent Mental Health Group (BMHG) (1986) *The Irish Experience of Mental Ill-heath in London*, Brent: BMHG.

Bunreacht na hEireann, The Constitution of Ireland (1937) Dublin: Government Publications Office.

Camden Borough Council (1990) *The Voice of the Irish in Camden,*

Conference Report, London: Camden Council.

Camden Irish Conference Planning Group (1990) *The Voice of the Irish in Camden, Report of a Conference*, London: Camden Council.

Cara Report (1988) *Irish Single Homelessness in Lewisham*, London: Cara.

(1988) *Irish Single Homelessness in Southwark*, London: Cara.

(1989) *Irish Single Homelessness in Wandsworth*, London: Cara.

(1991) *Access to Housing for Single Homeless Irish People*, London: Cara.

Commission on Emigration and Other Population Problems, 1948–1954, Reports (1955) Dublin: The Stationery Office.

Ethnic Minorities Department and Hammersmith and Fulham Irish Support and Advice Centre (1989) *Ard Fheis '89, Report of a Joint Conference*, London: Hammersmith and Fulham Council.

Greater London Council (GLC) (1984) *Report on the Prevention of Terrorism Act in London and Report on Consultation with the Irish Community*, London: GLC.

(1984) *Policy Report on the Irish Community: Ethnic Minorities in London*, London: GLC.

Haringey Irish Community Centre (1997) *Working Towards Equality: Annual Report 1996–7*, London: Haringey Council.

Irish in Britain Representation Group (IBRG) (1986) *Survey into the Promotion of Irish Culture within Haringey School Curriculum*, London: IBRG.

Irish Liaison Unit, Haringey Council (1991) *Equal Opportunities: The Irish Dimension, An Agenda for Change*, London: Haringey Council.

London Irish Women's Centre (LIWC) (1985) *Report of the Second London Irish Women's Centre*, London: LIWC.

(1986) *Annual Report*, London: LIWC.

(1987) *Irish Women, Our Lives, Our Identity, Conference Report*, London: LIWC.

(1987) *Annual Report*, London: LIWC.

(1989) *London Irish Women's Conference Report*, London: LIWC.

(1988/9) *Annual Report*, London: LIWC.

(1991/2) *Annual Report*, London: LIWC.

(1993) *Roots and Realities, A Profile of Irish Women in London*, London: LIWC.

(1994) *Annual Report*, London: LIWC.

(1995) *Information for the Single Homeless and Private Tenants*, London: LIWC.

(1996) *Roots and Realities: A Profile of Irish Women in London in the 1990s*, London: LIWC.

(1996) *10th Anniversary Report*, London: LIWC.

(1999) *Irish Women and Mental Health – A People Ignored, Culture and Context, Conference Report, 1998*, London: LIWC.

London Strategic Policy Unit (LSPU) (1987) *The Irish Community: A Training Guide*, London: LSPU.

(1988) *Police Monitoring and Research Group, Briefing Paper no. 5*, London: LSPU.

National Economic and Social Council (NESC) (1991) *The Economic and Social Implications of Emigration*, Dublin: NESC.

Rule Books:

Congregation of the Sisters of St Louise (1927; 1984)
Congregation of the Sisters of St Nadine (1934)
Congregation of the Sisters of St Cecile (1962; 1984)
Congregation of the Sisters of St Mildred (1953; 1983; 1998)
Congregation of the Sisters of St Marie (1925)

Index